We
Americans

10,000 SAILORS, IN TRAINING DURING WORLD WAR I, FORM A LIVING STARS AND STRIPES.

PRECEDING PAGES: CITIZENS OF BRIDGEPORT, CONNECTICUT, SHOW THEIR PATRIOTISM IN A MAIN STREET PARADE DURING WORLD WAR I.

We Americans

Celebrating a Nation, Its People, and Its Past

Edited by Thomas B. Allen and Charles O. Hyman

Introduction by Spencer R. Crew
National Museum of American History

NATIONAL
GEOGRAPHIC

WASHINGTON, D.C.

FLANKED BY NAME AND FLAG IN THE MIDST OF WAR, A UNION SERGEANT MARKS AN AMERICAN MOMENT.

ISBN: 978-0-7922-7005-8

Library of Congress Cataloging-in-Publication Data

We Americans: celebrating a nation, its people, and its past /
edited by Thomas B. Allen and Charles O. Hyman; introduction by
Spencer R. Crew.
     p. cm.
  Includes index.
  ISBN 0-7922-7005-3
  ISBN 0-7922-7007-X (dlx)
  1. United States—History. 2. United States—History Pictorial
works. 3. National characteristics, American. 4. National
characteristics, American Pictorial works. I. Allen, Thomas B. II.
Hyman, Charles O.
  E178.6.W35 1999
  973—dc21   99-31275
                         CIP

Printed in the United States of America
12/WOR/2

contents

"…thoughts of home and my dear Father and Mother would almost overwhelm me with grief. As each step bore me farther from them, the unbidden tears would flow…."

—LAVINIA HONEYMAN PORTER
ON THE OREGON TRAIL

PIONEERS REST NEAR COLORADO SPRINGS ON THE WAY WEST.

The airs of heaven blow o'er me;

A glory shines before me

Of what mankind shall be—

Pure, generous, brave, and free.

       —JOHN GREENLEAF WHITTIER

IN AN AMISH COMMUNITY IN ILLINOIS, A FAMILY PRAYS ITS GRACE.

Music I heard with you

was more than music,

And bread I broke with you

was more than bread....

— CONRAD AIKEN

CHILDREN AND GRANDCHILDREN GATHER ON THEIR IMMIGRANT GRANDPARENTS' FARM.

You will come, with your slim, expressive arms,

A poise of the head no sculptor has caught

And nuances spoken with shoulder and neck,

Your face in a pass-and-repass of moods....

— CARL SANDBURG

A MASSACHUSETTS MADONNA MIRRORS HER GRANDMOTHER'S PORTRAIT.

foreword

Picturing
Our Past

BY JOHN M. FAHEY, JR.
President and CEO, National Geographic Society

In October 1888, the first issue of the National Geographic Society's magazine devoted 22 pages of text to the Great Storm of 1888. There were no photographs. But in snow-smothered cities and towns throughout the East, cameras were clicking, preserving personal moments of what people would call the Blizzard of '88. And millions of snapshots were to come, for in that same year George Eastman, a bank clerk turned entrepreneur, introduced the Kodak, a camera so simple that it would work for anyone who "could wind a watch."

Photographs at that time went into family albums or into frames on parlor walls, not onto the pages of publications like the new NATIONAL GEOGRAPHIC magazine. Technically, it could be done. In 1880 a New York newspaper had published a photo by transforming an image's blacks and whites into tiny dots engraved on a metal plate. On a printing press, this "halftone," as it was called, picked up ink in proportion to the density of the dots and transferred an image to the paper going through the press. In 1896 the NATIONAL GEOGRAPHIC became "an illustrated monthly," and Alexander Graham Bell, president of the Society, said he wanted, "dynamical" photographs—"pictures of life and action—pictures that tell a story 'to be continued in our text.'"

By the turn of the century, photos and text began regularly appearing together in magazines, books, and newspapers. Still in the future, however, was the idea that photographs could contribute to an understanding of the past. History usually filled pages with unaccompanied words, carrying on the British scholars' maxim: "Pictures are the books of the ignorant." It took a while for historians to discover that images of ordinary events could help us interpret the past.

Today, photography is hailed by such historians as Daniel Boorstin, winner of the Pulitzer Prize, former Librarian of Congress, and Director of the Smithsonian's National Museum of American History. "The picture," he writes, "has a depth and clarity and ambiguity not found in any historian's words." Boorstin believes that photographs bring people of the past "into the range of our eyes" and "into our own community."

That is what this book does, spanning the illustrated America—from daguerreotypist Jacob Byerly, who aims his camera on the first page, to the digitized images of the World Wide Web on page 380. Words and photos take you to the Great West and into the Civil War, out of the 19th century and into the 20th, stopping along the way to see moments of everyday life.

American history begins with portraits and sketches of colonial times, but photography soon arrives. As a measure of how much of our story has been photographed, consider this: Daniel Webster, born during the Revolutionary War, appears on daguerreotypes. He looks stern and hollow-eyed, wearied by his efforts to save the Union from civil war. We know now that Webster looks that way because, during the long exposure, a hidden brace held his head in place and bright skylights darkened his eye sockets.

The daguerreotype was a French import that quickly became an American phenomenon. Within a decade after Jacob Byerly opened his pioneering gallery in the United States in 1842 there were some 10,000 more daguerreotypists' galleries in the country. From daguerreotypes and tintypes came enduring American images. We know the face of Frederick Douglass, the escaped slave who led abolitionists. And we can see the hand of an abolitionist, branded with SS for "slave stealer" (page 140). Then come the faces of war-bound boys of North and South, eyes wide and peering, trying desperately to see their futures. Many go into battle carrying tintype images of their sweethearts or kin.

The invention of the collodion wet plate in 1851 ended the era of the daguerreotype and ushered in modern negative-and-print photography. Daguerreotypists like Mathew B. Brady adapted swiftly. He produced portraits, including one of Abraham Lincoln that seemed to look into the Great Emancipator's soul. When the Civil War began, Brady and his "operators" immortalized scenes of death and horror that men had seen in every war but had never so preserved (pages 162-167). Oliver Wendell Holmes, Sr., who went to the Antietam battlefield in search of his wounded son, later saw photographs of the place where nearly 23,000 men had fallen in a single day. "It is so nearly like visiting the battlefields to look over these views," he later wrote, "that all the emotions excited by the actual sight of the stained and sordid scene, strewed with rags and wrecks, came back to us."

After the war, photographers headed West, recording a new chapter in American history and luring Easterners to lands long imagined and now visible. Viewing stereopticons and large prints made from glass plates, Americans saw mountains etched on endless horizons, mammoth canyons, steam gushers soaring from cracks in the earth. Photographers, hired to document the building of railroads, left a visual chronicle not only of the tracks and the trestles but also of the crews, native-born and immigrant workers building the way westward (page 91).

Photographers also accompanied federal mapping expeditions into the West. They loaded heavy, cumbersome cameras on mules, trekked deserts and mountain passes, set up tents in windswept wilds, developed large glass wet plates, and got them home intact. William Henry Jackson speeded up his developing with hot water from Yellowstone's hot springs. His breathtaking views of Yellowstone helped prompt Congress to create the world's first national wilderness park.

As the 19th century ended, photography passed from the hands of professionals with their bulky cameras and glass plates to amateurs clicking their Kodaks and one-dollar Brownies, capturing images on flexible film. At the same time, photography entered the mainstream of journalism and government. In 1901, traditionalists hailed the *New York Times* because "it does not print pictures." In 1904 the *Times* began regularly illustrating news with photos and never stopped.

In 1919 the National Geographic Society organized its photographs, along with albums of travel snapshots contributed by members. Now the Society's Image Collection consists of more than 10 million photographs and original artwork. Many of the photos in this book—such as the World War I photos on pages 216-221—come from our original collection. Many others come from the National Archives. In Washington, not far from where this is being written, the National Archives is exhibiting 100 years of its outstanding photographs. The pushcarts on page 187 are in that exhibit, as is Dorothea Lange's photo of a man on a breadline (page 231). In that instant she shows us the absolute reality of the Great Depression.

The National Archives describes the photographs in its exhibit as time machines, allowing us to "look back in history, freeze a moment in time, and image ourselves as part of the past." As you read this book, I hope that its images will fire up your own imagination and take you to the American past, to discover who we are and how we got here.

AT THE BOSTON NAVY YARD IN 1873, A MARINE GUARDS THE ORIGINAL STAR-SPANGLED BANNER.

BY SPENCER R. CREW
Director, National Museum of American History

Preserving Our Past

The past is a wondrous and intriguing realm, full of the people, events, and things that can answer the questions asked by those of us who want to better understand history: Why did people make the choices they did? Why did a certain chain of events lead to a particular outcome? The past becomes less mysterious when we approach it for information through writings, official records—and artifacts, the things left behind when people and generations pass away. Historians call these artifacts "authentic, primary historical material." Here at the National Museum of American History we have more than three million representations of this historical material.

We collect, preserve, and study them to offer visitors a special relationship with history. We want our visitors to realize the power of contact with objects from the past. The stories connected with these objects offer a wonderful means of understanding the moments of glory and despair, progress and miscalculation, or failure and perseverance that are all part of the American story.

One of our largest objects is the Star-Spangled Banner, a tangible link to a critical moment in our history. In September 1814 this flag flew over Fort McHenry in Baltimore as a 24-hour bombardment of that fort by the British came to an end. The banner's presence, which marked the survival of the fort and its garrison, was significant. The independence won in the Revolutionary War was still in jeopardy. A British victory in Baltimore might have lead to the defeat of the fledgling nation. Francis Scott Key understood all this when he looked that morning—"and our flag was still there." Inspired, he penned the words of what would become our national anthem.

The survival of the fort and the flag, captured in Key's song, changed the ways Americans thought about their flag and themselves. It was no longer just a military emblem but rather a symbol of American patriotism and fortitude.

It represented the new democratic form of government that our nation espoused and our growing importance as an international presence. In many ways the emergence of the United States as a world power over the next two centuries had its foundation in part in the survival of Fort McHenry and the flag that flew over it.

While the Star-Spangled Banner evokes thoughts of patriotism and national pride, other objects signal important technological moments. Two artifacts in the museum—the *John Bull* locomotive, built in 1831, and the Xero Alto computer, created in 1973—represent such moments. One dramatically demonstrates the application of an important breakthrough. The other illustrates more halting steps taken toward the future.

The *John Bull* is the world's oldest complete and operable locomotive. It and others like it were instrumental in launching the railway age in the United States. They sped up communication between cities, as well as transporting people and goods as fast as 35 miles an hour, amazing passengers and changing the ways people thought about travel and distance. The rapid evolution of bigger and faster locomotives helped fuel the economic and industrial growth of the United States during the latter half of the 19th century. As an artifact, the *John Bull* illustrates how significant technological changes can take place in a relatively short time.

The Xerox Alto illustrates a very different lesson about technology. The Alto emerged from research at the Xerox Palo Alto Research Center in the early 1970s. It was a fully operable, networked personal workstation, comparable to the desktop personal computers we now take for granted. The developers envisioned computers as tools that enabled people to work collaboratively. The Alto's simplified system included a mouse and connections that allowed the rapid exchange of information among users. While bulky and expensive, the Alto represented a significant breakthrough in computer technology.

But computers and word processing were so new that no one understood how to apply them effectively. It took a decade before the Macintosh began to apply the technology pioneered by the Alto. More than 20 years passed before the mouse gained widespread acceptance, followed by the idea of the World Wide Web. While innovations like the *John Bull* captured the public imagination, the Xerox Alto did not. Ahead of its time, the Xerox Alto failed because potential users were not ready to embrace its advanced technology. The Alto story is a reminder that progress is not inevitable and that our understanding of American history is enriched by the stories of successes and failures enmeshed within it.

Artifacts also are important as a way to understand the stories of ordinary people. The museum's Ipswich House is an excellent example of an object rich in history. Built in the nation's early years, it has survived the arrival of the 21st century, an artifact with a long story to tell.

The house's original owner, George Hart, lived in the seaport of Ipswich, Massachusetts. A cooper, Hart produced barrels for the local fishermen, farmers, coastal traders and merchants. In 1696, at the age of 27, he purchased a two-acre lot that included a small dwelling and a barn. By the time he married Elizabeth Wells in 1699, he had built a new house on the land. George and Elizabeth had four sons; two became coopers like their father.

One of the sons, Nathaniel, continued to live in the house after his mother's death and his own marriage. In the 1740s the Harts built a new, larger house on a different street. They moved the original dwelling and attached it to the new building as the kitchen wing. The new house had upstairs rooms and provided more space for the family. When George Hart passed away in 1752, the well-crafted house—with mortise-and-tendon joints, hand-wrought nails—reflected the improving fortunes of the Harts and many residents in the colonies. Furnishings included leather-covered chairs, mirrors, imported ceramics and glass pieces, as well as textiles manufactured in Europe.

We do not know how the Hart family felt about the growing tension between England and her American colonies, but we do know how a subsequent resident felt. Abraham Dodge, a West Indies merchant, trader, and sea captain, lived there with his wife, Abigail, two children, and their slave, Chance. After the battle of Bunker Hill in 1775, Dodge answered the call for soldiers and, accompanied by Chance, fought as an officer in the militia. While he was away, Abigail Dodge, with the help of her daughter and son, cared for the animals and grew food. Abigail passed away in 1781. Within a year, Abraham remarried the recently widowed Bethiah Staniford and moved her into his home.

Abraham's many months away from home, his irregular army pay, and wartime inflation all combined to hit his family hard. He died a debtor in 1786.

The Unisonic Calculator, made in Hong Kong in the 1970s, was an early hand-held calculator. Another Smithsonian artifact, it is a link in the evolution of devices designed to take the labor out of counting. Desk-top adding machines began appearing early in the 20th century. By the 1950s, electronic calculating systems had doomed the adding machine—as well as that tool cherished by mathematicians since the 17th century, the slide rule.

Among the most valuable possessions he bequeathed to his wife was the slave Chance, who was not given his freedom despite his loyal service during the Revolutionary War. Lacking documents, we do not now the fate of Chance and the other members of the Dodge household. Probably they continued to struggle forward, as did their new nation.

Josiah Caldwell, recently married to Lucy Lord, who was 17 years his junior, purchased the Ipswich house in 1822. Caldwell became enmeshed in the politics of the era. In the 1830s he held several public offices, including selectman and member of the General Court. He also was a Democratic nominee for the U.S. Senate. One of the leading citizens of Ipswich, he was a founder of local chapters of the Total Abstinence and the Anti-Slavery Societies.

The parlor of the Caldwell house was probably a frequent meeting place for these organizations. Here, as in other parts of the nation, people debated about the treatment of men and women who fled slavery. Opposition to slavery was especially strong in New England, where William Lloyd Garrison and other abolitionists were based. The Caldwells read the *Liberator* and *Uncle Tom's Cabin*, heard lectures by such former slaves as Frederick Douglass, and supported the Northern cause in the Civil War.

In New England towns like Ipswich, the end of the war meant not only the return of the men who fought for the North but also the continued growth of industry. In Ipswich, this growth centered on a cotton mill converted to produce hosiery. In 1880, when this and other Ipswich mills were employing hundreds of Irish-born women immigrants, Catherine Lynch occupied the Ipswich house. Irish and a widow, she earned her living as a laundress, sharing her home with her 25-year-old daughter Mary and two boarders, Nicholas Donovan and Agnes Wilkens, all mill workers. Catherine used the cast-iron wood-burning stove in the kitchen for boiling water and heating irons for the laundry as well as for cooking. She rented the house from John Heard, a merchant who lived in a mansion overlooking the Lynch house. Catherine had been the Heard family's private laundress in better times. Heard had become prosperous in the China trade but lost his fortune in the mid-1870s.

By the third decade of the 20th century, the Ipswich house's tenants were Andrew and Mary Scott. The couple lived in a downstairs apartment with their three children Roy, Frank, and Annie. Andrew was an itinerant farmhand who had moved to Massachusetts from Kansas and worked as a groundskeeper and

A treasure of the Smithsonian, Edison's incandescent light bulb (opposite) ushered in the electrical age. After trying many filaments—including coconut hair—he discovered in 1879 that a charred cotton thread would glow for 13 hours. The filament, now broken, in this 1880 bulb, is made of bamboo. The life rating was about 600 hours—not too much less than the 750-to-1,000 hours common today.

handyman for several area families. Mary enjoyed gardening and grew vegetables, which she canned. After Andrew died in 1945, she began working as a matron at the local high school.

Their son Roy graduated from Ipswich Manning High School in 1934, in the midst of the Great Depression. When Roy joined the Navy in 1942, his sister and her husband moved into the house. After four years in Pacific combat, Roy moved back into the house at 13 Elm Street, a war veteran who

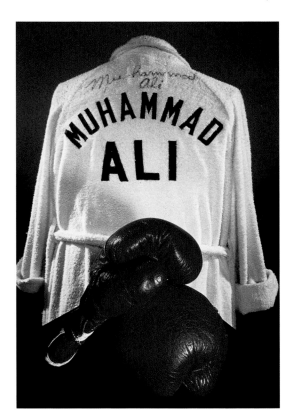

went from job to job—plumber, caretaker, fisherman. He left the house in 1961, when his mother died. He passed away in 1987 in a Massachusetts veterans' hospital.

Here at the museum, the story of the Ipswich House continues, embodying for all who learn about it a history that in many ways is a microcosm of the history of our country. Those who lived in the house reflect the patriotism of Americans, their concern about the political system, their role in the economic growth of the country, and their faith in the American dream.

This sense of optimism encouraged immigration to America in large numbers during the last quarter of the 19th century and the early decades of the 20th century. Immigration helped fuel the economic growth of the country, a growth that eventually propelled the U.S. to world economic and political leadership. But equal access to the privileges of citizenship has continued to nag at the nation throughout the 19th and 20th centuries.

African Americans, constantly pointing to the contradictions between theory and reality, finally caught the full attention of the country in 1954, when the U.S. Supreme Court, in *Brown* v. *Board of Education*, declared segregation in public schools unconstitutional. In 1955 came the Montgomery, Alabama, bus boycott, ignited when Rosa Parks refused to give up her seat on a city bus to a white man. The years of protest against discrimination and segregation continued. In 1960, four African-American students from North Carolina's Agricultural & Technical College walked into a Woolworth's store in Greensboro, sat at the whites-only lunch counter, and refused to leave until they were served. Their sit-in at the counter, the abuse they took, and the photographs of the sit-in further galvanized the civil rights movement, brought college students into the battle in ever increasing numbers, and led to many of the successes that culminated in the Civil Rights Act of 1964.

As an artifact in our museum, the Woolworth's lunch counter is a powerful piece of "authentic, primary historical material." It reflects the courage and determination of the North Carolina A&T students. It reveals the power hold of segregation and discrimination at that time—and the level of patriotism and commitment it took to loosen that hold. The counter also illustrates how the country engaged those issues and made changes when confronted with the contradiction of segregation in a nation founded on democratic principles.

The power of the lunch counter as an artifact highlights the role that objects can play in linking us to the past. Each artifact has a unique history. It may be its association with an event or individuals, its catalytic role in a critical moment, its creation at a key point. Or it may have other characteristics that make it historically significant—and interesting—to seekers of the past. Careful examination of the object and research into its heritage yield information about its importance in understanding our history. This information is not always easily acquired, for artifacts do not reveal themselves the way documents do. But the information produced by research can provide wonderful stories about the objects and the places and times in which they existed. These stories add immensely to our understanding of our history. They are an enriching addition to the more traditional research done by scholars investigating the past.

Another kind of research—into the American public's attitude toward history—tells us that Americans are indeed interested in the past. This interest is strongly connected to their personal associations with people and events, although it is not limited solely to those links. Artifacts in museums, along with the objects' stories, also have great resonance for the public. The direct link of these objects to people and events from another era is extremely important. It opens people to the excitement and energy that history can embody when presented at its best. The challenge is to transfer this fascination with objects and personal historical association to a larger stage that links historical moments with broader events and trends. To make this happen, it is crucial to present the stories with all the richness and wonder inherent in them.

The chapters in this book will present our past in just this fashion, revealing the history of this nation through the lives and extraordinary accomplishments of everyday people. Their collective efforts in the course of two centuries transformed a group of tenuously linked cities and communities into one of the world's most powerful nations. How that transformation took place is an exciting story that will reveal itself for you in the pages that follow.

To tell America's story with artifacts—officially, "authentic, primary historical material"—the Museum of American History preserves icons of American movies, television, and sports, such as Dorothy's magical red shoes from The Wizard of Oz, Kermit the Frog *from "Sesame Street" and "The Muppets," and boxing champion Muhammad Ali's robe and gloves (opposite).*

The New Land

A "fruitfull and delightsome land. . . . Heaven and earth never

agreed better to frame a place for man's habitation."

—CAPT. JOHN SMITH

BY EDMUND S. MORGAN

Becoming an American has never been easy. The Englishmen who first tried it, at Jamestown and Plymouth and Massachusetts Bay, found that they had much to learn and more to unlearn. Whether they came looking for a way to wealth or a way to righteousness, they had to begin by staying alive, by making a living. And making a living in the New World required a whole new set of ideas and attitudes.

The England that the settlers left behind had become a puzzle to its inhabitants. For a century people had been multiplying at a rate that almost surpassed the capacity of the island to support them. Jobs were scarce; the cost of food had soared. The government did what it could to spread work around. To hold down the number of artisans so that each would have enough business to support him, laws required youngmentoservelongapprenticeships before setting up in trade for themselves. Employers had to hire by the

year, not by the day or hour or job. It was illegal to practice more than one trade. Labor was divided, not for efficiency's sake but to multiply jobs. The making of a bow and arrow, for example, was shared by four workers: one who rough-hewed bow staves, a bowyer who finished them, an arrowhead maker, and a fletcher.

Some farming tasks, too, became the preserve of specialists. Many villages had but one plow and one team to pull it, and only after the plowman had done his work could the ordinary farmer or "husbandman" plant his fields. Whether a man

Theodore de Bry, Flemish engraver, never saw America. Yet his 1590 Indian "Town" resembles what early explorers reported: villages, often palisaded; huts roofed by bark, reeds, skins. Longhouses, some stretching 200 feet, held several families. Indians, mostly friendly (right), were described as tall and "of comely proportions."

PRECEDING PAGES
Santa Maria's sail bears a cross, as did her priests. Sunlight adds a hint of gold, the dream of Columbus—and of all Spain.

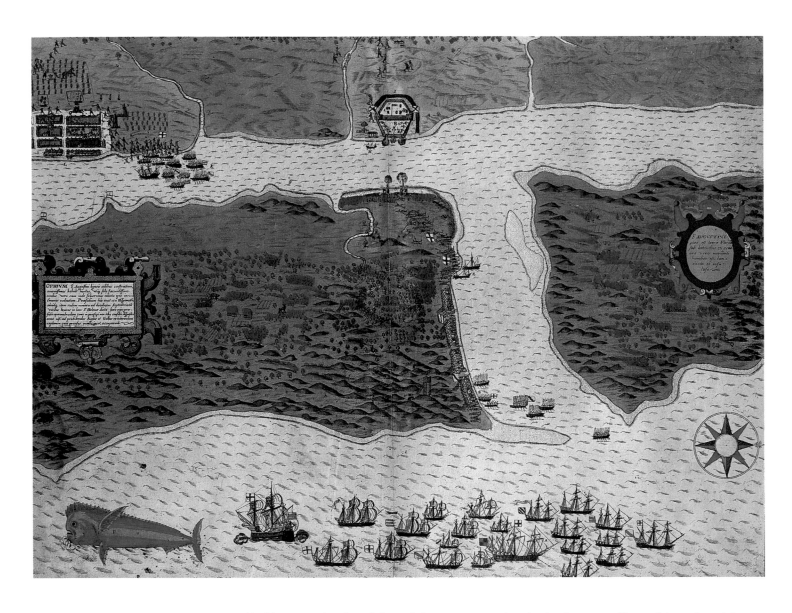

tilled his own land or labored for someone else, he had to coordinate his tasks with those assigned to others. They would resent, perhaps even prosecute, an overeager individualist who tried to do for himself a job that rightly belonged to another.

Farmland, like work, was scarce in England; it had to be used continuously and intensively in order to nurse from it as much food as possible. And few men could afford farmland. The island also had hilly, wooded lands too rough to till. To these wastelands, especially in the north and west, drifted men and women who could find no land or work elsewhere. They squatted and made do, living from scrawny gardens, wild nuts and roots, and animals that foraged in the woods. Not wild animals—only aristocrats could hunt—but the cows and pigs that an ordinary man might raise on the common land. At best he went hungry much of the time; at worst, he turned to thieving and ended up on the gallows. The number of thieves, rogues, and tramps rose ever higher. It seemed to John Winthrop, future governor of Massachusetts Bay, that the land "growes wearye of her Inhabitants."

He and other gentlemen looked to America to provide room for England's miserable surplus—as well as room at the top for themselves. To get here, poor emigrants had to sign on as servants, indentured to work several years for "the better sort" to repay the cost of passage. Masters and servants alike, whether set down on New England's rocky shores or Virginia's fertile Tidewater, confronted a land where past experience was a poor guide.

The English found a vast continent thinly peopled by the native Indians. The first Spanish conquerors in Central America had faced 15 or 20 million people who were intensive agriculturalists; by contrast, the English encountered only about 13,000 inhabitants in the Virginia area and probably no more than twice that many in all New England. The settlers quickly outnumbered the native peoples—already drastically reduced by the onslaught of European diseases caught from visiting explorers and fishermen on the coast.

For land-hungry Englishmen, the new continent seemed an answer to prayer, and in the end it proved to be so. The ambition of the ordinary Englishman was to own his land, and by the end of the colonial period most English settlers in America had achieved or were on their way to achieving that goal.

In 1776 approximately 90 percent of the 2.5 million Americans lived on farms, and most families owned their land. The scarcity of people made it necessary to husband labor, not land. The average farmer had to be a jack-of-all-trades, doing nearly everything for himself—however crudely—yet conserving his precious labor. Men and women alike had to learn new ways to take advantage of the novel situation.

Fortunately, teachers were at hand. The Indians had long since devised ways of making a living from the continent with a minimum of labor. One way was to treat land as a natural food preserve. Eastern tribes subsisted partly from hunting, and on large areas they let the game thrive, harvesting animals only as needed by stalking with bow and arrow, or sometimes by firing forests and encircling deer as they ran from the flames. Burned-over tracts sprang up with wild nut trees, berries, and beneath the soil were edible roots.

But most of what the Indians ate came from patches of land they tilled. In the forest near a village, families would girdle the trees on a few acres and perhaps build fires around the trunks to hasten their deaths. Then, without removing the trees, they scraped up the ground between and planted maize. All the Indians on the Atlantic Coast had acquired this plant, which had been developed in the Indian civilizations to the south. Corn is still perhaps the most sophisticated, highly bred

First portrait of America's first European settlement (opposite) shows St. Augustine huddling at upper left as Francis Drake's mighty English fleet assembles to torch the town. In 1586, Spain's outpost was only 21 years old. The Italian artist added the monstrous "Dorado fish" (dolphin). Castillo de San Marcos (above), looming over its tidal moat at St. Augustine, ended such depredations as Drake's. Started in 1672, its 30-foot walls of coquina, "shell rock," were some 12 feet thick and took a generation to finish.

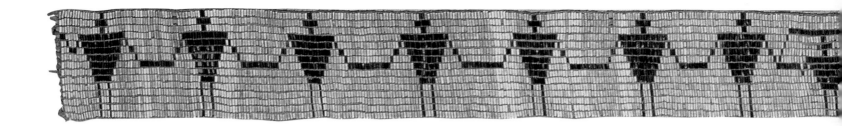

grain that people possess (so highly bred that it does not survive by itself in the wild). An acre or two planted in it, with beans and squash mixed in, could sustain a family for the better part of a year. The tribe would abandon a patch when its fertility gave out after a few years. It was easy to "clear" another one, Indian style.

Few white Americans became full-time hunters, for few had the needed skills; in England, hunting had been reserved for the aristocracy. Instead, the settlers often treated the cattle and hogs brought from England almost like game. Turned loose to fend for themselves, the animals still provided a reliable supply of meat and sometimes grew as wild as the deer they supplanted. Hogs especially multiplied rapidly, feeding on acorns. Cattle and hogs, the colonists' game, provided a more reliable meat supply than deer. But the Indians' corn proved a more effective way of getting bread than English wheat. Everywhere the settlers grew corn. An acre or two in corn and a few hogs in the woods gave people enough to eat and time to grow something extra for sale.

In Virginia and Maryland, the land proved ideal for a crop that brought high prices in the Old World—tobacco, which produced the first American boom. In 1619, two years after the initial shipment to London, the secretary of Jamestown Colony observed that "one man by his owne labour hath in one yeare, raised to himselfe [tobacco] to the value of £200 sterling." That was ten or twenty times what a farmer could expect to make in England. The price collapsed in 1629, but settlers continued to come and to plant tobacco. Throughout the colonial period the annual crop was worth as much as all other American exports combined.

Tobacco required a longer growing season and much more attention than corn. You sowed the seeds—so tiny that 10,000 fit in a teaspoon—in special beds sometime after the middle of January, transplanting the seedlings to the field in May or June. Thereafter you had to pick over the plants for worms. June was weeding time. When stalks grew a foot or more tall, you topped each plant; and to secure maximum growth, you snipped the suckers as they appeared. Harvesting began in late August. Plants were cut, wilted to limpness, then hung in open sheds to cure for several weeks. Finally, you packed the leaves tightly in hogsheads.

Tobacco was so demanding that one man could tend only a few acres. But a tobacco planter still needed a lot of land. The plants required rich soil but rapidly depleted its fertility. After three or four crops of tobacco, a field still might grow

New World's early explorers found no great cities north of Mexico. In eastern forests, where soaring trees blocked sunlight, scattered bands of natives lived. European newcomers with metal tools and weapons, burdened by odd habits, beliefs, and desires, shook the natives' natural world like an earthquake. Wampum (above) did not suit Europeans. But tell them gold lay beyond those hills, and they would go away. They craved land—not just to use but to own. They sought fealty to their God. And they brought disease. Smallpox (opposite) flayed off the Indians' skin, and, said Plymouth's William Bradford, "They die like rotten sheep."

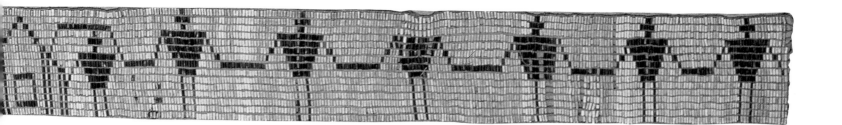

passable corn for a few years. Then it was allowed to return to forest. Eventually, fertility returned to the worn land. The cycle might take 20 or 30 years. By the usual calculation, for a tobacco plantation to stay in continuous operation required fifty acres of land for each working hand, though only two or three acres per hand was under tobacco at any one time.

As tobacco profits rolled in, planters invested in more labor, and the family farm grew into the plantation. In the early period planters bought English, Irish, Welsh, and Scottish servants. Increasingly, after the 1680s they bought slaves from Africa. By the end of the colonial period, 40 percent of Virginia's population consisted of slaves.

The most profitable plantations, on Virginia's broad rivers, had direct access to the London market through oceangoing ships that docked at their doorsteps. Their owners frequently marketed inland planters' crops and imported and sold them manufactured goods. Great mansions facing the James, York, Rappahannock, and Potomac rivers still bespeak the elegance that primitive agriculture, abundant land, and forced labor brought to the lives of the first gentlemen of Virginia.

For every big riverside plantation, there were dozens of small farms back from the rivers. On them lived the ordinary men and women, raising large families in

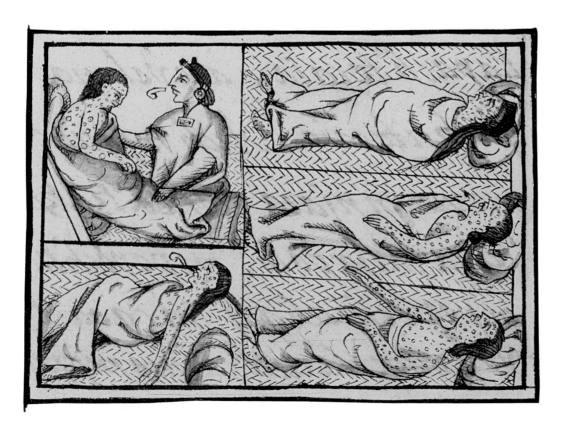

crude houses, built by simply placing posts in the ground and attaching boards to them. Later the farmers learned to cut timber to build crude log cabins, helped out by the children as they grew old enough. Living with plenty to eat, if not in comfort, they shocked European visitors by their uncouth manners, surly independence, and slovenly farming methods.

Tobacco also grew fairly well in part of the Carolinas adjacent to Virginia. Farther south, the settlers found stands of pine growing in a soil that would support little more than a meager food supply. But they could tap the pines for sap, which was crude turpentine. About three years after the wounded trees died, their wood, processed in a kiln, yielded tar and pitch, valued for keeping ships tight and dry.

The vast swamplands of coastal South Carolina at first seemed worthless and were bypassed for pinelands. Then someone had the notion of trying rice in swamps. Rice culture became America's most intensive agriculture, for waters that fed the swamps apparently renewed their fertility, and they could be cropped continuously. But rice never rivaled tobacco in value. Nor did indigo, another crop grown by Carolina planters. The plant was prized as the source of a blue dye.

North of Virginia, where the climate, soil, or terrain did not favor crops that Europeans craved, no one made a fortune from farming. But there, as in the South, land shaped people's lives, giving thousands of ordinary men a security and independence few of their ancestors could have known. They paid something in neighborliness, for the American farm was large enough to isolate a family from casual daily contacts with neighbors. In New England a unique religious dedication combined with a stubborn, rocky soil to keep people living and working together for a time in tightly knit villages. Gradually, though, the endless land drew families away to farms remote from the village. Self-sufficient, they produced a small surplus of cattle and hogs, dairy products, corn, and wheat to take to market. Though lonelier than his European counterpart, a man could well "rest satisfied, and thank God that my lot is to be an American farmer, instead of a Russian boor, or an Hungarian peasant."

Most of the artisans who came to the New World quickly shifted to farming. Some of the best, however, stuck to their hard-earned skills and clustered together in the towns and cities that gradually grew up along the coast. A number of men, hardier than most, had no taste for the farm and took to the sea. The eastern

continental shelf, especially the Grand Banks off Nova Scotia, teemed with fish. Indeed, for a century before the Atlantic coast of North America attracted any settlers, fishermen had sailed there in the spring from England, France, Spain, and Portugal—to return in the fall loaded with well-salted cod for the tables of their less daring countrymen. American fishermen could reach the fishing grounds in smaller ships than the French and English, who had to make the Atlantic voyage. The smaller size made it easier for Americans to maneuver on the Banks and to bring the daily catch ashore to be dried and salted. As a result, they were able to take over a large share of the "dry" fishery in summer, as well as to supply the local market with fresh fish in winter.

Working the sea was no surer a way to wealth than working the land. Most fishermen died poor. Even whalers, who logged thousands of miles for their more valuable prey, seldom died rich. Nor did the young men who manned ships carrying commodities between the colonies and Europe.

Yet it was the sea and ships that offered men in America the greatest opportunity for profit. Even in the tobacco country, the biggest profits came not from

News of mastodon bones found near Newburgh, New York, inspired Charles Willson Peale, artist and collector, to buy up the dig, take over, and excavate the world's first skeletons of the extinct animal. To keep the site from flooding, he rigged a chain of buckets powered by a huge treadmill. It turned as spectators walked inside. Peale (at right in painting) portrayed himself supervising.

Old notions, old crafts in a new land

Yankees fought winter cold by filling a warming pan with glowing embers and passing it across the sheets of a feather bed. Another way to warm up: With parental approval, lass and lad could find privacy in the bed—with an upright bundling board between them. For "lewd and unseemly behavior," a Boston sea captain was clamped in the stocks to be derided by his neighbors. He'd broken a law by kissing his wife publicly on a Sunday, just after ending a three-year voyage. At birth, a Pennsylvania Dutch newborn received a baptismal "fraktur" (named for its German penmanship), containing solemn thoughts and gaily adorned. At death, stone cutters cheered the soul heavenward with carved feathers and wings to suggest its flight, and cherubs to escort it.

Here lyeth Buried

growing the crop but from marketing it. Virginia's great planters were as much merchants as agriculturalists. In South Carolina, the large rice and indigo planters, also doubling as merchants, made Charleston the only commercial city of any size south of Maryland.

Trade had been one reason for founding colonies in America. When the Indians discovered that the white man would exchange blankets, guns, hatchets, and rum for the skins of beaver, they filled canoes with pelts and brought them down

the lakes and rivers in sufficient quantity to make the fur trade a principal activity on the Hudson. From beaver pelts Europeans made felt hats. New York continued as a center of the fur trade long after the English took over the colony from the Dutch in 1664, for the beaver, though widely available in America, was most plentiful in the interior. In New England, where no easy waterway led to the interior, the fur trade flourished only briefly.

But New England was not short on good harbors and good trees for building ships—huge oaks for timbers, white pine for masts and spars. Abundant raw materials made it possible to build ships for half what they cost in England; here a man could acquire one, or an interest in one, with far less capital. New Englanders had hardly arrived before they began building not only small fishing boats but also ocean-going vessels. Captains in the growing seaboard cities often turned merchant and sent younger men off to peddle their wares throughout the globe.

Merchants found their best commercial opportunities in the sugar plantations of the West Indies, which began to flourish about the time that the New England colonies were getting established. It was sugar, not, as so often supposed, the slave trade that attracted the New England merchants to the islands. Not that their scruples precluded human cargo. In the 17th century the Dutch and the English Royal African Company monopolized the trade. During the 18th century New England merchants did deal in slaves on a small scale, but the principal carriers operated out of Bristol and Liverpool. The slave trade amounted to only a small fraction of New England's commerce.

New England supplied the sugar islands of the West Indies with wood staves and headings for their sugar casks, with horses and oxen to power the sugar mills, and with food for both slaves and their masters. Land in the islands was too valuable to be used for much besides sugar. New England's small farmers contributed salted beef and pork as well as live animals and corn. New England fishermen specialized in "refuse fish," the poorer grades that sugar planters wanted for slave food. On the return voyage the New Englanders brought back molasses, the syrup left over from the first crystallization of sugar. They thus traded refuse fish for refuse syrup, and they distilled that into a rum that many people considered refuse also! New England rum sold—for pennies that the poorest man could afford—in enormous quantity throughout the mainland colonies.

Yankees, though notoriously aggressive traders, did not dominate colonial commerce. The merchants of New York and Philadelphia were an equally numerous and ubiquitous tribe. And they all had to compete with English merchants. Moreover, British policy limited the markets open to the colonists. Under the Navigation Acts of 1660 and 1663, tobacco, indigo, sugar, and other colonial products from the West Indies could be carried only to England or to another British colony. European goods could be bought only in England, which meant that English merchants and manufacturers had a virtual monopoly on the expanding American market. But colonial ships were given parity with English ships in imperial trade; foreign ships were excluded. Colonial merchants were therefore able to compete with merchants of the mother country in carrying goods everywhere the laws permitted—and sometimes where they did not. Colonial captains bought and sold goods of every kind in ports all over the world, from Surinam to Istanbul. And merchants sometimes realized tremendous profits.

By the mid-18th century, Americans who were not slaves or Indians enjoyed a degree of prosperity that would have been hard to match in most places in the world. The British imperial system worked because it seemed well suited to the needs of people who lived in the different interdependent parts of it. It was not a

Jamestown, the first lasting English settlement, barely survived feckless mistakes by London's Virginia Company. Fiery John Smith persuaded his sick, starving companions that it was not unseemly for gentlemen to work. Wattle-and-daub huts like these reconstructions (above) then arose within a fort. Despite Indian raids, fires, and outbreaks of disease, Jamestown hung on for 92 years as Virginia's capital. In 1699, Williamsburg took over. Puritans built early and well, as indicated by the Whipple House (opposite), which has stood in Ipswich, Massachusetts, since 1640.

Of poems and plantations

Phillis Wheatley, a slave who wrote poetry, was returning from London in 1773 after arranging for the publishing of her book of poems—the first book ever published by an African American. On the voyage, she wrote a long poem called "Ocean," with lines of eloquent fantasy:

"The King of Tempest thunders o'er the plain, and scorns the azure monarch of the main...."

Wheatley, shipped from Africa at seven, was sold to a Boston family. She learned to read and write, devoured the classics, and at 13 had a poem published in a Boston paper. Her lot was far from usual for a slave. Most went to great plantations like this one, pictured in primitive art (left). Its great house faces a river— a highway for communication and commerce. Other buildings for storage, milling, maintenance, education of children, and Sunday sermons, make the plantation self-sufficient, a village in its own right. Weeping willow at lower left symbolized mourning, so the painting may memorialize the owner.

perfect system. The interests of one part were sometimes sacrificed to those of another, and the interests of all the colonies were subordinated to those of England. But the laws were not too strictly enforced; they could be bent to prevent serious inequities.

In 1764 the system began to come apart. England had hitherto borne the brunt of the expenses of administering and protecting the empire, and during the Seven Years' War with France, which had just ended, those costs had helped to double the national debt. In that war England had wrested Canada and the eastern Mississippi Valley from France. The colonists would benefit; they were prosperous. And it seemed reasonable, at least in England, to make them pay by levying taxes.

But taxation was one form of subordination to England that the Americans refused to accept. Their view of the matter was that English customs duties and trade restrictions already exacted a fair contribution from them. They insisted that they could be taxed only through their own legislative assemblies. They had in Parliament no representatives who would know how large a tax burden they could bear, who would themselves have to pay the taxes imposed, and who could affect decisions with their votes. If Parliament could tax the colonists a little, it could tax them a lot. It might take as much from them as they took from their slaves!

Laden with cod, coastal fishermen moor in a New England cove where catch is dried, salted, and shipped to market, perhaps to the West Indies in trade. This big (up to 200 lb.) abundant fish was vital to Yankees. It fed them, fertilized their crops, fostered shipbuilding, hence commerce. No wonder they called it "Sacred Cod."

Denying that Parliament had any right to tax them, the colonists tried to make the members change their minds. To reinforce their assemblies' protests, they decided to bring pressure on English merchants and manufacturers. So many English workers got a living out of making goods for export to the colonies that an American boycott of those goods might seriously impress the mother country. And so it did.

In response to Parliament's Revenue Act of 1764 and the Stamp Act of 1765, merchants of several colonial cities agreed not to import English goods until the acts were repealed. The Stamp Act was repealed and the Revenue Act modified. Yet Parliament did not give up. Neither did the colonists. Between 1767 and 1773,

Parliament levied taxes on tea, glass, paint, and paper, and the colonists responded with agreements not to import these products. When Americans finally created the Continental Congress to coordinate their continuing struggle against Parliament, the delegates adopted an even broader agreement against trade with England. And local vigilance committees enforced it.

The boycotting of British goods turned out to be the first step toward a fundamental change in the way Americans made a living. Until the boycotts, they had generally avoided manufacturing on any extensive scale except for products requiring heavy raw materials that they possessed in abundance. They built ships and they smelted iron, for they had both ore and the large quantities of wood needed for smelting it. The colonies in 1776 were actually producing one-seventh of the world's iron. But apart from iron, ships, and rum, they considered manufacturing a poor way to use their time. Parliament's attempts to tax them made them begin to wonder about that.

Once war with Britain began, Americans had to make their own clothes and tools and weapons or else find a new source of supply. In total output these efforts at manufacturing were small, but they fixed in the American mind the need to be more self-sufficient, not simply as individuals but as a nation. The Declaration of Independence was a proud gesture; but when the military and political battles had been won, would Americans be able to sustain independence against a hostile world? Unless they had the means to make for themselves the goods they had formerly bought from abroad, might they not be held in economic, and perhaps ultimately political, bondage?

The argument gained weight when Americans went on a buying spree after the Revolutionary War, indulging themselves in the "baubles of Britain"—goods they had done without as long as the war had lasted. British merchants, happy to recover old customers, extended credit liberally. Americans found themselves heavily in debt to the people from whom they had just broken loose. No-import movements bloomed anew, along with societies to promote domestic

Hybridized American tobacco caught on quickly in England when first shipped from Virginia in the early 1600s. Plantations like this soon sold all they could grow, but the growing was tricky. A crop depended on topping, cutting plants, wilting and curing leaves, all at the right time. And, as colonists learned, the soil must be rested.

Slaves for new land, new profits

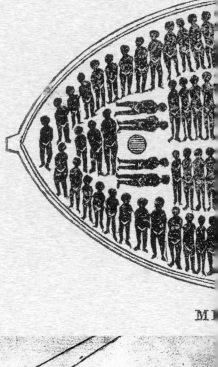

The sale of human beings first occurred in America when a Dutch warship hauled in to Jamestown in August 1619 "and sold us twenty Negars" in exchange for much needed supplies. Jamestowners may have treated them as indentured servants who served for a specified term before being freed. (The 1775 agreement below indentured a carpenter for four years.) But as profits rose for crops like tobacco, the status of the African slaves who did the work sank. Virginia laws mark the milestones. 1659—the word "slave" used in legislation; 1662— the child of a slave is also a slave; 1705—slaves deemed real estate. Plan of a slave ship (top) displays a coffin-size space for each man: women and children got less. Built to carry 500 slaves, this slaver packed in more than 600. On another slaver (right) crewmen pass buckets of food through the fence that separates men and women. The sickliest slaves often were tossed overboard—alive. As many as one in five died during the passage. In 1790 the first U.S. census reported the slave population at nearly 700,000, with 75 percent in the southern Atlantic states.

MI

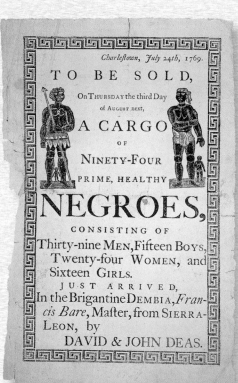

Charlestown, July 24th, 1769.

TO BE SOLD,

On THURSDAY the third Day of AUGUST next,

A CARGO

OF

NINETY-FOUR

PRIME, HEALTHY

NEGROES,

CONSISTING OF

Thirty-nine MEN, Fifteen BOYS, Twenty-four WOMEN, and Sixteen GIRLS.

JUST ARRIVED,

In the Brigantine DEMBIA, *Francis Bare*, Master, from SIERRA-LEON, by

DAVID & JOHN DEAS.

This Indenture, Made the Fourth Day of August in the Twenty Ninth Year of the Reign of our Sovereign Lord George the Third King of Great-Britain, &c, And in the Year of our Lord, One Thousand Seven Hundred and fifty five Between William Buckland of Oxford Carpenter & Joiner

Thomson Mason of London Esqr of the one Part, and

Witnesseth, That the said William Buckland for the Confideration herein after-mentioned, hath, and by these Presents do nant, Grant, and Agree to, and with the said Thomson Mason Affigns, That He the said Wm nant Servant, well and tru

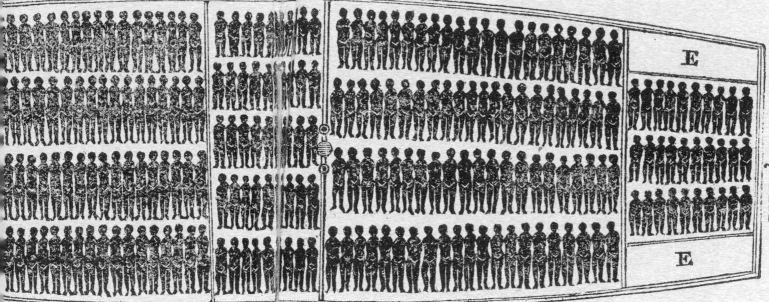

ROOM. BOYS' OOM. WOMEN'S ROOM. GIRLS' ROOM.

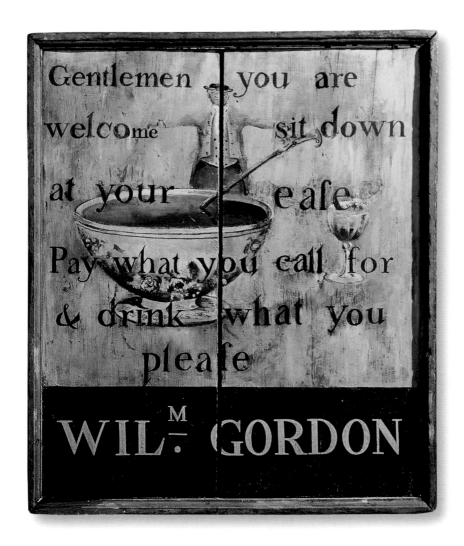

manufacturing. But what Americans needed most was a stronger central govern-ment to keep them from the folly of falling into debt and dependence on England or any other country.

The adoption of the federal Constitution of 1787, establishing a strong new national government, did not in itself guarantee a more independent economy. There were still those who thought that America could make her way in the world most effectively by concentrating on what was most economically profitable—agriculture. Disagreements over this and other matters would split the country into opposing political parties. But while politicians and the rest of the country argued, a new element had entered the picture, an element that changed the mean-ing of manufacturing.

The word "manufacture" is today indelibly associated with machinery. In 1780 the word still meant what the word's roots imply: to make by hand. When Amer-icans argued about manufacturing things themselves, they were talking about making things by hand. But in England an inventor, Richard Arkwright, had devised a way of spinning cotton into thread that was stronger than cotton thread spun by hand. Strong enough so that cloth could be made entirely of cotton (hith-erto it had to be mixed with linen). The invention was a closely guarded secret, for it enabled England—and England alone—to produce cotton cloth that was light,

cheap, and durable. But such secrets do not keep indefinitely. In 1789 a young Englishman named Samuel Slater, who had worked for six years with Arkwright's machine, arrived in New York posing as a farm laborer. He carried details of the machine in his head (an early instance of industrial espionage), and in 1793 in Pawtucket, Rhode Island, Slater built one for a firm started by the Brown family, the state's wealthiest clan of merchants. In the same year inventor Eli Whitney, a Connecticut man visiting in Georgia, devised the first cotton gin to separate cotton fibers from the seeds.

Thus, with an idea stolen from the former mother country, combined with Yankee ingenuity, the American industrial revolution began, hard on the heels of the political revolution. Overseas commerce would continue to attract American entrepreneurs in the years ahead. But the debate as to whether the United States should devote any of its energies to manufacturing was settled by the threads that wound out of Samuel Slater's machine. It would be many years before manufacturing took the place of agriculture as the principal way to make a living in America. The very invention of the cotton-spinning machinery would turn the Southern states not to manufacturing but to growing cotton. But in the end the machine would triumph, even on the farm itself. As the 19th century opened, a decade after Slater built his first mill, the transformation had already begun.

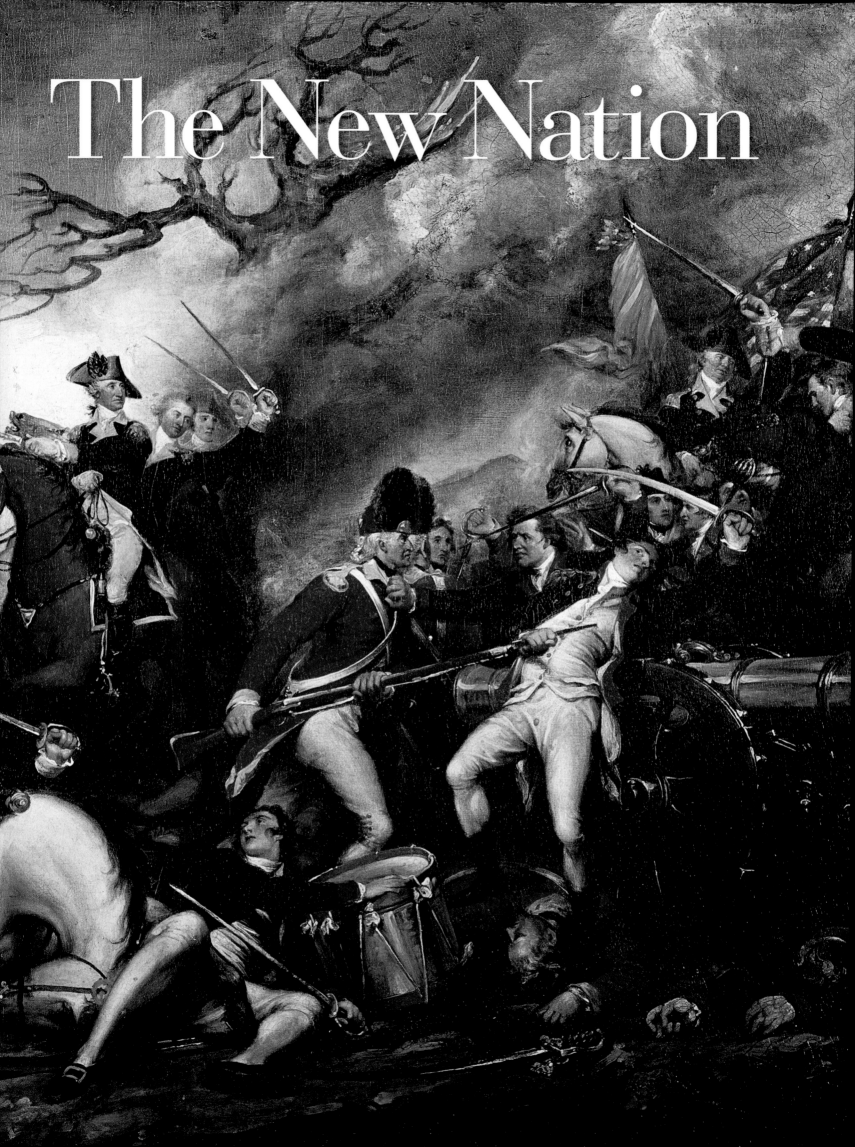

The New Nation

"O! ye that love mankind! Ye that dare oppose not only

the tyranny but the tyrant, stand forth!"

—THOMAS PAINE

BY EDWARDS PARK

Boston's Old State House (opposite), built to serve the crown, was on King Street in the fall of 1774 when Gen. Thomas Gage warned London that his small army, entrenched in Boston, could no longer maintain British rule. After the Revolution, the State House changed its address to State Street.

PRECEDING PAGES

Yankee John Trumbull crammed his "Death of General Mercer at the Battle of Princeton" with heroic posturing. The Americans won.

Horseflies buzzed through the open windows of Philadelphia's State House to pester the delegates. All who later looked back on those meetings in the heat of summer in 1776, recalled the oratory, often of earthshaking importance, being punctuated by occasional slaps. But no annoyance could deter the Second Continental Congress from voting to form a new nation out of 13 British colonies—a concept so daring that delegates risked eventual hanging by even mentioning it. That young, red-haired Virginia delegate, Thomas Jefferson, had put it into carefully crafted words, penning it out at his specially made portable desk. He had declared that our America no longer belonged to Great Britain. We were "Free and Independent."

The approval of the Declaration of Independence on July 2 stirred John Adams of Massachusetts, a man of sudden enthusiasms and despairs, to write to his beloved Abigail that the day "ought to be solemnized with Pomp and Parade, with Shews, Games, Sports, Guns, Bells, Bonfires and Illuminations from one end of this Continent to the other from this time forward forever more." The date for this celebration was later pushed to the Fourth of July. The actual signing of the document by most of the delegates and their presiding officer, John Hancock of the fabled signature, did not occur until August 2.

The idea of actually breaking away from the mother country had seemed unthinkable even after muskets blazed and men died in April 1775, and again in June at Boston's Bunker (really Breeds) Hill. The debate over independence was officially kept from the public, but of course word leaked out, and Philadelphians, walking past the State House, glanced at it with worried eyes. Independence was not only a frightening thought; it was presumptuous. As it was being debated, the

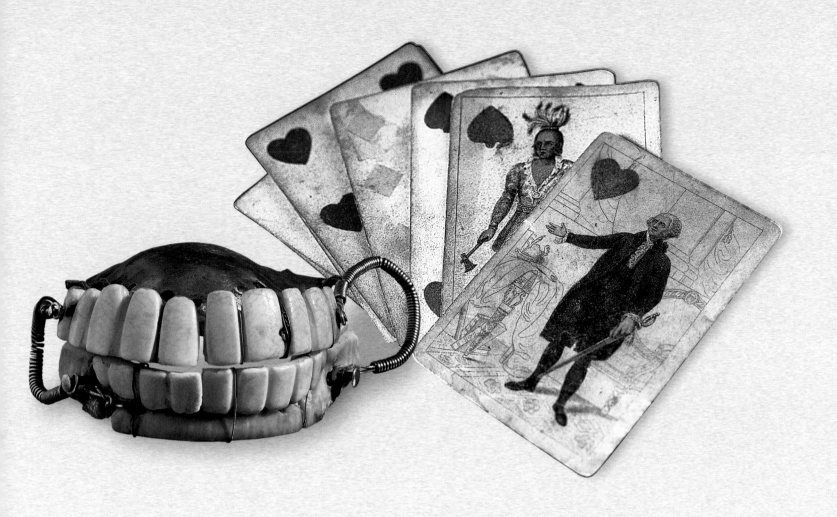

The little luxuries of colonial life

A splendid quilt evokes Sunday morning serenity in a New England village: Parishioners gather from homes around the tree-lined common, greet each other, and file into church (to writhe furtively in discomfort for perhaps a three-hour sermon). Work like quilting would be taboo on the Sabbath, as would playing cards. Even New Englanders, told that cards were "the devil's picture-books," would likely succumb to a deck with George Washington on the ace of hearts. He gestures toward his false teeth, one of several sets he tried in his battle against abscesses that began when he lost a tooth at 22. John Greenwood, judged America's finest dentist, carved these teeth of walrus or hippopotamus ivory set in gold, warning the President that their discoloration was "Ocationed either by your soaking them in port wine, or your drinking it." The granddaughter of an early governor wore the brocaded slipper for her wedding. Had she been of German descent, she might have kicked it off during the feast. Then, if some young blade snatched it, tradition had her buy it back with a bottle of wine before she could start the dance.

largest transatlantic fleet ever seen—more than 400 British ships—arrived off New York with more than 30,000 redcoats and German mercenaries. And, as the resolution was being approved, this mighty army was successfully invading the New York area. It seemed likely that "the child Independence…now struggling for birth," as Boston's firebrand, Sam Adams, described it, would miscarry.

Though the word "independence" was seldom heard until the summer of '76, the notion of freedom, of liberty, was as old as British America, as ancient as Britain herself. In its name, our forefathers came here. And it was as free subjects of the crown that we'd aired our complaints about what we considered parental injustice over taxes and harsh parental punishments for our rebelliousness. Actually, we colonists had left home so long ago and lived so far away that we could be considered a separate race. At first we'd faced a host of troubles barely known in Britain, from tropical heat to arctic cold, from gnats to tomahawks. We'd stuck it out, even prospered. And our environment shaped us into a new people, different from our British relatives.

We looked different. Plenty of good food and hard work had tended to make our country people—the large majority of us—taller and huskier than the folks back home. George Washington, at nearly six-feet-three, usually towered above admiring visitors, who wrote impressions of him. But several of his officers and many of the buckskin-clad riflemen in his army also topped six feet.

We spoke differently. We'd first come here with the varied accents of the shires and regions where we were born. Puritans of New England, for example, usually came from East Anglia—the counties of Suffolk, Norfolk, Essex, and others where their faith was strong—bringing with them their native 17th-century speech. It tended to forget the "r" when it occurred before a consonant. Back in England, that speech habit faded over the years. But not in New England. (Modern Yankees still complain that it's "hahd to pahk near Hahvahd Yahd.") Similarly, many Virginians came from England's southwestern counties, bringing their own words and accent—soft and drawn out. That changed in England but not here. Our language was flavored by the Scots and Irish; it picked up German, French, a great many Dutch, and, later, Spanish words; and it bewildered the rest of the world with Indian place-names.

We had a different outlook. Three thousand miles of ocean, which took about a month to cross, forced us to solve our own problems without waiting for parental decisions. We Americans had faced troubles together and respected each other

"If a nation expects to be ignorant and free…it expects what never was and never will be," wrote Thomas Jefferson, champion of public education. From the earliest days Americans fostered schooling, starting with three- or four-year-olds learning from hornbooks (above), so named because transparent horn guarded lessons from grubby hands. The New England Primer (opposite) was an alphabet of Puritan maxims for 17th-century pupils, who learned it by rote and had it "good dinged into 'em" by rod. Their forebears had left an England where schools abounded and literacy was soaring. After the Revolution, literacy in America was probably higher than it was in England.

A   In *Adam's* Fall
We Sinned all.

B   Thy Life to Mend
This *Book* Attend.

C   The *Cat* doth play
And after flay.

D   A *Dog* will bite
A Thief at night.

E   An *Eagles* flight
Is out of fight.

F   The Idle *Fool*
Is whipt at School.

with little regard for social status. We had gained independence, in fact, about a century and a half before we declared it. Our nation's first sire was the Atlantic Ocean. "Proteus rising from the sea" should take his bow along with George Washington.

By July 1776, about a third of us fully supported our Declaration of Independence. Another third opposed it. The rest wanted only to be left alone. But the Revolution's battles and their effects struck at all our daily lives as randomly as summer storms. Picture a subsistence farm wrenched out of the stony soil of New Hampshire. The farmhouse is small and sturdy, its walls sloping inward a few inches as they rise, to better bear the weight of snow. Sheds, privy, and barn are all attached to the house, so most winter chores can be done without plowing through drifts.

Father—tall, bony, leather-tough—pastures a few sheep and cattle, pens hogs and chickens, plants corn and sometimes buckwheat. He usually consults stages of the moon for various phases of farmwork. He wonders if that really matters, but at least it can't hurt. He probably sets out his corn the old-fashioned way, in

rows of little hummocks. And he may remember with a grin the rhyme to explain the traditional five kernels:

> *One for the cutworm, one for the crow,*
> *One for the woodchuck, and two to grow.*

The boys do the milking; the girls churn butter, make cheese, help Mother with the cooking. Whoever happens to pass the chicken coop gathers a few fresh eggs. The family eats well. Mother sometimes bakes an apple pie for breakfast, and there's always a pot of baked beans kept warm on the hearth. Deer and occasionally bear offer a change. Bear meat, at least down in Virginia, is "very savory," according to that most entertaining diarist, William Byrd II. He recalled a chaplain who "lov'd it so passionately that he would growl like a Wild-Cat over a Squirrel."

Sometimes the New England wartime farmer and his son drive cattle and perhaps an oxcart of produce to market. They walk, because horses are scarce—thanks to the cursed cavalrymen of both armies. They hope to find a Tory buyer who might pay them real money. The paper money issued by Congress, the continental currency, is…well…"not worth a continental." Their chances of finding

With that purpose, the Boston News-Letter, *the first regular colonial newspaper, began publishing in 1704—"by Authority," meaning British censorship. News of the fighting at Lexington and Concord in 1775 was carried by post riders (above) to newspapers in New York and Philadelphia, city of "B Franklin, Printer," as he signed himself. During a stint in London he worked on this press (opposite). He conceived the cartoon (bottom) of Britannia, colonial limbs amputated, awaiting a fatal thrust from a New England avenging the Stamp Act. The* Pennsylvania Journal *reacted by "expiring," at least for a while. And the* Massachusetts Spy *ran a derivative of Franklin's "Join or Die" as an appeal for unity.*

Tories would be better around New York, but Father has heard tales of the "cowboys" down there—thieves pretending to be either patriot or Tory partisans who'd kill them in a minute to get their cattle. Father's glad to be safe in this strongly patriot colony. Or is it a state?

One night he's wakened by a messenger calling out the militia. Though it's lambing time, he's compelled to obey the summons of his militia captain. He dumps his tasks on those unsung heroes, his wife and children, slips on a linsey-woolsey smock, snatches up his musket, powder horn, and cartouche box for spare flints. He adds a chunk of corn bread—"johnnycake," probably a corruption of journey cake—and hurries off with his neighbors. They know that their long, wearying hike will end in terrifying salvos of artillery and a vast array of redcoats advancing with glittering bayonets.

Officers will beseech the militiamen to stand their ground, to fire, reload, fire again. Then they'll probably run if the redcoats don't. If Father survives, he won't be too sure who won. But he'll have finished another little part of the American Revolution, and home he'll come to a joyful and admiring welcome. Until the next call, he's free to get on with his clearing and planting, his reaping and storing, his shearing, milking, fattening, and butchering. He and his family prefer small steps toward survival rather than those vast, vague dreams of nationhood down in Philadelphia.

The life of this northern family is nearly duplicated on small farms in the South, though some crops are as different as the climate. To the Virginian farmer, the idea of joining up with those strange, distant Yankees to form a nation is hard to swallow. But the great plantations have long amassed wealth, which helps pay for the war.

Picture an old Maryland tobacco plantation—early Georgian house shaded by tall trees, facing a serene inlet, or creek, of Chesapeake Bay. Call it Rose Cove. The planter, well fed and well dressed in the London fashions of a few years ago, wonders if he can keep this family property in these days of warfare. For a hundred years merchant ships have slipped in and moored at the long pier, which bridges the silted shore and reaches deep water. As sailors unload whatever furnishings the mistress of Rose Cove has ordered from London, slaves roll great hogsheads of tobacco—four feet tall, nearly the same in diameter—from the barns to the

Wise and witty, Ben Franklin's precepts included: "Eat to live, and not live to eat." And "If you would know the Value of Money, go and try to borrow some."

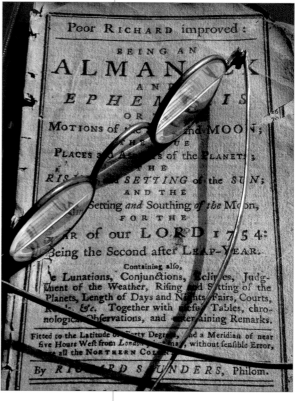

Dozens more appeared for a quarter-century in Ben's Poor Richard's Almanack. Such toil tired his eyes, so he invented these bifocals. "Man of the Signs" (opposite), his limbs and body areas labeled by the zodiac, embellished the 1760 Almanack.

The Anatomy of Man's Body as govern'd by the Twelve Conſtellations.

♈ The Head and Face.

♊ Arms
♌ Heart
♎ Reins
♐ Thighs
♒ Legs

♉ Neck
♋ Breaſt
♍ Bowels
♏ Secrets
♑ Knees

♓ The Feet.

To know where the Sign is.

Firſt Find the Day of the Month, and againſt the Day you have the Sign or Place of the Moon in the 6th Column. Then finding the Sign here, it ſhews the Part of the Body it governs.

The Names and Characters of the Seven Planets.
⊙ Sol, ♄ Saturn, ♃ Jupiter, ♂ Mars, ♀ Venus, ☿ Mercury, ☽ Luna, ☊ Dragons Head and ☋ Tail.

The Five Aspects.
☌ Conjunction,　☍ Oppoſition,　＊ Sextile.
△ Trine,　□ Quartile.

The American Rattlesnake presenting Monsieur his Ally a Dish of Frogs.

British cartoon of 1782—a year after Yorktown ended serious warfare—depicts the rattlesnake America presenting a dish of dead frogs to "Monsieur," its elegantly laced and bewigged friend. Caption warns Britons to "part these Allies," or conquer them both. The Treaty of Paris, ending the war, had not yet been signed.

pier, flattening the ground to make a road, a "rolling road." Profits depend on the planter's factor, his British agent who arranges to ship and sell tobacco. But war with Britain has wrecked this smooth operation. If independence is the outcome, will the old trade ever return?

In early days, a ship's captain sometimes swapped his items, perhaps a Chippendale sofa, for a hogshead, or maybe only a couple of hands—bundles of leaves—of tobacco. Not a farthing was exchanged. This bartering helps account for the shortage of hard cash now that it's badly needed. Military supplies, for example, are at a premium. Troops of both armies scour every plantation for horses, harnesses, food, firewood. American soldiers usually "impress" them, with a promise to repay or return. But as Gen. Nathaniel Greene writes to Thomas Jefferson, "In war it is often impossible to conform to all the ceremonies of law and equal justice." British troops, of course, simply seize what they need as spoils of war.

Prices are soaring, bringing hardship to the poor, staggering even the rich. All have been looking toward Philadelphia with trepidation, as debate droned on about independence. In theory, fine. In practice? Those tied to Britain by trade already expressed disapproval in an early vote in Congress. Maryland (tobacco) and South Carolina (rice and indigo) shouted "Nay" to independence. In recent years, nearly 100 million pounds of Maryland and Virginia tobacco has gone to England, most

TO HIS EXCEL.Y GEN.L | Mr. TRADE & Family or the State of ye NATION | WASHINGTON PAT·PAT·Æ.

This Plate is humbly Addrefs'd | | by His Obedient Serv.t Tho.s Tradelefs

Oh WASH'GTON is there not some Chosen Curse | Publifhd by Virtue of Parliament not this day in particular —Dec.r 1779 | "Red with uncommon Wrath, to BLAST "those MEN,
"Some Hidden Thunder; in the Stores of Heav'n. | | "Who owe "their Greatnefs to "their Country's RUIN?

of it to be sold to other European countries. Now the trade is over, and the owner of Rose Cove wonders how London, addicted to smoking, feels about it. The price for tobacco must be rising like a rocket.

He recalls hearing that over in Virginia, George Mason, author of the Virginia Bill of Rights on which Jefferson is basing his Declaration, seems sure to hang on to Gunston Hall. That plantation is like a small village: school, foundry, forge, shops for carpenter, cooper, shoemaker. Mason and another Virginian, Richard Harrison, have established a trading connection with the West Indies. From there, goods can be shipped to Britain—and all of Europe.

Soon, when callers drop in at Rose Cove (sometimes staying a week or two), they relish, as usual, the crabmeat and huge oysters on the dining room table, and the glasses of choice Madeira, the gift of a trading captain. But outside, instead of the cries of osprey, they hear the sounds of saws, adzes, hammers as yet another schooner takes shape. She will join the Bay's growing fleet of fast, quick-handling trading vessels—fine for running small cargoes to the Indies, perfect for a little privateering thrown in.

In the sixth year of the Revolution, the French suddenly turned the war's dark days as bright as their white uniforms. Ben Franklin's tactful tongue and wily

A ragged "Mr. Trade" and his scarecrow family are "reduced to Beggary" in war-ravaged America. This 1779 cartoon, "Published by Virtue of Parliament," levels a pen at George Washington, riding to hounds over barren meadows while cities burn. Such men, snarls the text, "owe their greatness to their Country's RUIN."

intellect were largely responsible for French aid. When at last the fine British army of Lord Cornwallis fell into a trap at Yorktown, in the summer of 1781, the French and Americans moved south from New England and New York to Williamsburg. The French ate so many frogs along the way, claimed bemused country people, that for years not a spring peeper sounded beside their route. At Virginia's former capital, they joined forces with Washington's Continentals. Clean, well-trained French soldiers and dashing cavalry troopers goggled the eyes of country folk. And the cannon! People stared at the big guns, new, accurate, and served by artillerymen who knew precisely how to use them. The French also brought a "war chest" for military funds. It was so heavy that, when set down in a first-floor room at a house in Williamsburg, it collapsed the floor and ended up in the basement.

On October 9 the allied guns opened fire in a siege on Yorktown. They say Washington fired the first shot. The guns roared until October 17. On that day a very brave drummer boy, clad in the scarlet of a British soldier, clambered up on his army's torn breastworks, frantically beating his drum amid the crash and whine of bursting shells. As gunners saw him valiantly sounding the drum call for a parley, they ceased fire. Yorktown citizens, driven out by the battle and sheltered by friends and relatives nearby, were startled by the sudden silence. Warily, they ventured homeward to see what had happened to their town.

Much of it had been devastated by the allied artillery. The story goes that during the thunderous bombardment, one of Yorktown's leading citizens and a Continental officer, Thomas Nelson, pointed out a tall house to the gunners, and told them to aim for it because it was a likely place for the British to set up their headquarters. How did he know? "Because it's my house," he answered. And it was bombarded, along with many other fine residences.

Other cities suffered damage during the long war, but with hordes of gifted carpenters coming home from the army, towns rang with the sounds of repairing and rebuilding. After peace was signed in 1783, Boston, its seaborne commerce barely afloat, found British merchantmen warping up to its docks laden with impractical gimcracks for sale to gullible Yankees. Sam Adams noted testily that the British hoped "to revive that foolish prediliction that we once had for British Manufactures and British manners."

Boston and other cities had reached a high level of urban comfort in their last days of colonialism. Lamps glowed at night along paved streets, well drained and

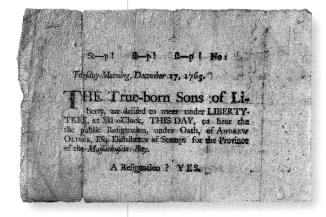

In a British cartoon, bestial Sons of Liberty tar and feather a customs agent for serving the crown, then give him more tea than any stomach could hold. The Sons alerted colonists to royal plans and actions.

A note, or printed squib like this, mobilized them. To break a Tory's will, patriots relied less on violence than on threats. Mention of tar and feathers could force a crown official to resign or take to the woods, for simmering pine tar, first mentioned during the Crusades, could kill him. Feathers were mere frippery.

The BOSTONIAN'S Paying the EXCISE-MAN, or TARRING & FEATHERING

Plate I.   London Printed for Robt Sayer & J. Bennett, Map & Printseller No 53. Fleet Street as the Act directs 31 Octr 1774

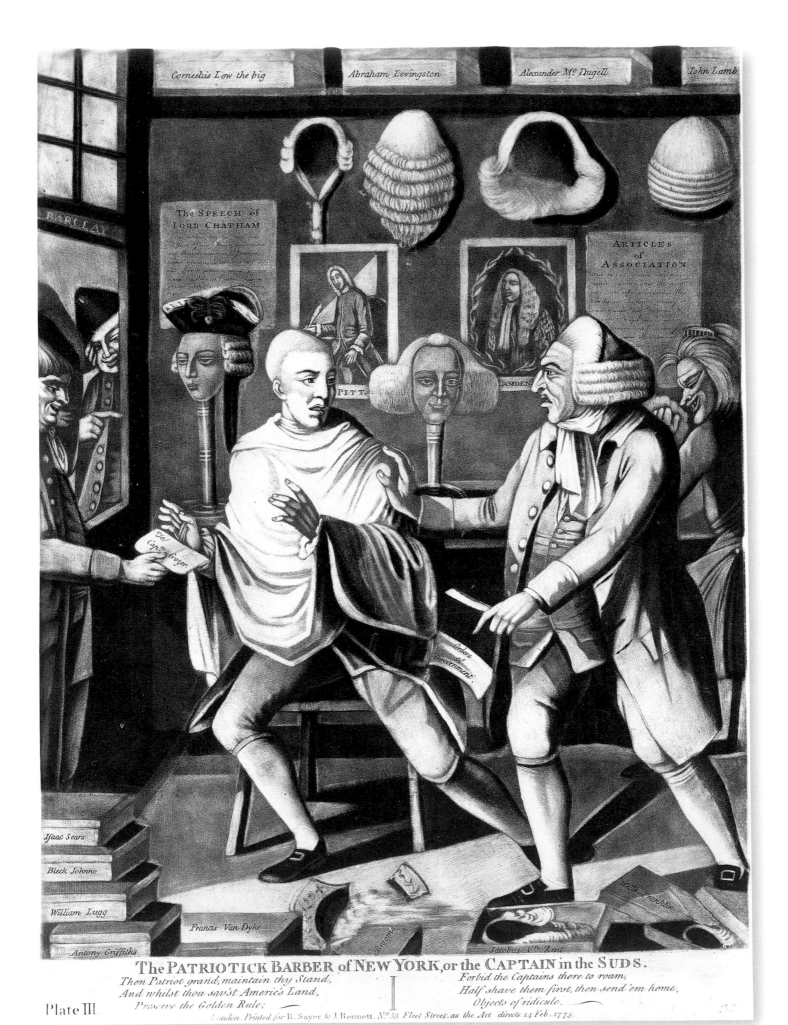

The PATRIOTICK BARBER of NEW YORK, or the CAPTAIN in the SUDS.

Then Patriot grand, maintain thy Stand,
And whilst thou sav'st Americ's Land,
Preserve the Golden Rule;

Forbid the Captains there to roam,
Half shave them first, then send 'em home,
Objects of ridicule.

Plate III.

London, Printed for R. Sayer & J. Bennett, No. 53 Fleet Street, as the Act directs 14 Feb. 1775.

often flanked by sidewalks, or at least a series of posts to safeguard people on foot from drays and carriages. Traffic was notoriously heavy on Boston's narrow streets (said to follow cow paths) and in Philadelphia, our largest city. Speeding was the main problem. Often pedestrians had to jump for their lives. And the noise! A student in Philadelphia wrote that "the thundering of Coaches, Chariots, Chaises, Waggons, Drays, and the whole Fraternity of Noise almost assail continuously our Ears." Ferries and "canows" eased pressure when streams were handy.

Urban populations had sagged during the war. Philadelphia, boasting about 40,000 in 1775, sliced that figure almost in half a year later. But with the peace treaty signed in 1783, trade with Britain resumed, and the cities rebounded.

By treaty, the Loyalist problem had to be settled. Many Tories had suffered egregiously at the hands of so-called patriots, who beat them, tarred and feathered them, vandalized and burned their homes. Those serving the crown got the worst of it. Governor Thomas Hutchinson of Massachusetts, a devoted American, traced his lineage back to the famous Anne Hutchinson, who was exiled from that colony in 1637 for her outrageously liberal religious views. In 1774 Thomas was also banished for stating with equal candor his staunchly Loyalist political views. So, for being every inch the king's man, upholding the crown's edicts with firmness, Hutchinson was labeled a tyrant and a peril to all humanity. He and other Loyalist Americans were hustled off to England, and there, as the historian G. O. Trevelyan wrote, "condemned to stand by, idle and powerless, while the two nations, which they equally loved, were tearing at each other's vitals." Poor, homesick Hutchinson noted that he'd "rather die in a little country farmhouse in New England than in the best nobleman's seat."

Many of these despised, but often heroic, people regained acceptance by their old neighbors and returned home. The poorer found freedom on the frontier, moving through the Appalachians on trails blazed by Daniel Boone. A number of well-to-do merchants, true to the king, went to live in Britain, often amid sniffs of disapproval by relatives because they were "in trade" and therefore not gentry.

Straining at ropes, levering, shoving with staves, New York Sons of Liberty topple the gilded George III from his domination of Bowling Green on July 9, 1776. People have just heard the Declaration of Independence. The city roars with cheers. The statue's gilt will fund the cause. Its inner lead, trundled to Litchfield, Connecticut, will make about 42,000 bullets.

Some, especially from the South, found havens in Bermuda and the Bahamas. A suggestion that Loyalists settle Australia fell flat when shiploads of British convicts, deported for petty crimes, tried to disembark, as usual, in America. Officials of the new republic turned them away. So convicts with little use for the crown headed for Australia, and Americans who had sacrificed and bled for it remained in limbo. A large number of loyal families resettled in Ontario and the Maritime Provinces of Canada.

Newly thriving trade brought a healthy flow of money to our shores. A new merchant class arose, rich and often a bit crude in the eyes of the old aristocracy. A Bostonian of impeccable family complained that "fellows who would have cleaned my shoes five years ago now rode in chariots." And at dancing schools, couples, puffy of physique and awkward of manner, tried to learn the grace required for the minuets and gavottes of the well-bred. Balls were frequent in Charleston. That charming city, built, so goes the saying, where the Ashley and Cooper rivers join to form the Atlantic Ocean, offered the coolness of sea air to rich planters from the humid inland. Under the moon, music wafted across broad lawns of great houses, as handsome blades and exquisite belles flirted over silver punch bowls. Poor folk, meanwhile, found joy in taverns.

Even staid old Philadelphia suffered "the wanton Frolicks of sundry intoxicated Bucks and Blades of the City." But more than street drunks engrossed its people. For debates hummed again in the Old State House as the new nation's best intellects constructed a constitutional government that would work for 13 states as diverse as New England in February and Georgia in July. Haggling, compromising, sending up trial balloons, trying to shoot them down, 55 delegates sweated through the hot months of 1787, and at last came up with the world's first written Constitution. At Ben Franklin's request, they all signed it, and the wise old sage, noting the sun painted on the back of George Washington's chair, remarked that he now had "the happiness to know, that it is a rising, and not a setting sun."

In 1789, George Washington began his term as first President, and in 1790 the states' ratification of the Constitution was completed. Six states wanted some specific guaranteed rights, and, after some debate, the Congress agreed to add ten amendments. They became known as the Bill of Rights, giving us our freedoms of religion, speech, the press, the right to assemble and petition, to bear arms, to get a speedy jury trial and, through curbs on the government's judicial powers, to get justice.

TO ALL BRAVE, HEALTHY, ABLE BODIED, AND WELL DISPOSED YOUNG MEN,

IN THIS NEIGHBOURHOOD, WHO HAVE ANY INCLINATION TO JOIN THE TROOPS,
NOW RAISING UNDER

GENERAL WASHINGTON,

FOR THE DEFENCE OF THE

LIBERTIES AND INDEPENDENCE
OF THE UNITED STATES,

Against the hostile designs of foreign enemies,

TAKE NOTICE,

THAT _Tuesday, Wednsday Thursday, Friday and Saturday at Spotswood in_ _Middlesex_ county, attendance will be given by _Lieutenant Reading_ with his music and recruiting party of company in _Major Shute's_ Battalion of the 11th regiment of infantry, commanded by Lieutenant Colonel Aaron Ogden, for the purpose of receiving the enrollment of such youth of SPIRIT, as may be willing to enter into this HONOURABLE service.

The ENCOURAGEMENT at this time, to enlist, is truly liberal and generous, namely, a bounty of TWELVE dollars, an annual and fully sufficient supply of good and handsome cloathing, a daily allowance of a large and ample ration of provisions, together with SIXTY dollars a year in GOLD and SILVER money on account of pay, the whole of which the soldier may lay up for himself and friends, as all articles proper for his subsistance and comfort are provided by law, without any expence to him.

Those who may favour this recruiting party with their attendance as above, will have an opportunity of hearing and seeing in a more particular manner, the great advantages which these brave men will have, who shall embrace this opportunity of spending a few happy years in viewing the different parts of this beautiful continent, in the honourable and truly respectable character of a soldier, after which, he may, if he pleases return home to his friends, with his pockets FULL of money and his head COVERED with laurels.

GOD SAVE THE UNITED STATES.

Want to join up? $12 bounty; handsome clothing; good food; $60 a year in gold and silver!
Here's how you'll use your musket by the numbers—11 positions, from "Poise" through "Fire"
to "Ram Down Cartridge." In action, you may be able to fire three shots a minute. Rifles
(opposite), German in origin, are slower—but deadly. Backwoodsmen swear they can hit
game so far away that they salt bullets to keep the meat from spoiling before they can get to it.

We weren't sure what, exactly, a presidency meant. Many of us instinctively turned back to the familiar notion of monarchy—an American King George. But Washington, who had risked his neck to get away from the other King George, was outraged at the idea. He tried to establish precedents that gave his position dignity, even a touch of awe, and more than two centuries later we still feel that the presidency is special—different from monarch or prime minister and presumably better than both.

We Americans had wide spaces to settle, especially after Napoleon sold us the huge French territory of Louisiana to finance his war with England. It stretched from New Orleans north to the source of the Mississippi and west to the Rockies. We were amazed at all we suddenly owned and sent Lewis and Clark to explore it. And we ordinary Americans probed it, too, crossing the eastern ranges into the Ohio country, the Bluegrass country, the Old Northwest (Illinois and Indiana), and along the great rivers to the greatest of all, the Mississippi.

West of the Appalachians, new buildings began clustering around taverns and stores, and towns were born. Travelers, by horseback or wagon, jammed crude roads that sometimes turned into almost bottomless mud. An Illinois stage driver swore that though he'd driven the same mule team for months, he didn't know what color the mules were, for all he could see of them was their ears. Some highways, like the famed National Road that ran west from Cumberland, Maryland, were graveled to keep big Conestoga wagons from sinking out of sight. Inns sprouted along such routes, offering generally poor food (washed down with corn liquor) and bedrooms, each with two beds for four people. Sexes were segregated, and, said an English traveler, the clientele was so filthy that "it is extremely difficult in this warm climate to keep free from bedbugs."

Travel by boat along waterways was far less arduous. Canals intrigued President Washington, and he foresaw them opening Ohio farmlands to eastern ports. Raised to be handy around the farm and generally surrounded by plenty of wood, we Americans could whittle anything, usually knew basic carpentry, and were fascinated by machines. In Britain, steam engines had developed steadily since Thomas Newcomen's 1712 mining pump, using steam in a cylinder. We soon were experimenting with steamboats, and an inventive artist, Robert Fulton, built one that chugged up the Hudson from New York to Albany, proving that such vessels could carry passengers and make a profit.

Fulton also came up with a submarine that sailed on the surface, then with mast collapsed, submerged and moved by manpower. He demonstrated it to a commission appointed by Napoleon. No sale. Fulton's was not our first submarine. During the Revolution, a Connecticut Yankee, David Bushnell, designed a submarine aptly named *Turtle,* to blast blockading British warships. It carried one man who pedaled and cranked his way, unnoticed amid floating debris, to his target vessel, then submerged in order to screw a mine against the enemy hull. He was unable to attach the mine. But the British ship moved uneasily away.

I n 1794, Congress appropriated money to build six warships for the protection of American merchantmen against the pirates off Africa's Barbary Coast. They did well, and our little Navy gained self-respect, even grudging admiration from the British. So when our nation drifted toward renewed warfare with Britain in the early 1800s, we Americans were not entirely despondent over our chances. Causes of the dispute? Partly anger at Britain's refusal to regard us as a separate nation. Continually battling Napoleon's France, Britain's navy denied us trade with much of Europe, and their officers felt free to board our ships in search of their own seamen who had deserted. Impressment and loss of trade roused our hackles. A new breed of young politicians, mostly from the South and the newly admitted western states—Kentucky, Tennessee, and Ohio—saw this as a perfect time to take on Britain, absorbed as she was with Napoleon. Their main goal was to acquire Canada.

We'd tried that in 1775 when Benedict Arnold, arguably our best fighting general before his defection, led a party of handpicked troops up Maine's Kennebec River and down Quebec's Chaudière—an all but impassable wilderness route to the shores of the St. Lawrence. They almost captured Quebec City, the bastion that held the key to all Canada. But not quite. Now the "War Hawks" of Congress, led by Henry Clay, wanted to try for that country again, and got the ear of President Madison. Before we quite realized it, we were at war.

The War of 1812, or "Mr. Madison's War," was generally disastrous. We like to remember the early victories of our Navy, especially the glorious triumphs of

Recruiting posters (page 70) didn't mention Valley Forge. In this bleak encampment near Philadelphia, Washington's Continentals wintered in 1777-78, building huts, huddling in ragged clothes, slowly starving while enemy troops lolled in the city they had captured. Farmers sold food to the British for sound money rather than to Americans for promises.

the 44-gun frigate *Constitution* ("Old Ironsides,"), now docked in Boston. We like to forget that British blockaders eventually bottled up our ships and captured several thousand of our privateer seamen. As for our army, we recall Fort McHenry's gallant defense of Baltimore, when Francis Scott Key wrote our national anthem, but we hate being reminded of the burning of Washington, the abject surrender of Detroit and Fort Dearborn (later named Chicago), and our failed attempts to invade Canada. Our only major victory, at New Orleans, is worth remembering, because we whipped a huge force of crack British troops, victors at Waterloo, and regained a lot of badly shattered honor. That battle proved nothing, because peace had already been signed in Europe. But no army invaded us again, and our nation earned a nod of respect from others.

A coach rumbles on cobbles near a Philadelphia hotel (opposite). The city played host to the Founding Fathers so well that John Adams feared he'd "be killed with the kindness" in drawing

Before the Battle of New Orleans, during the bleakest days of that senseless and despised war, bitter feelings arose in regions dependent on trade, especially New England. So badly did commerce suffer there that one Massachusetts town vowed its people were "ready to resist unto blood." Resist the British? No. The U.S. government!

When peace talks stalled and British troops occupied eastern Maine, New England's leaders met at Hartford, Connecticut, to seek ways to survive. The moderates prevailed, but ideas for signing a separate peace had been discussed, and even the word "secession" was whispered. Peace came before the Hartford Convention stirred any action by the Yankees. But perhaps the thought lingered. The word secession would be shouted half a century later.

A new peacetime. Again, our cities grow, and our ships now cover the globe. Visitors arrive from Europe to see what this odd thing—democracy—is all about. Perhaps they criticize our ways, our manners, our lack of culture, but they notice a special, enviable exuberance in us. For we are at last undisputedly Americans, a new breed. And we're on the move. Westward lies the great expanse that leads to the Pacific. We'll settle it all. It's our manifest destiny.

rooms glinting in candle-light. Philadelphia was the national capital through the 1790s, while the city of Washington took shape.

Forging the Links

Enjoying stately travel on an Erie Canal boat, passengers escape stagecoach perils. "You push along so slick," said one, "there's no chance of getting one's neck broke...." To attract genteel customers, boat owners used horses rather than mules. They plodded at the speed limit: four miles an hour.

PRECEDING PAGES: *Steamboats, still plying the Mississippi into the 20th century, take on passengers and cargo at Memphis, Tennessee. Navigating the river in the steamboats' heyday, sounders yelled the depth—"By the mark, twain"—and gave river pilot Samuel Clemens his pen name.*

"It was kind of solemn, drifting down the big, still river, laying on

our backs looking up at the stars...."

— MARK TWAIN

BY WILLIAM H. GOETZMANN

"We rush like a comet into infinite space!" Former Congressman Fisher Ames of Massachusetts was dismayed when he learned in 1803 that President Jefferson had purchased Louisiana. Fourteen disparate states and territories now stretched across the continent. That fragile Union, so carefully nurtured by Federalists such as Ames, was about to be pulled apart, flung across the Mississippi and the "Stoney Mountains" to infinity. The mind reeled. Now, barely into the 19th century, it was clear there might never be a *United* States.

Unlike the Federalists, however, most Americans were optimistic. To them, as to Jefferson, the frontier was the future. A sense of national pride and cultural solidarity developed early in the 19th century. There was, after all, a national government in the new capital city of Washington, based on a specific national document, the Constitution, which was already an object of veneration. The people's representatives—senators from every state, congressmen from every district, and territorial representatives, however remote—assembled in the capital city to determine the course of the nation. Political parties tying these representatives together in common interests had begun to emerge. A Supreme Court under Chief Justice John Marshall had clearly established lines of federal authority. And the national role of the Presidency had been enhanced incalculably by George Washington, man and symbol. Both parties—Federalist and Democratic-Republican—and most regions of the country were agreed upon a common currency and a national bank, as well as the need for roads and a national defense.

Poets and orators, preachers and educators—speaking in English, the national language—proclaimed the ties that bound Americans together as "one people under God." However, the process of tying the nation together was technological as much as political, intellectual, linguistic, and symbolic. Technology's task was nothing less than subduing a continent, much of which was still a wilderness. Most machines, gadgets, and techniques took on a peculiarly American style: lighter, cheaper, faster, easier to build, more specialized, and not designed for permanence.

On the earliest trails, many of them enlarged Indian paths, travel was difficult and dangerous. It was practically impossible to transport a heavy load, especially across the Appalachians to the "Western" settlements. It took a man on horseback nearly three months to struggle from Massachusetts to the Carolinas, if he made it at all; gangs of bandits preyed on lone travelers along the gloomy forest trails. Horses, wagons, and stagecoaches carried the itinerant peddler, the mail or post rider, the traveler, the circuiting preacher, lawyer, doctor, judge. Nearly every rural family depended on the horse.

Stagecoaches took some of the risk and discomfort out of overland travel and added a measure of speed. "We were rattled from Providence to Boston in four hours and fifty minutes," wrote one traveler in 1822. "If anyone wants to go faster he may send to Kentucky [for a Thoroughbred] and charter a streak of lightning!" Roads were almost uniformly bad; as late as 1904 only 7 percent of public roads in the United States were surfaced.

The bulk of traffic went by sea. Sloops and schooners plied the coastal lanes, sometimes turning inland up Chesapeake Bay, the Potomac, the Cooper, or the Hudson to stop at scattered river towns or planters' wharves, take on cargo, and deliver the news. Beyond the mountain barrier, traffic also moved on water, but the shortest distances weren't always straight lines. To trade with the East on any large scale, settlers had to ship their goods down the Mississippi, across the Gulf of Mexico, and up the Atlantic Coast. They felt they needed transmountain roads, and they blamed Eastern capital and the new government for keeping them in isolation by ignoring repeated demands.

From the beginning American entrepreneurs and statesmen foresaw the West as a great inland market and source of raw materials. They realized the precarious nature of a Union cut in half by the Appalachian Mountains. In 1806 Congress finally authorized a National Road from Cumberland, Maryland, to Wheeling, then in western Virginia; it was completed in 1818. But when Congress approved federal funds in 1817 to connect Washington with the Southern states and aid in other "internal improvements," President Madison vetoed what he thought was an undue extension of federal power. By then, most Southerners agreed with the

Oceangoing vessels and Chesapeake and Ohio Canal boats crowd Washington's port of Georgetown in the mid–19th century. An aqueduct across the Potomac connected with Alexandria, Virginia. As work began on the C & O Canal in 1828, 40 miles to the north entrepreneurs were beginning the end of the canal era by founding the Baltimore and Ohio, the nation's first major railroad.

King Cotton's long reign

Drawn to the fertile bottomlands and plains of Alabama and Mississippi early in the 19th century, migrants founded the Cotton Kingdom, making fortunes with slave labor and Yankee Eli Whitney's gin, which extracted seeds from cotton fibers. Next came farmers who had worn out the soil by growing tobacco in the Carolinas and Georgia. While the kingdom flourished in the 1840s, so did antislavery sentiment in the North. After the Civil War, King Cotton still reigned: Like these cotton pickers of about 1870 (opposite), many former slaves eked out a living on the old plantations. Cheap black labor also kept this tobacco factory humming in Richmond, Virginia (above).

President: If the government subsidized roads, it would most likely get the funds through a tariff system that would raise the price of foreign goods exchanged for Southern cotton. Many Northerners agreed. Their own roads were relatively good, and they feared losing even more of their population if emigration became easier. Many a desperately needed federal road bill was detoured forever by sectional rivalries and constitutional debate.

Thus most roadbuilders had to risk their own capital. In 1794 a 62-mile toll road was completed between Philadelphia and Lancaster, Pennsylvania—"which was very much wanted," noted one observer, "as the Old one is very bad, indeed." The new one was America's first macadamized road, "a masterpiece of its kind," said another writer, "…paved with stone the whole way and overlaid with gravel." Its success helped touch off a turnpike craze as builders laid ribbons of gravel or plank, or a rough corduroy of logs, along some crucial route, but this one was among the few that made money. Maintenance was expensive, and toll-gates (where, upon payment, an attendant turned a pike that barred the way) were too easily cir-

A stern-wheeler at Vicksburg, Mississippi, unloads cotton from Brierfield, the plantation of Jefferson Davis, who became the president of the Confederacy. Many steamships on the Mississippi River sank on snags and bars or were destroyed by fire or explosion. The restless river also claimed Brierfield itself, boring a channel that transformed the riverside plantation into an island.

cumvented. In the 1830s the boom fizzled.

Very early, Americans began to think of building canals. In 1804 Simeon DeWitt, surveyor-general of New York, became intrigued with the possibility of connecting the Hudson River with the Great Lakes via a canal through the Mohawk Valley. In 1817, thanks to strong support by DeWitt's cousin, Governor DeWitt Clinton, the New York Assembly authorized construction of the Erie Canal. A handful of self-taught engineers drew up the plans, designed the locks and aqueducts that carried "Clinton's Ditch" over obstructions, and supervised every detail of construction. Thousands of English, Welsh, and Irish immigrants earned their living digging the Erie Canal. Completed in 1825, the canal opened up remote western New York, facilitated travel on the Great Lakes, and launched settlements on their shores as far west as Green Bay and infant Chicago.

The canal brought settlers to upstate New York and spawned a wild, polyglot boom in the towns along its banks. Rome, Troy, Utica, Lockport, and Buffalo became Wild West towns of the day—and eventually the prime target for preachers whose fire and brimstone inspired the nickname, the "burned-over district." The Erie Canal channeled the trade and emotional allegiance of the Old Northwest into New York City, making it the nation's largest port. The city rapidly assumed a commanding role in finance, in commerce, in Atlantic shipping, and, by the 1840s, even in literature and other forms of culture.

The success of the Erie Canal caused a canal-building boom across the country. Canals joined Boston and Lowell, Providence and Worcester, New Haven and Massachusetts' Northampton. The Chesapeake and Ohio Canal linked Cumberland, Maryland, and Alexandria, Virginia. Richmond tapped the West via the James River and Kanawha Canal. The Delaware and Chesapeake bays were connected, and a mainline canal, complete with inclined planes and a portage railroad over the Alleghenies, flowed all the way from Philadelphia to Pittsburgh. The Ohio River was joined to Lake Erie, and an even longer waterway flowed from Toledo, Ohio, to Evansville, Indiana. Fast-growing Chicago reached out to the Mississippi with a canal to the Illinois River. Hundreds of smaller waterways served as feeders to the great canals.

By 1840 Americans had built 3,326 miles of canals. But by then, because of financial collapses and increasing competition from railroads, canal building had all but ceased. Many states defaulted on bond issues, and boomtowns along the towpaths became backwash country villages. Only a few canals, such as the Erie, continued in heavy use.

Even before the building of the Erie Canal, there appeared on the Hudson an invention that would revolutionize water transportation: the steamboat. In August 1807 Robert Fulton proved the commercial value of his craft, popularly called the *Clermont,* by taking passengers from New York to Albany in 32 hours; a sailboat might take four days. Fulton did not invent the steamboat. But from his shallow-draft designs, drawn with an eye to western rivers, emerged an ideal vehicle for tying the country together.

Fulton saw the steamboat as a "cheap and quick conveyance to the merchandise on the Mississippi, Missouri, and other great rivers which are now laying open their treasures to the enterprise of our countrymen." His company proved the steamboat's practicality on western waters in 1811 when the *New Orleans*

"One cannot see too many summer sunrises on the Mississippi," Mark Twain wrote. Artist George Caleb Bingham reflected Twain's sentiments in this 1847 painting, "Lighter Relieving a Steamboat Aground." The boatmen have removed cargo so that the steamboat in the distance can float free. Bingham, a Whig, thus dramatized his party's call for federal funds to dredge rivers.

steamed from Pittsburgh down the Ohio and Mississippi, bound for the boat's namesake city. In Missouri those on board suddenly found themselves in the midst of the great New Madrid earthquake, the worst ever observed outside a volcanic region. As they watched in horror, riverside bluffs caved in, islands were swallowed up, great waves rose and fell, and the channel was utterly obliterated. Ashore the ground rippled and cracked, trees flailed like buggy whips, buildings fell in splinters. The shocks continued for two weeks. The *New Orleans* steamed right through it all. Three years later, she hit a stump and sank, but by then she had pioneered regular service on the Mississippi. By 1815, steamboats were traveling *up* the Mississippi as well as down.

Some 740 riverboats steamed on western waters by 1850. A revolution had taken place. The West began to control its own economic destiny and draw closer to the East via the river roads. "Steam navigation colonized the West," wrote former Senator James H. Lanman of Connecticut. "Steam is crowding our eastern cities with western flour and western merchants, and loading the western steamboats with eastern emigrants and eastern merchandise. It has advanced the career of national colonization and national production, at least a century!" Another American rhapsodized that a steamboat "brings to the remotest villages of our streams, and the very doors of the cabins, a little Paris, a section of Broadway, or a slice of Philadelphia…."

Steamboats faced a gamut of perils. Between 1811 and 1850, some 44 collided, 166 burned, 209 blew up, and 576 hit obstructions and sank. New technologies, such as the Oliver Evans high-pressure steam engine, Henry Shreve's flat-bottom steamers, and even planned obsolescence (a steamer built to last only five years) produced the fragile grandeur of a nation in a hurry. Steamboats, almost unknown in Europe, were monuments to a kind of ingenuity, symbols of grand days full of life on the Mississippi, floating democratic amalgams of merchants, planters, Indians, gamblers, immigrants, soldiers, and ubiquitous American con men.

If steam worked well on water, why not on land? As early as 1804 Oliver Evans chugged around Philadelphia in a strange, watertight wagon rigged with a paddlewheel astern. Evans' wagon, intended as a river dredge, was America's first steam-driven land vehicle. In 1825 John Stevens built the first American steam locomotive. It was a toy that rattled to nowhere on a circular track at his Hoboken, New Jersey, estate, but it fueled a growing interest in railroads. Four years later,

Colorful westering stagecoaches like this one were scrupulously built and decorated in Concord, New Hampshire. Each coach had its own color scheme and decoration. The shop owner smashed any flawed part "before the eyes of the workmen," so they would know that "no sham work was allowed." It took three or four craftsmen about three weeks to build a Concord coach.

The Pony Express: a wild short ride

WANTED—YOUNG, SKINNY WIRY FELLOWS NOT OVER EIGHTEEN. MUST BE EXPERT RIDERS, WILLING TO RISK DEATH DAILY. ORPHANS PREFERRED.

With that ad in March 1860, the Pony Express began its gallop across Western history. When 19-year-old Richard Egan (opposite) asked for a furlough to get married, he was excused from only one ride. Early riders lingered in the West (right), and some became famous. Buffalo Bill Cody was a rider at 15. James Butler Hickok became "Wild Bill" after a shoot-out while working for Pony Express. A division chief reputedly killed 26 men. He cut off a victim's ear, tanned it, and made it a watch fob. Getting business with posters (left) and deliveries (the letter above carried word of Lincoln's election westward), the Pony Express succeeded. But after only 19 months the telegraph killed it.

Horatio Allen, with no previous experience, demonstrated an English locomotive called the *Cambridge Lion* on a hair-raising, three-mile run through the woods of Pennsylvania.

In 1830 Peter Cooper built and ran the one-and-one-half horsepower *Tom Thumb*, first locomotive to pull a load of passengers in America. It ran on tracks of the newly formed Baltimore and Ohio, one of five railroad companies organized by then. That same year the South Carolina Railroad Company unveiled America's first scheduled steam railroad train. *The Best Friend of Charleston* drew the train between Charleston and nearby towns for six months, then blew up when a fireman sat on a safety valve to silence its irritating hiss.

The earliest trains rolled on wooden rails surfaced with long straps of iron. The straps tended to work loose and curl up under the weight of a passing train, sometimes thrusting up through the floor of a coach— to the consternation of its passengers. Then Robert L. Stevens designed the T-shaped iron rail, safer, stronger, easier to lay. A uniquely American technology began to take shape from the ground up. Europeans laid rails on granite blocks, but Americans quickly switched to wooden ties; they were cheaper and gave a softer ride. American railroads often routed tracks along lines of least resistance, with many twists and turns to climb mountains or dodge obstacles. Some turns proved too tight for heavy, fixed-axle British locomotives. So in 1831 John B. Jervis developed an idea to mount the front wheels in a truck that swiveled to take the sharpest curve.

The American passenger car with its boxlike interior made it difficult to segregate people into class accommodations. Elite Europeans disliked associating with the common people, their pets and small livestock—odors and all. But Americans had no time for niceties. They were in a hurry to get where they were going—especially to get on with exploiting a continent.

The government, now less wary of "undue extensions" of its power, assisted the railroads with a land grant subsidy: 6 alternate sections of land per mile of track, a section being 640 acres. The railroads, which in turn could sell the granted land, launched a massive campaign to lure immigrants out West to build up commerce along the tracks.

In crews that included Irishmen, Chinese (in wide straw hats, below), Indians, and Mexicans, rail workers traveled with their jobs (opposite). In precision moves often supervised by former Union officers, crews pounded ties and plates into position. Then 12 men trotted to the ties with rails 30 feet long. Spike drivers hit each spike three times— ten spikes to a rail—and America moved westward at four rails a minute.

Men of the Northern Pacific proudly pose with visiting families on a bridge over Mosquito Creek in Washington's Cascade Mountains. Soon abandoned when the route shifted to a two-mile tunnel, the spindly bridge symbolized the haste of railroad builders; masonry structures came later. Real railroad wrecks inspired deliberate ones, like this one (opposite, lower), staged in 1896 by William Crush, a railroad official. While some 50,000 Texans watched, two locomotives touched cowcatchers, backed two miles apart, lurched ahead as crews jumped clear, and rammed each other at full speed. Both boilers exploded, killing three and injuring dozens.

With astonishing rapidity, railroads laced America, driving most canals out of business and rivaling or complementing the steamboats. In 1860 the United States was crisscrossed with 30,626 miles of railroads; by 1890, there were nearly 200,000 miles. Railroads made possible the great cattle industry of the Western plains as railheads reached out to meet Texas cattle trails in such Kansas towns as Dodge City, Ellsworth, and Abilene. Railroads made great marketplaces of Kansas City, St. Louis, and Chicago, which became an immense inland port—the place where railroad and steamboat met the Great Lakes and eventually the sea.

The railroad had indeed linked America. It transported people to all parts of the country. It carried the mail and, through Montgomery Ward catalogs, the city's products into the country, gradually connecting country life with city life and reducing the importance of the one-street country town. It also brought Great Plains natural resources into the hinterland, forever altering the Indians' way of life. It made far-off California feel more a part of the Union, though discrimination in freight rates—charging more for one commodity or locale than another, and more per mile for short hauls than for long—made the South feel less so. The railroad created great companies and concentrated great wealth as railroad magnates gobbled up small lines, rigging rates and fares.

Most important, the railroad was a dramatic, visible symbol of national union. After 1869 a citizen or even a foreigner could travel anywhere, through all the states and territories, coast to coast, north or south, without passing through customs or a passport or visa check, as one did in Europe. There was no better evidence of union.

In the heyday of developing transportation systems, a startling idea came to fruition: the notion of the message arriving before the messenger. In 1832 Samuel F. B. Morse, a young American painter with sketchy knowledge of electromagnetism, became convinced that messages could be sent over wires for long distances. But his first instrument could span only a short distance before its signal petered out. By 1837, aided by the discoveries of Princeton physicist Joseph Henry, Morse had invented a system of relays to reinforce fading pulses; now he could telegraph a message accurately over any distance. After years of persuasion, Congress in 1843 voted $30,000 to build an experimental line—a wire strung on poles, with glass drawer knobs as insulators—between Baltimore and Washington. On a spring day in 1844, couriers sped to the capital by train with the news that the Whig convention in Baltimore had nominated Henry

TEN MINUTES FOR REFRESHMENTS.

An 1886 cartoon lampoons the dawn of American fast food: railroad passengers gulping and going during a stop. Train stops usually lasted twenty minutes—though a ten-minute stop, as in this tableau, did happen. Lunchroom owners bribed trainmen to leave early so that food, paid for but not eaten, could be served to the next halted, hungry, and hurrying passengers.

Clay for President. Morse's wire beat the messengers by more than an hour.

The possibilities of Morse's invention were quickly grasped. Henry O'Rielly, an outspoken Irish-born promoter, built 8,000 miles of telegraph line through communities all the way to the Mississippi and the Great Lakes. Newspapers began transmitting Mexican War dispatches over what O'Rielly called "the lightning wire." In 1848 newspapers, banding together for collective use of the wire, formed the Associated Press. Eight years later all the telegraph systems joined in one monopoly called Western Union. In 1861 a telegraph wire was strung from New York to San Francisco, reducing the time between the coasts from days to seconds. The Pony Express was rendered obsolete. The price of gold on the San Francisco Stock Exchange, of grain futures in Chicago, of cotton at the New Orleans Exchange—all this and more could be instantly flashed around the nation, making the country a true national market.

On June 25, 1876, at the Centennial Exhibition in Philadelphia, visitor Dom Pedro II, Emperor of Brazil, picked up a strange device, patented only a few months earlier. He put the instrument to his ear and suddenly exclaimed, "I hear, I hear!" With Alexander Graham Bell's telephone, the message again preceded the messenger, but now in the message one could hear and feel the very presence of the sender. A new age of instantaneous, personalized communication had begun.

The transportation and communications revolutions seem to have linked people together, but whether this is really the case is still an open and important question. Transportation also split people apart, spreading Americans all across the continent, dividing families and ethnic enclaves, effacing local memories, promoting a kind of endless transiency that replaced lasting relationships with tangential and temporary ones.

The transportation revolution promoted the growth of large cities and an eventual clash between urban and rural values that still continues. Industries grew to giants, concentrating factory workers in cities where every day they could see about them the stark contrasts between wealth and poverty. The great railroad strikes of the 1870s sounded a strident warning of social conflict. The rise of the farmer against the railroads spurred the enactment of the Granger laws for "just, reasonable, and uniform rates" and resulted in the creation of the Interstate Commerce Commission in 1887, the first such federal regulatory body.

The profound social process of tying the nation together had been an ambiguous exercise that also seemed to drive it apart. Resolving this cultural paradox remains a major social question of our time.

383-"Jerk-line "twelve" on the old fright ro

The Great West

"Only to the white man was nature a 'wilderness'....To us it was tame....When the very animals of the forest began fleeing from his approach, then it was that for us the 'Wild West' began."

—LUTHER STANDING BEAR
Chief of the Oglala Tribe of the Sioux Nation

BY WILLIAM H. GOETZMANN

When Euro-Americans reached the Mississippi from the East, they confronted a new experience—a land so vast that few could imagine its true extent or its marvelous content. What Thomas Jefferson really bought in 1803 with the Louisiana Purchase was America's future and—in terms of people already there, also Americans—slightly over 9,000 years of history.

Historians and archaeologists have concluded that the high plains, reaching out from the Rocky Mountains onto parts of the Great Plains, formed the Pleistocene corridor through which, 15,000 to 25,000 years ago, early people migrated south from Canada amid the great glaciers. These first Americans valiantly hunted huge woolly mammoths, giant bison, camels, miniature horses, deer, antelope, and giant cave bears, the most dangerous prey of all. They used spears, with wonderfully crafted points (called Clovis Points after the place in New Mexico where the first ones were found), stone and even ice clubs, as well as the ingenious atl-atl that could hurl a projectile right through a giant deer or antelope. They are believed to have decimated the game wherever they were. And this, as much as the recession of the glaciers about 9000 to 8500 B.C., caused a change in the megafauna.

Most scholars believe that the Great West is the site of the earliest settlers in North America. Indians, or "First Americans," came some 60 centuries later, when the Great Plains were uplifted and drier than the last days of the Ice Age with its tremendous meltwater covering. The hunter-gatherer peoples in the Rocky Mountain area and the Cahokia moundbuilding peoples moved onto the plains. Mounds to the west and in the Deep South were outposts of the great Cahokia civilization and perhaps that of the Ohio-Mississippi Valley moundbuilders, whose snakelike structures and smaller mounds could be found as far east as Virginia, where Jefferson did his archaeologizing.

Promotional guides contained more raves than directions. "The loveliest… country on earth," exclaimed Hall J. Kelley in his 1831 book on Oregon— a place he had never seen.

PRECEDING PAGES
The rig is a "jerkline twelve"—a dozen horses, long reins, and a strong-armed man. The freight road is somewhere in the Great West.

Tribes from all directions peopled the Great Plains with Americans. The Sioux or Lakota, pushed out by the Ojibway from Minnesota, made the Missouri River country their hunting grounds. Apache moved south from Canada onto the western Great Plains. Then, pressed by the Lakota, Cheyenne, and Comanche, the Apache moved into what the white men would call the Southwest. After the revolution generated by the introduction of the horse from Spanish Mexico in the 1740s, the Comanche, in alliance with the Kiowa, commanded much of the southern plains.

The Shoshone, the Crow, and the Blackfeet dominated the northern Rockies, while Ute and Apache commanded the southern Sierras. In the Northwest, along the Columbia River, were Gros Ventre, Flathead, Nez Perce, Chinook, Walla Walla, Yakima, Salish, and Clatsop. These tribes often traded with the fierce Tlingit and Haida to the north in Canada. A whole Columbia River Basin trade system existed, with river tribes trading salmon for ingeniously carved weapons and canoes, as well as fantastically decorated shawls and blankets. A significant number of these items crossed over the northern Rockies to the sedentary tribes of the Missouri River.

To Euro-Americans, the Great West seemed a vast and empty space, but they knew a good deal about the country. The Spaniards were familiar with Arizona as far as the Grand Canyon. They knew of Zuñi, Pecos, Laguna, Acoma, and other pueblos. They knew about the Great Plains and some of its rivers. Farther west, the Spaniards had established Santa Fe, a trading center with the Utes. Out of Santa Fe, in 1776, Padres Domínguez and Escalante had marched north through the Ute country via the San Juan River and the Colorado all the way to Utah Lake, just south of the Great Salt Lake. Padre Eusebio Kino traced a trail west from Arizona to California. Missions were planted in Texas as far east as present-day Nacogdoches.

In the far north French explorer Pierre La Vérendrye and his son had come down the Souris River out of Canada in 1738, reached the northern Rockies, and established trade with the Mandans on the Missouri. François Antoine Larocque, out of Canada, explored the Yellowstone River. Traders from St. Louis probed far up the Missouri. On the eve of Lewis and Clark's journey, traders in St. Louis knew the Indians of the upper Missouri tribes and plains as far as the Laramie Range. They knew of the Yellowstone, the Powder, and Bighorn rivers, and from Indians they had heard about volcanic marvels on the upper Yellowstone.

Outpost on the Oregon Trail, Fort Laramie was a magnet for both pioneers and Indians, who traded pelts for dry goods, beads, tobacco, and alcohol. Families on the trail spent four to five months in canvas-topped wagon homes (right). On the Santa Fe Trail, New Mexico artists transformed a pioneer's discarded oyster tin into an ornate frame for a religious image (far right).

Blackfeet encamp on what had been their hunting grounds—until much of it became Glacier National Park in 1910. Here Pikamakan (Running Eagle), a warrior woman, fought alongside Blackfeet men and led a band that stole Sioux ponies. Blackfeet, a strong tribe that dealt aggressively with white men, tried to keep whites from trading guns to small, unarmed tribes.

Far to the west, Spanish exploring vessels had mapped the Pacific Coast as far as Alaska. In 1792, Capt. Robert Gray aboard the *Columbia* had discovered the river that bears his ship's name. In the most important expedition of all, Alexander Mackenzie first crossed the North American continent in Canada in 1793. Mackenzie's trek indicated the enormous width of the continent—and alerted Thomas Jefferson to a potential threat to the American fur trade from the British Hudson's Bay Company. In 1803, he sent Meriwether Lewis and William Clark on their own epic journey across the continent through territory claimed by the Spaniards.

Even before Lewis and Clark returned, fur traders and trappers were heading up the Missouri in their wake. For the next 35 years, intrepid fur traders and trappers called "mountain men" explored virtually every part of the Great West in search of beaver. They were in competition with Hudson's Bay, whose fur brigades penetrated deep into the heart of the West.

In the winter of 1824, two American mountain men, Jedediah Smith and Tom "Broken Hand" Fitzpatrick, heard from Crow Indians about an easy path over the Continental Divide—the South Pass below the Wind River Range. This made possible the Oregon Trail used by tens of thousands of white emigrants heading for greener or more golden pastures in Oregon and Gold Rush California. The California Trail was largely the result of the heroic efforts of another mountain man, Joseph Walker. He led his men from the Rocky Mountains over the California Sierras via Mono Pass to Tuolumne and all the way to San Francisco. They were the first white men to see Yosemite's silent vastness. After reaching San Francisco Bay, Walker realized that Mono Pass was not adequate for California-bound emigrants. He moved south through California and, rounding the southern end of the Sierra via Kern River and Walker's Pass, found a natural, easy route.

The mountain-man era was not entirely heroic. In 1837, a steamboat heading for Fort Union on the upper Missouri carried smallpox to the Mandans, almost wiping them out. At trading posts all over the Rocky Mountain West and out among the tribes bordering the Missouri River, the dread white man's disease decimated Indian tribes. Then another more lasting and insidious plague overtook the West—white man's whiskey.

After the mountain-man era so thoroughly dislocated the Indians' West, the Era of Manifest Destiny took its quasi-religious place in the minds of white Americans, who saw themselves as Anglo-Saxons destined to rule the continent. The white Americans' invasion of the Great West was the product of many

104

"...the whites are many and the Indians few"

The Apache chief Cochise, who fought for more than a decade against the "white eyes," acknowledged the reality of the bloody "Indian Wars," which ended in white conquest of the West. Another Apache, Geronimo (opposite), spent his last years in a federal prison, with such interludes as riding in Theodore Roosevelt's inaugural parade and appearing at the 1904 World's Fair. White Elk, a Cheyenne warrior, sketched one of his kills—spear against rifle (right) at Little Bighorn, where Indians wiped out George Custer and his men in the most famous of all battles; other sketches show the stripping and mutilation of the soldiers. Custer was found naked but not scalped. After the battle, the Army found a bugle (above) near an officer's body, his bugler lying across him.

Relics of a double deadly war

A man-topped mountain of skulls like this one at the Michigan Carbon Works symbolizes the near extinction of the buffalo—and the Indians that the animals sustained. "Ten years ago," said a U.S. Army officer in 1882, "the Plains Indians had an ample supply of food….Now… they are…without food, shelter, clothing, or any of those necessaries of life which came from the buffalo…." Herds that "darkened the whole plains" before the eyes of Lewis and Clark were killed off to starve Indians and to feed the builders of the transcontinental railroad. Bones and skulls were shipped to plants to be crushed into fertilizer.

visions: geopolitics vis-à-vis rival Britain; imperialism; a mania for land by speculators; farming and ranching; dreams of city and town building; flight from social disgrace; a "civilizing mission"; religious competition; bankruptcy; a search for a better life by starting over; racism; a belief in Anglo-Saxon superiority; a lust for gold; the ambition of youth. And if the pull was strong, so was the push— away from mudsill status and poor land, or even a jump ahead of the law: G.T.T., "Gone to Texas."

The first hero of this new era was young, handsome, Lt. John C. Frémont, who eloped with a powerful senator's daughter in one of the great romantic episodes of a romantic era. Frémont traced and mapped the main emigrant route via the Platte River and the trappers' South Pass, pointing the way West as he dramatically climbed one of the highest peaks in the Wind River Range and planted an American flag atop it.

In 1843-44 Frémont, now a captain, led a party of mountain-man explorers all around the Great West, mapping it with the help of Charles Preuss, a German cartographer. Preuss's seven-section emigrant map was the most important key to the Great West and was copied by dozens of emigrant guidebook compilers. Even the Mormon leader, Brigham Young, was led to Salt Lake Valley "guided by the light of Frémont's travels."

The war with Mexico (1846-48) introduced many a young man to the Southwest and Mexico. It also secured the vast territory that became California, Arizona, New Mexico, Utah, Nevada, Colorado, and Texas as far as the Rio Grande. In January 1848, James Marshall discovered gold at Sutter's Mill in northern California. President James K. Polk, holding a small nugget in his hand, announced the find and started a rush to California. More than 300,000 argonauts, as they called themselves, departed for California by ship around Cape Horn, via the jungles of Central America, and overland via trails that began as far south as Mexico. Some parties took "shortcuts" that landed them in Death Valley or in snowy Donner Pass, where cannibalism was forced upon them.

San Francisco boomed overnight. Two hundred ships were abandoned by their crews. Vigilantes went wild. Chinese men came in great numbers. Gold camps sprang up along every stream in the Sierras. Claim jumping and shoot-outs and lynchings became so common that codes of law had to be developed on the spot. Wells Fargo connected the gold towns and San Francisco and carried huge amounts of gold that became either robbers' loot or bars and coins made at the San Francisco mint. John B. Trask's map of the California goldfields became an instant

Cowboys and Indians shoot and ride in "A Dash for the Timber" by Frederic Remington. His paintings and sculptures—a mix of frontier legend and galloping realism—endured to become America's imagined West. His friend President Theodore Roosevelt said of Remington that, thanks to him, "The soldier, the cow-boy and the rancher, the Indian, the horses and the cattle of the plains, will live...for all time."

Acting in a 1913 film, Buffalo Bill Cody (opposite) dramatizes an 1876 encounter with Cheyenne warriors. Cody, a Pony Express rider and an Army scout, earned his nickname by killing thousands of buffalo for railroad workers. As a showman, he inaugurated the "Wild West" show; one starred Geronimo (above), who became a celebrity after his surrender in 1886. Sharpshooter Annie Oakley (right) picked off a hundred flying targets in Buffalo Bill's circus of a show, which from 1883 to 1913 entertained believers in a mythic West.

best-seller. Poorly paid soldiers deserted in droves to become rich. The need for a transcontinental railroad became obvious. Towns up and down the Mississippi vied to be the eastern terminus of the road even as gold and silver fever led miners over the Sierra to Nevada, where "Pancake" Comstock gave his name to the mother lode in silver. Mines spread from Montana to Arizona and Colorado. Carson City, Butte, and Denver bloomed almost immediately. The times also spawned such ghost towns as Gold Fields, Nevada, and Robbers' Roost in Montana.

As early as 1855, under orders from Secretary of War Jefferson Davis, five transcontinental railroad routes had been explored by the U.S. Army's intrepid topographical engineers. Their magnificent 12-volume report proved nothing. But the lobbying of Massachusetts-born Thomas C. Durant, builder of the Rock Island Railroad and organizer of the Union Pacific Railroad Company, produced passage of the Railroad Acts of 1862 and 1864. The acts guaranteed the Union Pacific $16,000 to $48,000 in federal subsidy per mile of track, plus extensive land grants. The route went along the North Platte or Mormon Trail and over the Laramie Mountains through a pass discovered in 1866. This route was further explored as far as Ogden, Utah. Then Jack Casement, an ex-general, began directing crews of Irish immigrants in the art of laying rails fast. Along the way they created "Hell-on-Wheels" towns, where life was truly wild and whiskey flowed freely.

MISS ANNIE OAKLEY, THE PEERLESS LADY WING-SHOT.

Out in California, the route for the future Central Pacific Railroad was decided in 1860 in "Doc" Strong's Dutch Flat drugstore by Doc and railroad engineer Theodore D. Judah. Strong had located a huge inclined ramplike landform over the western Sierra Mountains all the way to Donner Pass. From there, the route was straightforward to Truckee Pass and then out into Nevada's Great Basin via the rich Comstock mining region. Judah lobbied the federal government for funds from an office in the U.S. Capitol while financiers Leland Stanford, Charles Crocker, Collis P. Huntington, and Mark Hopkins formed the Central Pacific Railroad Company, which was included in the Railroad Acts. When in 1869 the two lines joined at Promontory Point, Utah, a new mechanized era began. Unlike the Indians who depended on special environments, white Americans had devised ways not merely to adapt to natural conditions but also to transcend and alter them in major ways.

"unlearned and illiterate…"

"…with but few wants and meager ambition…," said a screed against cowboys in a Kansas newspaper in 1871. Their "diet is principally Navy plug [tobacco] and whiskey" and "each one generally has killed his man….They drink, swear, and fight…." Glamorized in dime novels for Eastern tenderfeet, cowboys in reality lived a grimy, dangerous life, reflected in this photo made in some dusty Western town. Driving cattle herds from central Texas to Kansas railheads, they risked death by rattlesnake, stampede, lightning, rustlers, Indian raiders, and drowning. To keep themselves awake in the saddle, they rubbed tobacco juice on their eyelids. From a chuck wagon (above) came a steady diet of beef, beans, and thick black coffee "strong enough to float a pistol." About 9,000 of the West's 35,000 cowboys were African Americans, many of them former slaves seeking a hard kind of freedom in the West.

Military strategy in the years after the Civil War was concerned with controlling the Plains Indians to ensure the safety of the railroads. The major strategist was Gen. William T. Sherman. He envisioned the railroads ferrying troops quickly and dividing the buffalo herds upon which the Indians depended for food, clothing, and shelter. Meantime, the Indian Bureau had developed the reservation system. In large part, the army's task became keeping Indians on their reservations, which did not include the best hunting grounds. What became known as the Indian Wars broke out first in western Kansas, when the Cheyenne would not give up their traditional hunting grounds. Large numbers of tribes, starving and freezing, were forced to break out of reservations and hunt the buffalo and other game.

The army built forts all over the West to guard the reservations, strategic trails, and railroad towns. Traders out of these forts plied the Indians with whiskey and repeating rifles. Indian agents also proved dishonest, cheating Indians out of beef rations, ammunition, and other supplies. Lt. Col. George Armstrong Custer reported the atrocities, bringing about the resignations of the Secretary of War and the Secretary of the Interior.

The army pursued Indians with a vengeance. In 1864, Col. John M. Chivington, a militia officer, led an attack on peaceful Black Kettle's band camped at Sand Creek, Colorado. Despite Black Kettle's display of peace signs and an American flag, he and his people were slaughtered. Custer, on a cold November morning in 1868, defeated the Cheyenne at the Battle of the Washita in western Oklahoma.

In 1869, the Fifth U.S. Cavalry and a unit of Pawnee scouts, led by Maj. Eugene Carr and including William F. Cody as chief scout, came under attack by Tall Bull's Cheyenne and a large band of Lakota. The Cheyenne trampled the Pawnee and tried to run off Carr's horses. Carr pursued the Cheyenne relentlessly, hoping to free two female captives. In an attack on Tall Bull's camp, one of the captives was killed and the other was wounded. Carr and his men killed Tall Bull while the Pawnee massacred the women and children. An artist, Charles Schreyvogel, celebrated these exploits in a painting. Buffalo Bill Cody is shown rescuing the women; in fact he was far away at the edge of the camp.

Indians and whites alike saw the many battles of the Indian Wars as scenes of valor, reflecting what had become the martial spirit of the West. The climax came

For a cowboy at trail's end with four months' pay or a miner with a sackful of nuggets, Western boomtowns offered oases like the Cosmopolitan Saloon in Telluride, Colorado—

a mahogany bar, a poker table, a roulette wheel, and a lawman with a badge. Sometimes upstairs and never far away were the "soiled doves," like this nameless prostitute (opposite). She usually carried a gun or a knife in her purse, and she might cost $400, even $600, a night.

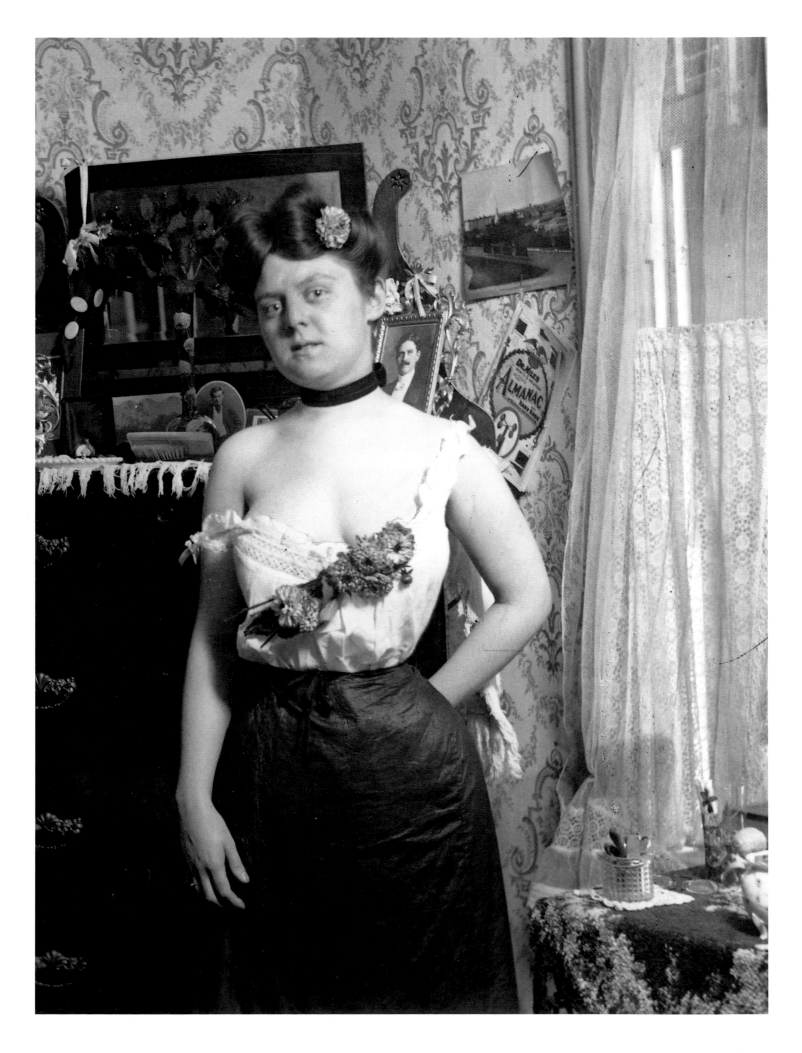

"Gold must be had"

That imperative drove a "forty-niner" to California in 1849. He had been "willing to brave most anything in its acquisition," he wrote, and like so many, he died seeking nuggets (above) hidden in the hills. By the end of 1849, some 80,000 people had headed for the storied gold. Ships advertised an "express"

trip (above)—a 13,600-mile, three- to six-month voyage from the East via storm-lashed Cape Horn to San Francisco. Boomtowns like Creede (right) sprang up in Colorado in the early 1890s, when silver and gold drew dreamers to the San Juan Mountains.

LOWER CREEDE.

Snow stairway
to golden hopes

*Discovery of gold in Rabbit
Creek in Canada's Yukon Territory set off a stampede that bot-
tlenecked at 3,500-foot Chilkoot
Pass (right) in 1897-98. About
30,000 people trudged up 1,378
steps carved in ice and snow.
Some Klondike-bound prospec-
tors who continued on to Alaska
included this woman (above).
Aided by her son, she sifts sand
for gold at Nome Beach. Canada
barred entry to Chilkoot climbers
who did not have a year's worth
of supplies. Chilkoot Indians,
hired as porters, said they often
made more money than the
gold seekers.*

PACKERS ASCENDING   SUMMIT OF CHILKOOT PASS.   '97.

Nebraska pioneer Sylvester Rawding and his family pose for an itinerant photographer in front of their sod home in 1886. Glass windows, livestock, and wooden doors proclaim prosperity. Settlers chopped sod strips into three-foot lengths and laid them like bricks. Wide-open ads (opposite) lured pioneers to the westering frontier.

at Little Bighorn on a hot, dusty afternoon in June 1876, when some 2,000 warriors—many using the traders' repeating rifles—killed Colonel Custer and 210 men of the Seventh Cavalry. The women finished the battle by stripping and mutilating the soldiers but sparing Custer.

The Indian Wars finally ended on December 29, 1890, when Gen. Nelson A. Miles and the rejuvenated Seventh Cavalry, together with a regiment of black troopers, wiped out a band of Lakota at Wounded Knee Creek in wintry South Dakota. During the wars, both Sitting Bull and Crazy Horse were also murdered while prisoners.

But what of those most distinctive characters of the Great West, the cowboys? Both the cows and the cowboys derived from Mexico. The cattle, let loose from missions or stolen by Comanche, multiplied into millions on the plains of Texas during the Civil War. The cowboys or buckaroos originated in the Mexican vaquero. After the war, ranchers rounded up hundreds of thousands of head of long-horned Mexican cattle. They were free for the taking, so Texas became a land of ranches and cowboys, many of them Mexicans and a number African Americans.

Jesse Chisholm first made the long cattle drive north to Abilene, Kansas, to meet the Kansas Pacific Railroad. His route up out of Texas came to be known as the Chisholm Trail. Then, as the Kansas Pacific Railroad and the Atchison, Topeka and Santa Fe spread out across the plains, carrying bib-overalled farmers and barbed wire, the trails moved westward. Charles Goodnight and Oliver Loving trailed their cattle to New Mexico Territory and Colorado. But most cattlemen and drovers headed first to such cattle towns as Dodge City, Abilene, Newton, or Caldwell. There, at the end of the long drive, the cowboys were paid off and went wild in gambling saloons and bordellos. The long drives only lasted from 1870 to 1890, an era punctuated by cattle wars and fights with sodbusters.

Away up north in Montana, ranchers also began to acquire Texas cattle that they fattened up and drove to cattle towns like Miles City and Deadwood or sold to the Army for Indian beef rations. British and Scot entrepreneurs invested heavily in Wyoming, Dakota, and Montana ranches. So did Theodore Roosevelt, who always wanted to be a real cowboy, but had to settle for President instead.

Out of the cowboy experience came rodeos, which were of Spanish origin. They first came into prominence in 1882 when Buffalo Bill Cody held a super-rodeo at his ranch at North Platte, Nebraska. Soon, after a brief career on the stage, Cody teamed up with a manager and created Buffalo Bill's Wild West Show, an extravaganza that relied on pure nostalgia.

In 1890 a Census Bureau report declared in a footnote that a "continuous frontier no longer existed." In 1905, Frederic Remington put it another way, writing eloquently of his thoughts in the 1880s and 1890s: "I saw men all ready swarming into the land. I knew the derby hat, the smoking chimneys…and the thirty-day notes were upon us in a restless surge. I knew the wild riders and the vacant land were about to vanish forever.…I saw the living, breathing end of three American centuries of smoke and dust and sweat."

Nature itself had been overpowered by a mechanized business civilization. But thanks to such preservationists as George Bird Grinnell, John Muir, and Roosevelt, the necessity of saving whatever Western wilderness was left, as well as preserving the Indian past, became issues that carried well into the 20th century. Back in 1864 Lincoln had granted California the Yosemite Valley and the Mariposa Grove of giant Sequoias to be held in public trust "inalienable for all times."

The first national park was Yellowstone, created by Congress in 1872. It was nearly 20 years before more parks were established: Yosemite in 1890, Mount Rainier in 1899, Oregon's Crater Lake in 1902. In 1891, Congress had passed the Forest Reserve Act. By 1901, the federal government had reserved 46 million forested acres. In 1906, the all-important Antiquities Act, protecting Indian artifacts and pueblos on public lands, was passed at the same time that Mesa Verde became a national park.

One of the greatest struggles to create a national park took place in Jackson Hole, Wyoming. Ranchers rose up in protest, formed a posse led by portly motion picture actor Wallace Berry, and besieged the National Park Service. The Tetons finally became a national park in 1950. Struggles between preservationists and ranchers, Sage Brush Rebels, ski resort entrepreneurs, water companies, federal dam builders, mining and timber interests go on even today at the end of the millennium, more than 10,000 years after the Pleistocene people first traversed the icy West. These are issues of importance to all Americans, including the Indians, who must be numbered in the great tribe of "We Americans."

Farmland emerges from the vanished frontier as 32 mules harvest a wheat crop. The driver tossed pebbles at balky mules to remind them "they were working along with us."

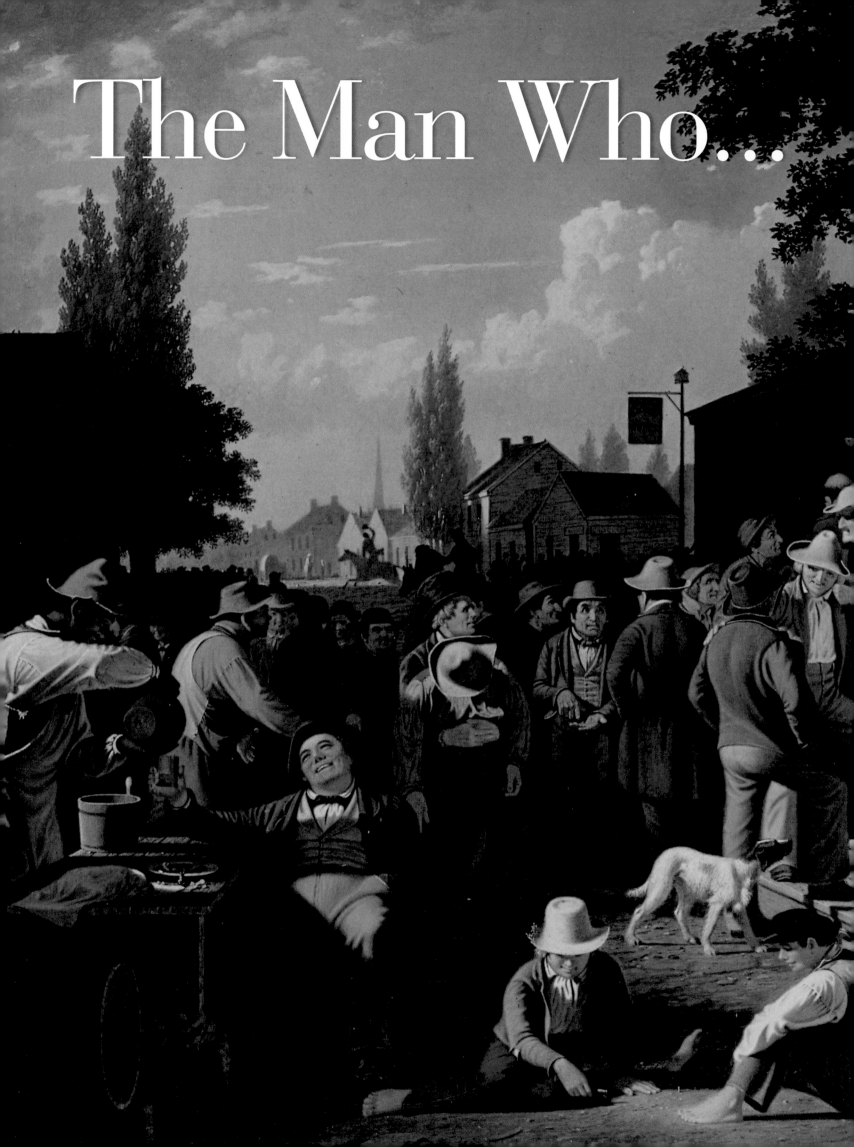

The Man Who...

"One man with courage makes a majority."

— ANDREW JACKSON

BY GEOFFREY C. WARD

Outweighed by Republican rival Benjamin Harrison in 1888, Grover Cleveland tipped the scales in 1892 to win a nonconsecutive second term. In 1884 he drew Republican chieftains— "Mugwumps"—who defected on Cleveland's pledge to clean the house of Tammany. A snuffbox (right) suggests a Napoleonic Andrew Jackson.

PRECEDING PAGES
Well-lubricated Missourians gather for artist George Caleb Bingham's 1851 "County Election."

"Politicks at the present time are the all-engrossing topic of discourse," wrote a young New Hampshireman named Benjamin Brown French as the presidential election got underway in 1828. "…In the ballroom, or at the dinner table, in the Stagecoach & in the tavern; even the social chitchat of the tea table must yield to the everlasting subject."

There was nothing new in that. Americans had always been intensely interested in how they were governed, even though at first most of them played little direct part in any of it: Candidates for President and Vice President were selected in private by congressional caucuses, and most members of the Electoral College who chose the winner were themselves picked by state legislators, not by ordinary voters. There were no party conventions, no mass meetings, no catchy slogans. All of the country's first six Presidents had been more or less polished aristocrats—two members of the same distinguished Massachusetts clan and four wealthy Virginia planters. James Monroe was reelected without any opposition at all in 1820, and until 1824 no one even bothered to keep an official count of the popular vote.

But now everything had suddenly changed. What alarmed Benjamin French and a good many others in 1828 was that for the first time in American history two full-fledged national parties were waging what seemed something like an all-out war on one another, a clamorous war of unsubstantiated charges, character assassination, and out-and-out lies. "I… tremble with apprehension that our Constitution will not long withstand the current which threatens to overwhelm it…,"

French wrote. "[T]he rancorous excitement which now threatens our civil liberties and a dissolution of this Union does not emanate from an *honest* difference, but from a determination of an unholy league to trample down an Administration, be it ever so pure, & be its acts ever so just."

French's alarm would have been understood by the Founding Fathers whose worst fears about their republic seemed to be coming true. They had been certain that the growth of political parties or "factions" would lead to demagoguery, mob rule, and dictatorship. It was the task of politics to repress factional division, they argued, and Presidents were meant to be selfless, nonpartisan patriots who embodied the hopes and dreams of the whole people. To help insure the election of such paragons, they hoped the vote would remain a privilege, limited exclusively to men of means, property-owning, tax-paying citizens who had an economic stake in calm and stability. And they assumed the whole business would be conducted in a staid, dignified manner befitting its importance to the country.

But the country grew much faster than its founders had imagined it would, and by the 1820s, beginning with Ohio, the new Western states adopted constitutions that granted the vote to all white males over 21, whatever the contents of their pocketbooks. Older states, worried that the greater freedoms offered in the West would lure away their citizenry, dropped their property ownership requirements, too. By 1828, in every state but one, the people—not the legislature—picked the presidential electors. The vote was fast becoming a right, not a privilege.

Four men had run for President in 1824, all of them at least nominally members of the original Republican Party founded by Thomas Jefferson. One of three Americans then lived west of the Alleghenies. Most of them had favored the candidacy of Andrew Jackson, a blunt, self-taught military hero from Tennessee whom they considered one of their own. Jackson received the largest number—but not a majority—of both the popular and electoral votes, yet lost the Presidency to John Quincy Adams in the House of Representatives. Both Jackson and his supporters were enraged, convinced they had been the victims of a conspiracy among aristocrats seeking power to pursue their own selfish ends.

Charging that a "corrupt bargain" had thwarted the people's will, Jackson's supporters vowed revenge. Organized as a new national Democratic Party, they were determined to turn out an unprecedented popular vote and put their man in the White House four years later. Jackson himself played no active part in their

Ballyhoo bandwagon touts William Henry Harrison in Philadelphia (opposite) and across the land. In 1840, Whigs won the first presidential campaign that buried issues under images—especially log cabins, promoted in many forms as the symbol of a homespun man. No matter that the hero of Tippecanoe (a minor skirmish) was in fact an aristocrat born at Berkeley, a Virginia plantation. Commemorating a more subdued political era, a pitcher presents Liberty crowning Washington with laurels (above.)

efforts. It was still considered unseemly for a man to appear to want the job too much. "I have no doubt if I was to travel to Boston where I have been invited that would insure my election," he had told a friend during the 1824 race. "But this I cannot do. I would feel degraded the balance of my life." Still, he did now consent to travel by steamboat to New Orleans to commemorate the 13th anniversary of his victory over the British in 1815 on the grounds that this was a purely patriotic occasion. He was rewarded with an outpouring of affection and gratitude.

Then Jackson returned to his plantation home near Nashville, refused all requests for his views on any topic, and let his lieutenants go to work behind the scenes. Perhaps the ablest was a diminutive New York politician named Martin Van Buren, whose air of mystery and shrewd organizing skills earned him the nickname the Little Magician. With his help, the Jackson campaign was launched simultaneously all across the country on July 4, 1827. Americans had never seen anything like it. "The *Hurra Boys* [are] for Jackson...," one disgusted Adams man complained, "and all the noisey *Turbulent Boisterous* politicians are with him." There were torchlight processions and mass meetings that drew thousands to hear orators praise their hero and charge his opponent with everything from being overly fond of "kingly pomp and splendour" to pimping for the czar of Russia. There were free cookouts, too, from which those too fastidious "to grease their fingers with a barbecued pig or twist their mouths away at whisky grog" were urged to stay away.

Jackson's toughness in the face of the enemy had won him the nickname Old Hickory. So local Democratic chapters were Hickory Clubs and steeples, signposts, and street corners all over the country sprouted hickory poles in his honor. "Planting hickory trees!" one New England editor wrote. "Odds nuts and drumsticks! What have hickory trees to do with republicanism and the great contest?"

President Adams and his supporters were caught off guard. Adams considered himself a statesman, not a politician. He hated electioneering. "The fashion of peddling for popularity," he called it, "by travelling around the country gathering crowds together, hawking for public dinners and spouting empty speeches." Adams' men denounced Jackson as a murderer for having executed deserters during his campaign against the Seminole Indians; the legitimacy of his marriage was questioned; posters charged that he was the bastard son of a prostitute.

Carnival of democracy yields a sideshow's worth of gadgets and gimmicks for 19th-century voters. Masters of the outsized gesture, Whigs in 1840 get a 12-foot paper ball (opposite) rolling from town to town for Harrison—and, urging followers to keep the ball rolling, coin a phrase. More muted crowing, for James Buchanan, characterizes an 1856 campaign ribbon, adorned with the Democratic Party's symbol of the time. Cartoonist Thomas Nast later created enduring party animals: donkey for Democrats, elephant for Republicans.

Nothing Adams supporters did seemed to matter. Jackson won an easy victory. To the American people in every part of the country, he had come to seem the living symbol of the self-made, democratic spirit of the age. So many of them surged up the stairs of the Capitol to get close to him at his inauguration that a cable had to be stretched across the staircase to hold them back. And so many more elbowed their way into the White House at the reception afterward, breaking windows and smashing crockery, that some feared the mansion itself would collapse. "I never saw such a mixture," said Associate Supreme Court Justice Joseph Story. "The reign of KING MOB seemed triumphant." But Jackson men loved it: "It is beautiful. It is sublime," said Francis Scott Key, composer of "The Star-Spangled Banner." Even

Benjamin French, who had been so frightened by the recent presidential race, soon entered politics as an enthusiastic Jacksonian Democrat.

For all its tawdry excess and cynical manipulation, the 1828 campaign had demonstrated the people's resolve to have a more direct voice in the choice of their Presidents. When Jackson ran for reelection four years later, both he and his opponent, Henry Clay, were chosen by the nominating conventions of their respective parties. In 1832, the Jacksonians again out-marched and out-organized and even out-fed the opposition. "If we tell Democrats we have great strength," one Clay champion complained, "*they reply by swallowing a pig. If we show them our gains in the Senate, they reply by devouring a turkey. If we point to our two-thirds majority in the House, they reply by pouring off a pint of whiskey or apple-toddy.* There is no withstanding such arguments. We give it up."

Jackson's opponents—they now called themselves Whigs, after members of the British antimonarchist party—failed again in 1836, and Martin Van Buren, the canny but uncharismatic operative who had helped engineer Jackson's first victory, was elected to succeed him. Although the country soon fell into a depression, the Democrats still seemed invincible: By 1839, when Philip Hone, a wealthy, well-connected Whig and former mayor of New York, ran for the state senate, political allies told him to forget it. In the current political climate, they said, "No gentleman can succeed."

Hone's friends were right—he was soundly beaten—but the Whigs were learning. By 1840, the depression had still not lifted, and bitter voters had begun to blame "President van Ruin" for their distress. To run against him, the Whigs nominated an old soldier of their own for President, William Henry Harrison of

Ohio, with Senator John Tyler of Virginia as his running mate. Then the Democrats played into their hands. When a Democratic editor airily dismissed Harrison as the kind of man who would be content if given enough hard cider to "sit the remainder of his days in a log cabin," Whig strategists saw a way to turn the Democrats' own tactics against them.

This time, they would present themselves as the party of the plain people. They would paint Van Buren as the pampered son of privilege and their man as the repository of Jacksonian virtues. Harrison was, in fact, a wealthy man who had been born in a handsome brick house, not a log cabin. He was not a notable soldier, either; his victories over the Indians at Tippecanoe and the Battle of the Thames had been due more to overwhelming numbers and able subordinates than to his own tactical skill. And he was distinctly unsteady in his views: At first his handlers forbade him to so much as write a letter, for fear he would inadvertently alienate one group of voters or another. Then, when the Democrats began to ridicule him as "General Mum," he delivered 23 innocuous speeches, the first ones ever made by a presidential candidate. The speeches are remembered best for the ostentatious swig from a barrel labeled "hard cider" he was instructed to take halfway through each one.

Whigs outdid the Democrats this time. They staged more processions and organized bigger rallies, gathering "17 acres of men" on the Tippecanoe battlefield to cheer their hero and putting a mammoth log cabin at the corner of Wall and Prince streets in lower Manhattan. Whigs wrote more campaign songs and slogans, too, and they inundated the country with specially made bric-a-brac—mugs and teapots, handkerchiefs, medals, women's brooches, all embazoned with Harrison and his supposed cabin. And party spokesmen relentlessly dinned his slogan, "Tippecanoe and Tyler Too," into the voters' ears, day and night.

"The question is not whether Harrison drinks hard cider," complained the poet

"Whistle-stop" campaign chugs into town, with President Andrew Johnson at the rail. Stephen Douglas gained the attention of voters in one-horse towns with thunder from a rented cannon aboard his train. Spreading with the railroad, whistle stopping flourished until politics took wings. On the stump, Rutherford B. Hayes (opposite), along with every other candidate, learned the value of pressing the flesh, even among citizens whose gender or age denied them the vote.

William Cullen Bryant. "…The question is what he and his party will do if they obtain power." But few seemed to care as Whig orators mounted an all-out assault on the unpopular President. Van Buren, whose origins were actually humbler than Harrison's, was denounced as a perfumed dandy who had turned the White House into a "PALACE *as splendid as that of the Caesars*" and wasted "the People's cash in FOREIGN…GREEN FINGER CUPS, in which to wash his pretty, tapering, soft, white lily-fingers, after dining on fricandeau de veau and omelette soufflé." It

was cheap, inaccurate, unfair—and hugely effective, the most vivid possible evidence, as one Whig editor admitted, that "passion and prejudice, properly aroused and directed, [would] do about as well as principle and reason in a party contest."

Van Buren won more popular votes than he had four years earlier, but many more Americans had gone to the polls this time—some 80 percent of all qualified voters—and they gave Harrison a narrow win, which he did not savor for long. He died of pneumonia within a month of his inauguration, and John Tyler, the first Vice President to succeed to the Presidency, had to endure Democratic jibes as His Accidency. But the Whigs had beaten the Democrats at their own game. "They have at last learned from defeat the art of victory!" the *Democratic Review* lamented. "We have taught them how to conquer us!" For better or worse, the two-party system was here to stay.

For a mostly rural population with few other amusements, political campaigns provided Americans with entertainment as well as edification. "To take a hand in the regulation of society and to discuss it," the French visitor Alexis de Tocqueville noted, "is [the American's] biggest concern and, so to speak the only pleasure an American knows….Even the women frequently attend public meetings and listen to political harangues as recreation for their household labors."

Women may have attended rallies but precious few dared even think of voting on election day. They were then confined to what was called "woman's sphere," expected to devote themselves entirely to the moral uplift of their children and the well-being of their husbands. By custom, women were barred from the pulpit and the professions, prevented from attending college, not permitted even to speak at public meetings. By law, they could not own or inherit property; could not serve on a jury or sue or testify in court. The premise underlying all this blatant dis-

Politics, Tammany Style

Tammany Hall, which became synonymous with big-city political corruption after the Civil War, began in New York in 1789 as the Society of St. Tammany, a nonpartisan club for craftsmen. When Irish-Catholic immigrants fleeing the potato famine booked ships to New York (opposite) and flooded into the city after 1845—over the protests of many Protestants—Tammany, a Democratic stronghold, made them welcome. Tammany men stole or stuffed ballot boxes from time to time. But they owed most of their success to poor voters, who had nowhere else to turn for a load of coal to get through the winter, for a job with the city, for help with obtaining citizenship, or for a basket of food at Christmas. Tammany's most infamous boss was William M. Tweed (shown as a bloated vulture in the above cartoon by Thomas Nast). He controlled the city from 1866 to 1871, siphoning off at least $20 million in bribes and kickbacks before he was finally sent to prison. George Washington Plunkitt, a subsequent Tammany leader, thought blatant thieves like Tweed were fools. Asked to account for his own large fortune—he had started out as a lowly butcher's apprentice—he saw nothing for which to apologize: "I seen my opportunities," he said, "and I took 'em." Headquarters, Tammany Hall (above), became a burlesque theater.

PAINTED BY J. NICHOL.   DRAWN ON STONE BY T. H. MAGUIRE LITHOGRAPHIC ARTIST TO THE QUEEN   PRINTED BY M & N. HANHART.

OUTWARD BOUND.
The Quay of Dublin.

Published by Henry Graves & Co. 6, Pall Mall, London May 24th 1854 & Williams Stevens & Williams Broadway New York.

"…in politics the middle way is none at all."

—JOHN ADAMS

crimination was the widespread belief—shared by most men of the time and a good many women as well—that while women were inherently more virtuous than men, women were inherently inferior in their ability to reason.

In 1848, when Elizabeth Cady Stanton and four other women dared issue their *Declaration of Rights and Resolutions* that "all men *and women*" were "created equal" and had the right to the vote, they were met with ridicule and patronization. "A woman is nobody. A wife is everything," said a Philadelphia newspaper. "A pretty girl is equal to ten thousand men, and a mother is next to God, all powerful….The ladies of Philadelphia…are resolved to maintain their rights as wives, Belles, Virgins and Mothers, and not as Women." It had been 72 years since the Declaration of Independence declared that governments derived "their just powers from the consent of the governed." Yet half the population was still barred from the polls by an accident of birth—and it would be 72 more years before American women became full citizens.

Benjamin Brown French moved to Washington in 1833 and went to work as clerk in the House of Representatives. So he had a chance to watch firsthand as Congress and the Executive Branch worked together under the two-party system, successfully dealing with the most vexing questions of the day: whether the federal government belonged in the banking business; whether it should impose protective tariffs or make internal improvements; or annex Texas; or wage the war with Mexico that brought California and the Southwest into the Union.

Far from being divisive, as the Founding Fathers had feared, the two-party system actually served to hold the country together during those years. For all its clamor and vulgarity, the system provided the country with a wide-open forum for national debate and encouraged creative compromise of issues that might otherwise have torn the country apart. Since both parties were national rather than local or regional organizations, each had to be careful not to favor one section over another. Nor could either afford to adopt extreme positions on any issue for fear of scaring off elements of the coalition it needed to hold together in order to win or maintain power.

But there was one divisive question for which no amount of public oratory, no carefully crafted cloakroom maneuver seemed able to provide a satisfactory answer: What was to be done about slavery? It was preeminently a moral issue and therefore resistant to compromise. The ownership of one human being by another—in a country that claimed to be built upon the proposition that all men were "endowed

THE BALLOT IS DENIED TO WOMAN

Darkening blot on a nation's conscious-ness, denial of the ballot to half its adult population persisted beyond World War I, despite state enfranchisement as early as 1869, in Wyoming Territory. Above, equal rights advocates Victoria Claflin Woodhull and her sister Tennessee Claflin are barred from a New York ballot box in a drawing that appeared in their pamphlet "One Moral Standard for All." Beyond polling places, "a hateful oligarchy of sex" kept women from pulpits, profes-sions, and active roles in public life. Some clergymen even maintained that equality for women was contrary to God's will.

AM I NOT A MAN AND A BROTHER?

THE NEGRO'S COMPLAINT.

Forc'd from home and all its pleasures,
 Afric's coast I left forlorn;
To increase a stranger's treasures,
 O'er the raging billows borne.
Men from England* bought and sold me,
 Paid my price in paltry gold;
But though slave they have enroll'd me,
 Minds are never to be sold.

Still in thought as free as ever—
 What are England's rights (I ask)
Me from my delights to sever,
 Me to torture, me to task?
Fleecy locks and black complexion
 Cannot forfeit Nature's claim;
Skins may differ, but affection
 Dwells in White and Black the same.

Why did all-creating Nature
 Make the Plant for which we toil,
Sighs must fan it, tears must water,
 Sweat of ours must dress the soil.
Think, ye Masters iron-hearted,
 Lolling at your jovial boards,
Think how many backs have smarted
 For the sweets your Cane affords.

Is there, as ye sometimes tell us—
 Is there one who reigns on high?
Has he bid you buy and sell us—
 Speaking from his throne, the sky?

Ask Him if your knotted scourges,
 Fetters, blood-extorting screws,
Are the means which duty urges
 Agents of his will to use?

Hark! He answers—Wild tornadoes,
 Strewing yonder sea with wrecks,
Wasting towns, plantations, meadows,
 Are the voice with which He speaks.
He, foreseeing what vexation,
 Afric's sons would undergo,
Fixed their tyrants' habitation
 Where his whirlwind answers—"No!"

By our blood in Afric wasted,
 Ere our necks receiv'd the chain—
By the miseries which we tasted,
 Crossing in your barks the main—
By our sufferings, since ye brought us
 To the man-degrading mart,
All sustain'd with patience, taught us
 Only by a broken heart—

Deem our nation brutes no longer,
 Till some reason ye shall find
Worthier to regard, and stronger
 Than the color of our kind!
Slaves of Gold! whose sordid dealings
 Tarnish all your boasted powers,
Prove that ye have human feelings,
 Ere ye proudly question ours.

He that stealeth a man and selleth him, or if he be found in his hand, he shall surely be put to death.   Exodus xxi. 16.
* England had 800,000 Slaves, and she has made them FREE.   America has 2,250,000!—and she HOLDS THEM FAST!!!

Sold at the American Anti-Slavery Office, 143 Nassau Street, New-York.

"Slavery is the great and foul stain upon the North American Union," wrote John Quincy Adams in 1820, but slavery produced profits in North and South. By 1850 slave-grown cotton comprised three-quarters of all American exports. In Southern slave markets (right) just before the Civil War, a prime field hand went for $1,800, a "handsome mulatto" woman for $2,000 or more. But for the small, determined band of abolitionists, slavery was, in the words of William Lloyd Garrison, "a covenant with death and an agreement with hell…." Abolitionists showered the country with tracts (top left) and risked their lives to spirit slaves out of bondage along the shadowy network known as the Underground Railroad. In 1844, Florida lawmen seared "SS" for "Slave Stealer" into the palm of Jonathan Walker (bottom left), after he was caught trying to smuggle seven slaves to freedom by sea.

Guns boom at Fort Sumter, and the "house divided against itself," as President Abraham Lincoln had reluctantly predicted, tumbles. The issue of slavery had already redrawn political fence lines, giving rise to Martin Van Buren's third-party Free Soilers, destroying the Whigs, splitting Democrats in two, and bringing into being a new, antislavery organization—the Republican Party.

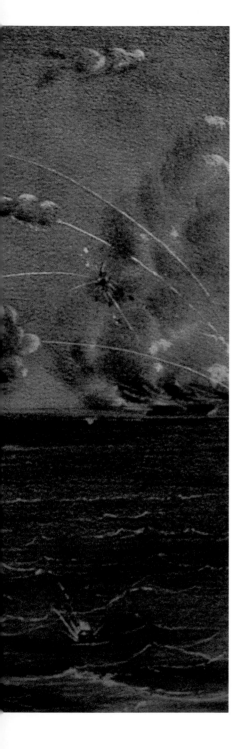

by their Creator with certain unalienable rights"—was either right or wrong. "There was never a moment," wrote the essayist John Jay Chapman, "when the slavery issue was not a sleeping serpent. That issue lay coiled up under the table during...the Constitutional Convention in 1787....Thereafter slavery was always in everyone's *mind,* though not always on his tongue."

From the first, American statesmen had sought to sidestep the issue, determined to avoid an open clash that might threaten the Union itself. Northern states had barred slavery since 1804, and in the Missouri Compromise of 1820 Congress had forbidden the spread of slavery farther north of 36° 30' north latitude. Most of those who opposed slavery hoped it would eventually die what a young Illinois Whig named Abraham Lincoln called "a natural death." But it did not die, and Southerners were determined to strengthen their hand by spreading it farther west.

Beginning in 1848, the serpent of slavery began slowly to uncoil until no one could pretend it wasn't there. The vast new territories seized from Mexico were the immediate cause. The South insisted they be open to slavery; the North wished them to become free states. In a gingerly compromise in 1850, Congress permitted California to enter the Union as a free state, and at the same time strengthened the Fugitive Slave Law, requiring federal agents to help slave owners hunt down runaways. Tensions grew but the Union still held.

Then in 1854 the most powerful man in the Senate, Democrat Stephen A. Douglas of Illinois, proposed that the 1820 compromise in effect be rescinded: Settlers in any new territory should be allowed to vote slavery up or down. To slavery's enemies, this seemed the final straw. If Douglas's Kansas–Nebraska Act was passed, they argued, Congress would give up the power to speak for the whole nation on a matter in which the whole nation had an abiding interest. Slavery's progress toward extinction would be stopped.

Sectional loyalty now overcame party loyalty; no compromise seemed possible. "Perhaps it is as well that it should [pass]," wrote French just before the vote was taken, "& let the question be forever settled. The Union will be in danger...but I trust that the Power which has so long sustained it will save it."

The bill was passed. But the issue would be forever settled by civil war. Even before the shooting started, the two-party system, whose birth French had chronicled in 1828, had been utterly transformed. The struggle over slavery would split the Democrats into Northern and Southern factions by 1860, and it would shatter the Whigs completely, as antislavery "Conscience Whigs" flocked to the brand-new Republican Party.

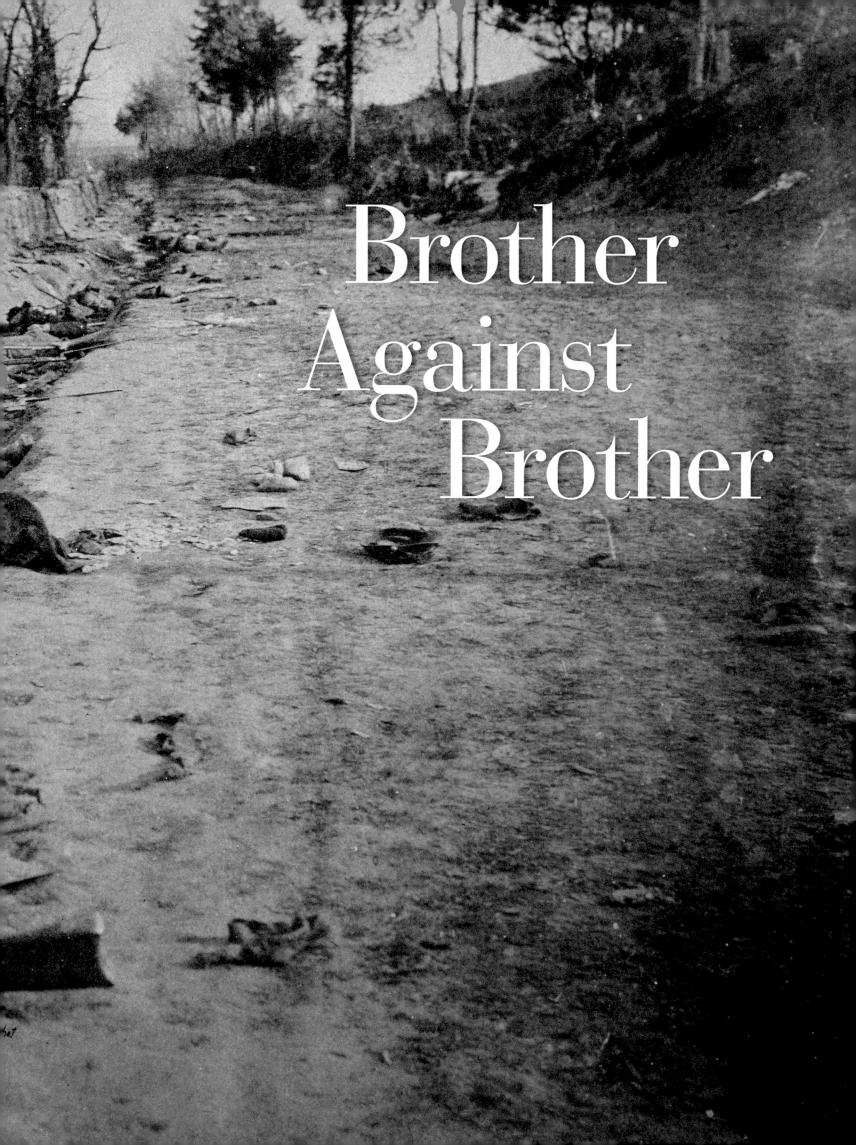

Brother
Against
Brother

"They were going to look at war, the red animal—war, the blood-swollen god."

—STEPHEN CRANE

BY DAVID HERBERT DONALD

"So Civil War is inaugurated at last," New Yorker George Templeton Strong wrote when he learned that the Confederates had attacked Fort Sumter on April 12, 1861. "GOD SAVE THE UNION, AND CONFOUND ITS ENEMIES. AMEN." When news of the firing on Sumter reached Georgia, it aroused a different emotion in the Reverend Charles Colcock Jones. "All honor to Carolina!" he exclaimed. "I hope our state may emulate her bravery and patriotism—and her self-sacrificing generosity.... The conduct of the government of the old United States towards the Confederate States is an outrage upon Christianity and the civilization of the age...."

Neither Strong nor Jones were typical of the civilian population of their hostile sections. The New Yorker—son of a prominent attorney, an honors graduate of Columbia College (later Columbia University), and a partner in a profitable Wall Street law firm—was too conservative to be representative of anything more than a tiny New York elite. Jones, for his part, was an equally exceptional Southerner. His ownership of three plantations—with some 3,600 acres and 129 slaves, in Liberty County along the coast south of Savannah—made him one of the wealthiest men of the area. A Presbyterian minister and a product of seminaries at Andover and Princeton, he could have had his choice of Southern pulpits. Instead, he elected to spend most of his active years as missionary to the slaves of his region.

But if Strong and Jones were exceptional men, their responses fairly captured the reactions of their rival sections to the outbreak of the Civil War. Both Strong and Jones recorded the remarkable unanimity of sentiment that developed in the North and in the South after the hostilities began. In the North, loyalty to the Union welled up. The streets of New York, like those of most Northern cities, were thronged with volunteers. Stopping one young recruit, the son of a farmer

Johnny Clem, a drummer boy at nine, had his drum smashed by a Confederate shell at Shiloh. He shot a Reb at Chickamauga. Unlike 600,000 soldiers on both sides, he survived the Civil War. He stayed in the Army and retired as a major general, just missing World War I.

PRECEDING PAGES
Confederate soldiers lie where they fell on Marye's Heights in Fredericksburg, Virginia, in May 1863.

147

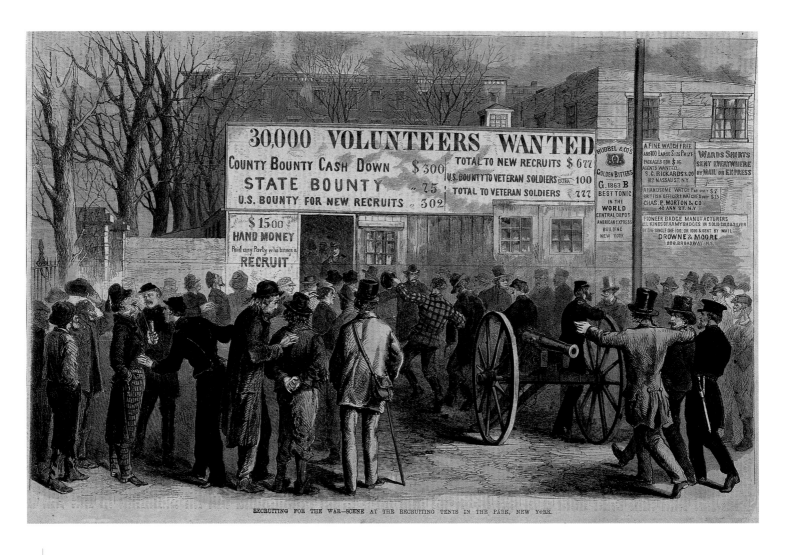

RECRUITING FOR THE WAR—SCENE AT THE RECRUITING TENTS IN THE PARK, NEW YORK.

Volunteers rushed to enlist when the war began. "It needed only the first man to step forward…be patted on the back…and cheered…," says an account of a recruitment rally, "when a second, a third, and a fourth would follow." State recruitment offices like this one in New York offered cash bonuses. Many an underage lad hid the number "18" in his shoe and solemnly swore he was "over 18."

who lived near Rochester, Strong asked why he had hurried to join the army. "I voted for Abe Lincoln," the lad told him, "and as there is going to be trouble, I might as well fight for Lincoln." Strong saw in the flags displayed a symbol of Northerners' "perfect unanimity, earnestness, and readiness to make every sacrifice for the support of law and national life."

Southerners too were ready to make every sacrifice. Men of the Confederate states rushed to enlist in the army. "The anxiety among our citizens is not as to who shall *go* to the wars, but who shall stay at home," noted the Georgia politician Howell Cobb. In the Jones family, Charles Colcock Jones, Sr., a 56-year-old minister with impaired health, had to remain at home, but he encouraged both his sons to join the army. His physician-son Joseph, with skills needed by the civilians of Augusta, nevertheless concluded "he could not reconcile it to his conscience to remain quietly in professional pursuits when his country was imperiled." His brother Charles, who was mayor of Savannah when the fighting broke out, could easily have avoided military service by accepting another term. But he also enlisted "as a matter of personal duty and of private example….The service will be arduous, involving sacrifices great in their character; but I am of opinion that my duty requires it, and I will go."

Whether in the Union or the Confederacy, those unable to enlist wanted to assist the soldiers in every way they could. Mary Jones, wife of the minister, pledged that she and her household slaves at Montevideo, the Joneses' 941-acre plantation on the North Newport River, would supply complete uniforms for four Confederate volunteers. With the blessing of Mayor Jones, the women of Savannah held a fair in May 1861 and raised several thousand dollars for the benefit of Confederate soldiers. The mayor's cousin in Marietta, Georgia, teamed up with other women to provide uniforms for Cobb County volunteers. Some bought the cloth and thread, others cut patterns, and the rest sewed. "It is incredible how many garments can be made by machine and otherwise," she reported. "We furnished three companies [300 men] this week…."

Far more extensive and highly organized were the exertions of Strong's New York associates. The recent Crimean War had shown that, without proper sanitation and supplies, deaths from disease would probably exceed those from combat. Well-informed Northerners realized that the tiny medical bureau of the U.S. Army, headed by a doddering surgeon-general, was unprepared to cope with the impending problems. So a group of prominent New Yorkers formed a volunteer auxiliary association, which became known as the United States Sanitary Commission, to supervise the diet, hygiene, and hospital care of Union troops. In June 1861, at the second meeting of the commission, Strong was named treasurer. For the rest of the war he spent at least half his time at the commission's headquarters on Broadway. As branches sprang up across the country, he coordinated their fund-raising drives and saw that the money contributed was prudently and honestly spent. By the end of the war Strong had approved disbursements totaling $4,925,000. No hint of fraud ever touched his office.

Thanks in considerable measure to Strong's exertions, the Sanitary Commission was able to supply to Union troops those necessities that the incompetent army administration neglected. An admiring reporter listed some items stocked at commission depots close behind battle lines: "Stockings, shirts, drawers, trowsers…pillows for the head and for stumps of limbs, slings of various sizes, paper, envelopes, pencils, sponges…towels, brooms, buckets, bed-pans, crutches, drinking cups, matches, tobacco, pipes, liquors of different kinds, oranges and lemons, spoons, soft bread, oatmeal…farina, dishes of different kinds, tents, bedticks, shoes, slippers, beefsteak…canned fruits

Posters recruiting black troops came belatedly. Black volunteers initially were turned away because the Militia Act of 1792 barred nonwhites from the infantry. Congress revised the law in July 1862, and in September the Union Army mustered its first black troops. By mid-1863 about 179,000 black soldiers— three-fourths of them from slave-holding states— enlisted. Their officers usually were white.

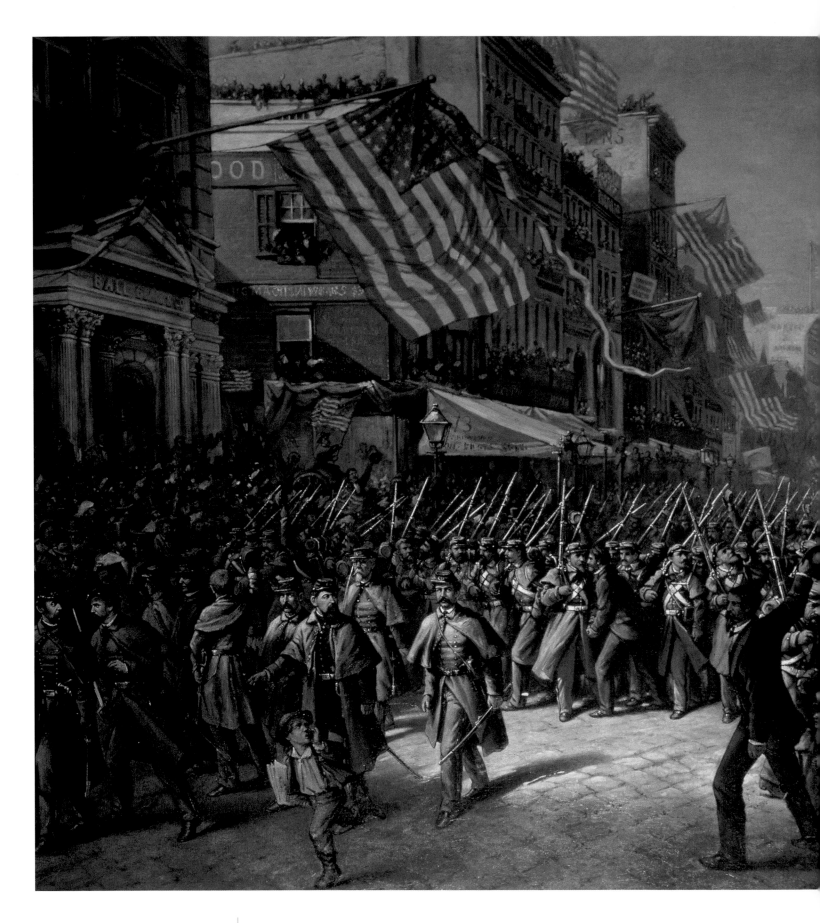

Down Broadway marches the proud Seventh New York Militia on April 19, 1861, a week after the Civil War began. Two years later, when President Lincoln issued his first draft call, soldiers of the Seventh were on New York streets to quell mobs—"like a company of raging fiends"—in antiblack, antidraft riots that killed more than a hundred people.

and vegetables, dried fruits, pickled onions…candles, soap, canes, fans."

Strong frequently had to go with other commission members to Washington to cut through red tape so that these supplies could reach the fronts. Visiting the Army of the Potomac on the peninsula between the York and James rivers during Gen. George B. McClellan's 1862 thrust toward Richmond, Strong was horrified to discover "men…lying on bare hospital floors and perishing of typhoid who could be saved if they had a blanket or a bed, or appropriate food and…hospital clothing instead of their mud-encrusted uniforms." He vowed he would help correct this situation, even if he had to neglect his law practice and lose half his income. Before the end of the war he could take rightful pride in the success of the commission. "I believe," he recorded, "…that we have saved more men than have been lost in any two days' fighting since the war began. Thank God that a miserable, nearsighted cockney like myself can take part in any work that…helps on the national cause."

Devotion to the national unity was not confined to men. Northern women—like those in the Confederacy—freely contributed time, energy, and money to the cause. Strong's wife, daughter of one of the wealthiest and most aristocratic lawyers in New York, felt the same impulse to serve as did her husband. In 1862 she volunteered to help nurse the wounded from the disastrous Peninsula Campaign, and, to her husband's considerable surprise, found that she enjoyed the "Bohemian life" of a nurse. Her superiors commended her "cordial acquiescence in drudgery."

Not all women were willing to play the traditional roles that conservative males like Strong expected of them. Indeed, the war considerably accelerated the women's rights movement. Organizing the Women's Loyal National League to promote the twin causes of Union and emancipation of slaves, Susan B. Anthony and Elizabeth Cady Stanton achieved a degree of political influence they had never had before. Working independently of the Sanitary Commission, Clara Barton—later to found the American Red Cross—did heroic service in getting medical supplies to the front and in ministering to the wounded. After a day in an Army hospital following one of the major battles, she wrote, "I wrung the blood from the bottom of my clothing before I could step, for the weight about my feet."

Of course not even the most dedicated civilian, whether in the North or the South, could devote all his or her time and energy to supporting the national cause. Even in the midst of death and desolation, family life revolved in the familiar cycles of marriages, births, and deaths. Especially in the North—except in the small portion touched by Confederate invasions—everyday life for civilians went

When days were Blue and Gray

From tintypes (photographs printed on thin metal) to toys, the Civil War swept through civilian life. "Daguerrean artists" produced countless images of waiting sweethearts and men off to war; this soldier (right) poses with his son. Children like him fought the war with toys; these wooden soldiers marched when a child pulled levers. No other war fostered such fervent songs. Southern sympathizers in Union-occupied New Orleans risked a $25 fine for singing "The Bonnie Blue Flag." But tunes knew no allegiance: A Northerner wrote the South's anthem, "Dixie"; and "The Battle Hymn of the Republic," with stirring words by suffragist and abolitionist Julia Ward Howe, stemmed from a Southern air. The Confederacy's myriad paper money—here with Stonewall Jackson's portrait (states also issued paper) was backed only by faith and fell steadily; the Union greenback (here the first U.S. paper dollar, issued in 1862) was often accepted in the South.

Harriet Beecher Stowe's novel dramatizing the cruelty of slavery first saw print as a serial in an abolitionist newspaper. Published as a book in 1852, it sold more than 300,000 copies within a year, spreading and strengthening anti-slavery sentiment in the North.

In the spring of 1862 at Cumberland Landing not far from Richmond, soldiers look down upon a panorama of Union might, produced by the highly industrialized North. Tucked in many a knapsack was a naughty "actress card" (opposite) from wicked Paris, where photography found a new niche. Advertised as "RICH, RARE, AND RACY," the cards sold for 50 cents each.

on at much the usual pace. Strong, for example, found that his work for the Sanitary Commission still left time for his many other interests: "energizing in Wall Street with reasonable diligence"; serving as vestryman for Trinity Church and as trustee of Columbia College; going to monthly meetings of the Century Club, where he enjoyed the company of such men as historian George Bancroft, political theorist Francis Lieber, and industrialist Abram S. Hewitt. And only the most desperate emergency could keep him from regularly attending opera and philharmonic concerts, for he was passionately devoted to music.

Still, the war did make a difference. Secession and the outbreak of hostilities precipitated a sharp depression in early 1861. By September, Strong declared he was "resigned to speedy and total insolvency. War, taxes, and cessation of business will have done their work before long." His view of the economy was unnecessarily pessimistic. By the middle of 1862 the North as a whole began to prosper. His father-in-law, Samuel B. Ruggles, who made a railroad tour of the Middle West that summer, better understood the temper of the times. Telling Strong of the huge wheat and corn crops he had seen, Ruggles said he was confident "of our national wealth and ability to feed the world." He predicted that he would live to see "King Cotton dethroned and King Breadstuff crowned as his successor." Buoyantly optimistic, Ruggles tried to interest his son-in-law in the newly chartered Union Pacific Railroad.

The fast-growing petroleum industry, which sprang up after Edwin L. Drake successfully drilled for oil near Titusville, Pennsylvania, in 1859, also fascinated Ruggles. He gave Strong 10,000 shares of Kenzua Petroleum Company stock, but his son-in-law failed to catch his enthusiasm. "My stock has cost me nothing, so I have nothing at stake," Strong wrote, "and any oil of gladness that may flow therefrom, if only half a pint, will be so much clear gain."

Strong, suspicious of quick profits, viewed disdainfully the extraordinary prosperity evident throughout the North by 1863. He held himself aloof from the

newly wealthy "shoddy aristocrats"—so called because some had made their fortunes by selling the government uniforms made of shoddy, the sweepings from floors of woolen mills and cutting shops. Held together with glue, the stuff made passable cloth until exposed to the first rainstorm. Strong was disgusted by the contrast between the deprivation he witnessed on the battlefield and the conspicuous consumption exhibited by "the crowds of gents and giggling girls" who flocked to the newly opened Central Park on Sundays to display their expensive clothing, jewels, and carriages.

Failing to share in this prosperity, Strong, though wealthy, sympathized with those who were hurt by wartime inflation. Until the end of 1864, wages failed to keep up with prices and laborers suffered. Women workers were particularly hard hit, especially those whose husbands were in the Army and could contribute little to support their families. Inequity and deprivation gave life to the nearly defunct labor movement, and newly formed unions often threatened work stoppages to get higher wages. With a tolerance exceptional in a man of his background, Strong noted on November 12, 1863, "Workmen and workwomen of almost every class are on strike (and small blame to them)...."

Strong's tolerance, however, did not extend to workers who challenged the government's war policies. To many workingmen, the administration in Washington appeared uninterested in their problems, while it showed profound concern about those of blacks in the South. Lincoln's Emancipation Proclamation of January 1, 1863, seemed to many white laborers in the North less a humanitarian act than an invitation for more and more freed slaves to pour into their cities and compete for jobs.

Discontent became open when the Lincoln administration resorted to conscription in order to maintain the armies in the field. The draft produced a riot in New York City that lasted from July 13 to 16, 1863, the worst of a series of such eruptions across the Northern states. A mob first attacked the enrollment officers who were drawing the names of draftees, then turned on the police, and further diverted itself in what Strong called "cowardly ruffianism and plunder" of stores and warehouses. Toward the African-American residents of the city the mob exhibited its most fearsome hostility. After sacking and burning a black orphan asylum, the rioters hunted down any black citizen unwary enough to appear on the streets and hanged to lampposts those they were able to catch. Loathing this "Irish anti-conscription

A standard Union Army mess kit looks more appealing than what was served on its plates. Soldiers ate so much greasy food and rancid meat that a doctor predicted "death from the frying pan." The recipe for Skillygalee: soak hardtack (biscuits known as "worm castles") in water and fry with salt pork. Sutlers— Army-approved vendors— sold Union soldiers such delicacies as oysters, along with whiskey, tobacco, and Bibles. Confederate soldiers (some, opposite, huddle at a fire) fared worse, drinking coffee brewed from parched corn or peanuts, living on ever diminishing rations, and supplied by a patchwork logistical system.

Nigger-murdering mob," Strong urged that it be "put down by heroic doses of lead and steel."

More than Northerners, civilians of the South found that the war affected every facet of their daily lives. Theirs was an agricultural society, primarily devoted to raising cotton and tobacco. When the war closed Northern markets and the Union blockade cut off European markets, bales and hogsheads piled up. Confederate authorities urged farmers to grow grain instead. Having the utmost confidence in Jefferson Davis, "our worthy President (at once soldier and statesman)," the Jones family willingly responded to this appeal. Cotton planting at 2,000-acre Arcadia, largest of their plantations, was limited in the 1862 season to one acre for every field hand. Charles C. Jones, Jr., wrote approvingly: "Every bushel of corn and blade of grass will be greatly needed for the support of our armies."

But the transformation of Southern agriculture could not prevent food shortages in the Confederacy. With so many men in the army, there were not enough hands to till crops, and the creakingly inefficient Southern rail system made it impossible to distribute fairly what food there was.

The Confederacy turned to the printing press to finance the war, issuing paper money in an endless stream. A Confederate treasury note with a face value of one

dollar was worth but 29 cents in gold by 1863, only 1.7 cents by early 1865. As the value of money fell, prices soared. "Living is ruinous, and exceedingly scarce," reported Mrs. Jones's brother from Rome, Georgia. "We have not had a piece of meat on our table for five days." Skyrocketing prices made Charles C. Jones, Jr., a beggar, and he wrote his parents "to send us anything to eat which you can spare from the place."

Nevertheless, the Joneses were comparatively fortunate. Those Southerners who had no country relatives to draw upon for food, and particularly those who lived on fixed incomes in the cities, fared worse. The situation in Richmond, capital of the Confederacy, was most critical of all. Overflowing with officers and civilian officials and their families, this old Southern town grew into a city overnight. But public services were virtually nonexistent. Housing was scarce and expensive. Food, regularly diverted from the capital to the nearby army, was in short supply. The chief of the Confederate Bureau of War, Robert Kean, complained that Richmond prices made his $3,000 salary worth about $300, and by October 1863 his family was reduced to eating only two meals a day. J. B. Jones, a clerk in the bureau, reported in May 1864 that shoes sold for $125 a pair, potatoes for $25 a bushel, and flour for $275 a barrel. "Such is the scarcity of provisions," he declared, "that rats and mice have mostly disappeared, and the cats can hardly be kept off the table."

"Detention barrels" encase four soldiers flanked by guards at a Union prison in Point Lookout, Maryland. Two may be Confederates who tried to escape; one or two may be Union men, possibly guards being punished. Prisoners suffered horribly on both sides. Smallpox killed 1,800 Confederates in Rock Island, Illinois. In Andersonville, Georgia, Union prisoners, forbidden shelters, starved to death in holes; 13,000 were buried in mass graves.

Gettysburg, July 3, 1863: Some 13,000 Confederates, commanded by Maj. Gen. George Pickett, charge the Union line, hitting it only here, at a point known as the Angle. The line held. The scene is from a 360-degree view—the Gettysburg Cyclorama—painted by Paul Philippoteaux from sketches, photographs, and interviews with survivors in 1881.

Until 1864, the Jones family in rural Georgia suffered comparatively little. They missed luxuries like tea, which was only available if smuggled through the Northern blockade, but Mrs. Jones asserted, "We will endure privations joyfully rather than yield an inch to the vile miscreants that are now seeking our destruction."

More serious was the shortage of salt, for without it they could not preserve and store meat. As increasing numbers of Georgians trooped to the coast to boil seawater and produce their own salt, they began to chop down trees and steal firewood from Maybank, the Joneses' 700-acre plantation overlooking the mouth of the Medway River. Early in the war, the Joneses needed clothing and blankets for their slaves. Since the few woolen factories in the South were busy with orders for uniforms, Mrs. Jones undertook the hard labor of weaving her own blankets, and her husband proudly reported that she "clothed most of the people" on the plantation as well.

The fate of these "people"—Southern planters rarely spoke of "slaves" but called them "the servants" or "our people"—was a matter of growing concern to the Joneses because a large portion of the Jones family fortune was invested in slaves. Along the Georgia seacoast, where federal gunboats could push up the hundreds of inlets and rivers almost to the doors of plantation houses, slaves were a particularly vulnerable sort of property. As early as July 1862, Jones learned that some slaves in Liberty County had run away to the Union boats. "The temptation of change, the promise of freedom and of pay for labor, is more than most can stand," he judged tolerantly.

That tolerance diminished after Lincoln issued the Emancipation Proclamation, which the Joneses viewed as "a direct bid for insurrection, as a most infamous attempt to incite flight, murder, and rapine on the part of our slave population." They began to look for a plantation in central Georgia, presumably safe from Union raids. At last they found one in Burke County, near Waynesboro, to which they sent most of the field hands.

Those whites who, like the Joneses, remained in the coastal area began to feel isolated and frightened. Since two-thirds of the voting population of Liberty County had enlisted and since most of the slaves had been moved inland, the countryside looked deserted. Mrs. Jones felt especially isolated after the death of her husband from "wasting palsy" in 1863. She was left almost alone in the plantations at Montevideo and Arcadia, with "not a white female of my acquaintance nearer than eight or ten miles." *(continued on page 168)*

Cameras capture "the terrible reality"

"The Dead of Antietam," Mathew Brady's 1862 exhibition of battlefield photographs, bestowed upon Americans what the *New York Times* called "the terrible reality"—as if Brady had "brought bodies and laid them in our dooryards…." Brady, a Washington photographer already famous for his portraits of eminent Americans, went on to create from the camps and battlefields a photo album that generation after generation of Americans still look through to fathom the Civil War.

A "spirit in my feet said, 'Go,' and I went," Brady (above) said, explaining why he headed for the war's first battle—Bull Run, in Manassas, Virginia, about 25 miles from Washington. After that, he rarely went to battlefields. But he did deploy a corps of photographers in portable darkrooms that the soldiers called "whatisit" wagons. The Confederacy had no Brady and left a legacy of relatively few photographs.

Most of what the war photographers captured was,

CONFEDERATE ARTILLERYMEN KILLED AT ANTIETAM LIE NEAR A FALLEN HORSE AND A GUN'S LIMBER. BEYOND IS THE SHELLED ÐUNKER CHURCH. A DEAD MAN'S SHOES WAIT TO BE FILLED AGAIN. BRADY'S BOX CAMERA (TOP) HAS A LENS THAT SUGGESTS USE FOR PORTRAITS, HIS SPECIALTY.

AT A UNION FORWARD COLLECTING POINT FOR CASUALTIES, WOUNDED SOLDIERS, INCLUDING SOME AMPUTEES, AWAIT EVACUATION.

MONTHS AFTER SOME 7,000 UNION TROOPS FELL IN THE 1864 BATTLE OF COLD HARBOR, FREED SLAVES INTER THE DEAD.

OPPOSITE TOP: AFTER THE BATTLE OF GETTYSBURG, EMBALMERS GO TO WORK; THESE SOLDIERS DEMONSTRATING COFFINS ARE ALIVE.

like most of war itself, routine and even dull. Brady's men made those images because it was easier to stay put than to pack up the wagon and follow the troops. Whatever their inspiration, those images take us back to enduring human moments: soldiers playing cards, writing letters, eating their hardtack and boiled beef, or staring into the lens, lonely and wondering.

A photograph began with coating a glass plate with chemicals and immersing it in solution. Now sensitive to light, the plate was inserted into a holder and then into a previously aimed and focused camera. The photographer then removed the lens cap and made a 5- to 30-second exposure, depending on the light. He had only a few minutes to remove the plate and get it into a developer pan in the wagon. Finally: two washes, a drying, and a coat of varnish.

On the battlefield, because the camera could not freeze action, photographers usually created somber icons of the dead. Sometimes they rearranged bodies to improve the composition or drama of a photo. For an image of a dead Confederate in a sniper's nest at Gettysburg, Timothy O'Sullivan dragged the body about 40 yards.

Brady put his label, "Photograph by Brady," on the works of the men he had hired. He amassed a collection of 7,500. The government paid him $25,000 for his photos in 1875. By then he was bankrupt. He died in 1896, poor and nearly forgotten.

Even so, she fared better than her daughter, Mrs. Robert Quarterman Mallard, whose husband in 1863 accepted a call to a church in Atlanta. Mallard and his family were just getting settled when Gen. William T. Sherman began his campaign to capture that bustling rail hub. Soon the city filled with refugees. Wounded soldiers poured in until stores and public buildings had to take the overflow from hospitals. For several months Mallard preached to the soldiers and left tracts at the hospitals, and his wife nursed the gravely ill. But when it became clear that Atlanta was going to fall, the couple fled to Montevideo, Georgia.

They did not find a safe haven. After capturing Atlanta, Sherman cut a swath across Georgia to the sea. The first Union troops, belonging to Gen. Judson Kilpatrick's cavalry, descended upon Montevideo on December 15. Arresting all able-bodied white males and enticing slaves to leave the plantations, soldiers went from house to house, ostensibly searching for weapons but actually seizing anything valuable they came across. They poked through every room at Montevideo, forcing Mrs. Jones to open cupboards and unlock trunks, and they made off with clothing, jewelry, and souvenirs. The soldiers stripped the storeroom of its sparse supply of cornmeal, bacon, and potatoes. Mrs. Mallard said they told her that "they meant to starve us to death." When Mrs. Jones begged the soldiers to leave enough food for the women and children, they laughed scornfully and dumped a quart or so of meal on the floor.

For three weeks the Union troops made life at Montevideo a nightmare. When not ransacking the big house, they prowled around the slave quarters, picking up what few valuables they could scrounge and making sexual advances toward the black women. The Jones household slaves proved clever at outwitting the succession of invaders. But not all slaves, even on the Jones plantation, remained devoted to their masters. "The people are all idle…seeking their own pleasure," Mrs. Jones

Civil War medicine: It began with the stretcher that carried a wounded man off the battlefield to the ambulance wagon that took him to the surgeon. If the ride did not kill him, the surgeon might. The saw was the instrument of choice, and amputation the most frequent operation. This one is staged (opposite) but realistic. Unaware of germs, surgeons probed with dirty hands. Medicine chests included opium, morphine, and marijuana. Whiskey was an anesthetic—as was "bite the bullet," on the theory that it would ease pain elsewhere.

complained. Disillusioned by what she considered faithlessness on the part of so many of the slaves she had treated indulgently, she turned against them bitterly. "I have told some…that as they were perfectly useless here it would be best for me and for the good of their fellow servants if they would leave and go at once with the Yankees."

By mid-January 1865, as Sherman's army moved north to the Carolinas, most of the Union soldiers in the Georgia coastal region disappeared. But the chaos and disorder they brought remained. If a planter and his wife left the area, vandals immediately stripped their house of everything movable. If they stayed on, they had to deal with uncooperative black men and women. In either case they were forced to alter profoundly their habits of thought. They had not merely to recognize that slavery was dead; they were forced to admit that their whole mythology about slavery as a benevolent institution, with which the slaves themselves supposedly were content, had been a tissue of lies. Living unprotected at Montevideo, Mrs. Jones captured the mood of these Southern whites: "Clouds and darkness are round about us; the hand of the Almighty is laid in sore judgment upon us; we are a desolate and smitten people."

Not a member of the Jones family ever questioned the merit of the Confederate cause, which, as Charles C. Jones, Sr., wrote, "exceeds in character that of our first [i.e., 1776] revolution." None ever doubted that it must be supported against "our malignant, unscrupulous, and determined enemy." Mrs. Jones spoke for her united family when she wrote: "I believe we are contending for a just and righteous cause; and I would infinitely prefer that *we all* perish in its defense before we submit to the infamy and disgrace and utter ruin and misery involved in any connection whatever with the vilest and most degraded nation on the face of the earth."

Similarly, George Templeton Strong gave his unqualified support to the government in Washington. At the outset of the war he was put off by Lincoln's appearance and manner: "Decidedly plebeian….his laugh is the laugh of a yahoo, with a wrinkling

Union soldiers' horses stand amid the ruins of Richmond, capital of the Confederacy. As the city was being abandoned on April 2, 1865, Confederates set afire their works and armories. The flames spread, destroying 900 buildings. On April 9, Gen. Robert E. Lee asked Gen. Ulysses S. Grant for a conference. They met at Appomattox, Virginia, where Lee surrendered.

of the nose that suggests affinity with the tapir and other pachyderms; and his grammar is weak." But after seeing the President several times, Strong judged him "a most sensible, straightforward, honest old codger" and rated him "the best President we have had since old Jackson's time, at least." By December 1863, when many Northern politicians were sniping at the President, Strong intuitively understood the mood of the Northern people: "Uncle Abe is the most popular man in America today. The firmness, honesty, and sagacity of 'the gorilla despot' may be recognized by the rebels themselves sooner than we expect, and the weight of his personal character may do a great deal toward restoration of our national unity."

These civilians felt that in God's good time peace would come and, along with it, a new sense of nationhood—separate for the South, as Confederates hoped; one united country, as Northerners expected. Paradoxically, both goals were to some degree realized. The war did enhance the American sense of nationality. The victory of the North meant that the nation's territorial integrity would never again be challenged. During the war, the functions of the government were enormously expanded, and the Chief Executive exercised power greater than ever before. Even while the fighting raged, the establishment of a national bank, chartering of a transcontinental railroad, opening of public lands to homesteaders, and creation of land grant colleges put government closer to people's affairs and strengthened the attenuated bonds of national unity.

But if the war promoted American nationalism, it also solidified the persistent sectionalism that had led to the conflict. After four years of war, Southerners and Northerners could not easily accept each other as members of a common country, or even as men and women sharing common human traits. Just as Southern whites came to think of pillaging and marauding Union soldiers as devils incarnate, so many Northerns developed a fierce hatred for the South and its inhabitants. In March 1865 Strong wrote what he would never have said four years earlier: "I almost hope this war may last till it become a war of extermination." A similar venom appeared in the response of one of the Joneses to the news of Lincoln's assassination: "One sweet drop among so much that is painful is that he at least cannot raise his howl of diabolical triumph over us."

It would take decades before these old rancors would fade, before old sectionalisms would meld in an expanding nation whose "new birth of freedom" Lincoln had predicted at Gettysburg.

1935: Shoeshine boys in a little Pennsylvania town listen, rapt, to a man who fought for the Union. In that same year, Supreme Court Justice Oliver Wendell Holmes, Jr., a wounded hero of the war, died, leaving an epitaph for his generation, North and South: "a man…should share the passion and action of his time at peril of being judged not to have lived."

Into the New Century

"The only history that is worth a tinker's damn is the history we make today."

—HENRY FORD

BY DAVID MINDELL

On August 11, 1911, just as he did every day, Joseph Cooney went to work as a molder in the foundry of the Watertown Arsenal outside of Boston. As he began working, Dwight Merrick showed up to observe him. Cooney refused to submit to Merrick's scrutiny, politely telling him, "Either you or I will have to be on the floor alone." Merrick would not relent. He called a manager, who summoned Cooney to his office. The workman would still not submit, and so he was discharged. As Cooney left the shop that morning, his fellow workers followed him, and soon they announced a strike.

Strikes were nothing new and indeed had happened regularly for decades in workplaces all across America. While not large, the strike at Watertown was no ordinary work stoppage. It was not against a large corporation but at a federal facility; the Watertown Arsenal made components for the Army's guns. And the workers were not responding to low wages or dangerous working conditions, the typical sources of friction in America's rough factories. Rather, they were reacting to something they found just as threatening to their well-being: a man with a stopwatch. This man, Merrick, represented what the workers at Watertown were struggling against: a new way of working and a new way of organizing work, called "scientific management" or "Taylorism," after its inventor, engineer Frederick Winslow Taylor. Taylor and his men represented a new profession, the "efficiency expert."

Taylor's methods, developed after years of study and experience in metalworking and machine shops, broke down each man's work into its fundamental parts—his individual movements and gestures. Each movement was carefully timed (what Merrick was doing to Cooney that day), and then recombined into a new whole that would represent the "scientifically" optimum task.

Disembodied forearm of a model of "Liberty Enlightening the World" thrusts through a ticket booth at Philadelphia's 1876 Centennial Exhibition. By 1900, French sculptor Frédéric Auguste Bartholdi's Statue of Liberty would blaze hope to millions of immigrants.

PRECEDING PAGES
A traffic jam, circa 1910, paralyzes Chicago's Loop. Trolleys, which replaced horsecars, are gridlocked.

This new version of the job would become the new standard by which each worker's performance would be measured. In the view of Taylor and his many followers, the new methods of "time and motion study," combined with other similar techniques, would not only improve efficiency and profitability but also help the workers find a more humane form of labor in the industrial world. "In the past, the man has been first," wrote Taylor, "in the future, the system must be first."

To the men on the factory floor, putting the system first threatened their autonomy and dignity. For them, the symbol of that threat was the man with the stopwatch. "We object to the use of the Stop Watch," they wrote to the Secretary of War, "as it is used as a means of speeding men up to a point beyond their normal capacity. It is humiliating and savors too much of the slave driver." Unlike workers in companies, workers at government facilities could appeal to politicians. So the Watertown strike initiated a series of congressional hearings. After a public investigation, Congress banned Taylor's methods throughout government facilities and in work under government contracts. More broadly, the Watertown strike epitomized the issues at stake as the 20th century dawned. As industry and technology changed, so did the nature of work, and both responded to changes in the workforce.

Workers and owners had struggled over control of the workplace since the first stirrings of industrialism. In the brief space of a hundred years, the dominant activity of most Americans had changed from farmwork, ebbing and flowing with the cycles of days and seasons, to wage labor, beginning and ending at the same time each day—labor often scheduled down to the minute by a master clock. Most Americans no longer owned the means by which they made their living. Many now worked in large industrial organizations, controlled and coordinated by a new breed of professionals called "managers." In the decades around the turn of the 20th century, these shifts became critical as never before. New technologies, from machine tools to telephones, were affecting not only what people made but also how they made products, along with the conditions under which they spent their working days.

And the workers themselves were different. In the early 19th century, the first factories at Lowell, Massachusetts, were staffed by young farm women seeking to supplement their incomes. By the end of the century, many workers were recent

"Huddled masses yearning to breathe free"—in Emma Lazarus' immortal verse—catch a breath of fresh air. Below decks, steerage passengers endured inhuman crowding on ships that might carry 3,000 men, women, and children at fares as low as $12.

immigrants, much closer to the economic edge, and hence more open to exploitation. As industry grew and the population changed, managers devised machines and methods to organize these new Americans and to control their activities. When the 19th century ended and the brave 20th dawned, professions and work patterns began to form that so define our modern world we barely notice them: large organizations, office work, management, and information processing. The tensions created by those upheavals reached their flash point when efficiency experts like Dwight Merrick timed and scrutinized workers like Joseph Cooney on the factory floor of the Watertown Arsenal.

This new industrial world and its new ways of working had their roots in the decades before the Civil War. Great factories, driven by waterpower, brought people together to work in large numbers as never before. For a while it seemed possible that America could avoid the dirty cities and social problems that industrialization, with its "dark, satanic mills," had wrought in Britain. Massachusetts textile mill towns like Waltham, Lawrence, and Lowell, began as model communities. Workers were required to attend church, keep to Christian behavior, and work six long days per week. Soon, however, the ideal broke down, amidst economic depressions and "speed ups" designed to press more work out of the same numbers of people and machinery.

The business of mass production began with guns, and in government-owned factories called arsenals (like the one at Watertown). Army officers were in charge. Legend had it that Eli Whitney, inventor of the cotton gin, "invented" the idea of "interchangeable parts," but others were pursuing the idea at the same time, including officers of the Army Ordnance Department and the skilled workmen at the Springfield Armory. These men, steeped in the routines of military life, sought to make their products adhere to the same disciplines.

Making each gun by hand, and carefully filing each part to a perfect fit, would no longer be acceptable. Now all parts, all guns had to be exactly alike, so any one gun could be repaired with pieces from another. As with soldiers, so with the components of machines: Interchangeable manufacturing required discipline and tight control, notions not always popular with the men who did the work with their hands, who thought of themselves as skilled artisans.

The logical next step from interchangeable parts was to interchangeable tasks and workers. Before, a skilled workman like a master armorer had great control over the products of his labor. Now any individual could easily be replaced by another.

Grasping tickets, vaccination cards, and bills of lading, immigrants arrive at Ellis Island (below), where hope mingled with terror. During medical screenings, dreaded "eye men" (left) flipped back lids to check for trachoma, a blinding and highly contagious affliction whose victims were usually deported. In 1913 came intelligence tests timed by stopwatches.

DUTCH

ALGERIAN

CHINESE

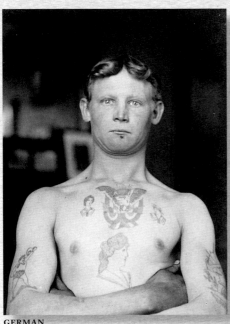

GERMAN

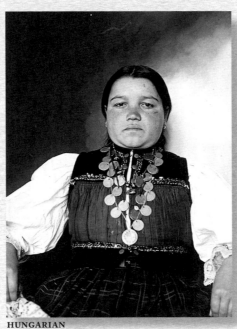

HUNGARIAN

RUSSIAN

Gallery of new Americans

As immigrants passed through Ellis Island early in the 20th century, officials had some of them photographed "in native dress." Although most immigrants came from Europe, Asia and the Middle East also provided new Americans. In 1907, during the high tide of immigration, nearly 900,000—about two-thirds of them male—entered the United States through the Ellis portal. Only 2 percent were turned away. Backed by "America for Americans" groups and some labor unions, the Quota Law of 1921 imposed a ceiling of 358,000 immigrants a year, with the total from any nation not to exceed 3 percent of its people in the United States as of 1910. In recent years, laws lowered the number of newcomers. But illegal immigrants and complex regulations blur actual numbers.

ROMANIAN (OPPOSITE)

"The sunlight never enters."

"A modern invention of the devil" to its tireless chronicler Jacob Riis, the turn-of-the-century tenement nevertheless functioned as a latter-day Plymouth Rock to countless immigrants. At New York's notorious Gotham Court (opposite)—"a packing-box tenement of the hopeless back-to-back type"—reporter Riis counted "not a native born individual… except the children." Unnoticed by most Americans, the pestilential tenements had mushroomed along with burgeoning cities, growing so crowded that several families might share a single room. An official report cited Gotham Court's "horribly foul cellars," and "infernal system of sewerage." Under such conditions, family life often disintegrated, leaving prostitution, criminal gangs, and legions of homeless young "street Arabs" behind; above, a dead horse provides passing entertainment for New York youngsters. Riis saw a pernicious cycle in play. He wrote, "The bad environment becomes the heredity of the next generation; given the crowd, you have the slum ready-made."

Inevitably, the artisans resisted the transformation, as when Thomas B. Dunn took over in 1829 as superintendent of the Harpers Ferry armory in Virginia. (An armory would be called an arsenal today.) In an effort to impose modern industrial practices, Dunn banned gambling, drinking, and unexcused absences from the armory shops, prohibitions that we take for granted today. One armorer, Ebenezer Cox, after being dismissed for such an offence, returned to Dunn's office and shot him dead. Cox was executed for the crime, but his fellow workers hailed the killer as a hero—a rebel against shop-floor control. More than a decade later, when a new superintendent tried similar reforms, such as mounting a clock on the factory wall, the workers reminded him of Dunn's fate. The clock was removed.

By the Civil War, the Army could produce hundreds of thousands of guns per year. Interchangeable parts allowed the armory to parcel out its production to private contractors, and then assemble the final guns at the arsenal. These shops had names that remain familiar today: Colt, Remington, Winchester, Pratt & Whitney. In 1865, the blessing of peace brought trouble to manufacturing, as production of guns went from its wartime highs to nearly nothing in 1867. Hurt the most from this shrinkage were the contractors—the numerous small machine firms that had arisen around the arsenals to produce these uniform parts. Now they were forced to find other business or go under. Many did go out of business, but a few found innovative uses for what they had learned while working for the Army.

What these firms had learned was not only a way to make guns but also a genuine philosophy of manufacturing. A British observer, much impressed, dubbed it the "American System." The American System of manufacturing depended on the heavy use of specialized machinery to mechanize workers' tasks, standardized jigs to hold oddly shaped parts, gauges to measure their conformity to close tolerances, and the production of identical products in very large numbers. In effect, these techniques displaced the skills of individual craftsmen, whom ordnance officers and superintendents saw as unreliable, variable, and difficult to control.

The more flexible manufacturers soon realized that the American System" could be applied to producing other types of machines, including those that could

Commerce spills into the streets of New York's Lower East Side (opposite), where 330,000 mostly Jewish immigrants were squeezed into each square mile by 1900. There and in count-

less other ethnic neighborhoods, a pushcart offered newly arrived greenhorns an alternative to airless sweatshops; many, though, regarded peddling as a last resort. Whatever the work, few families made enough money to spare their children long hours of toil; above, newsboys huddle at dawn near the Brooklyn Bridge.

To the endless whir of their sewing machines, "sweaters" assemble knickerbockers—"knee pants"—at 45 cents a dozen. Laws regulating factory labor failed to cover tenements, where most garments took shape. Some 20,000 strikers united in 1909 to set a precedent, while the deaths of 146 young women in the 1911 Triangle Shirtwaist Factory fire stirred public support for the industry's organizing. By 1913, union members from many lands (right) joined forces to voice their demands.

find a broad market in a peacetime economy. Companies adapted and refined the American System to make sewing machines, the 19th-century's ultimate domestic technology. (But the industry leader, Singer, was slow to adopt these production techniques, relying instead on another emerging business philosophy: marketing.) The changes affected the farm as well. Lewis Wilkinson, a veteran of the Colt armory and the Wilson Sewing Machine Company, took charge of the McCormick reaper works in Chicago in 1880, bringing armory practices and the American System to the manufacture of agricultural machinery. Production more than doubled in one year and continued to rise for a long time afterward.

In the 1880s, responding to a popular craze, small manufacturers soon turned to bicycles. They built on the American System, adding such new techniques as metal stamping, finishing, materials flow, and quality control to large-scale production. The Weed Sewing Machine Company in Hartford, Connecticut, produced the Columbia bicycle, using derivations of armory practice. Weed illustrates the great productive creativity of the time: During the last decades of the 19th century, the same factory produced firearms, then sewing machines, then bicycles—and, at the turn of the century, automobiles. The career of mechanic Henry M. Leland followed the same evolution: he developed manufacturing skills at the Springfield Armory making guns, brought them to Browne and Sharpe making machine tools, then to Wilcox & Gibbs making sewing machines. Leland eventually founded the Cadillac Motor Car Company and the Lincoln Motor Company.

Bicycles also presented one new manufacturing challenge not found in guns and sewing machines. For those earlier products, the basic problem was mostly making the parts; for bicycles, a bottleneck formed around putting the parts together. Because wheels required the stringing of spokes, a bicycle took up to 20 times as long to assemble as a gun. Assembly thus remained the last element to be put into the American System to transform it into modern mass production.

The American System, then, was the industrial background on which Henry Ford built to achieve his famous paradigm shift in the production of automobiles. The Model T, introduced in 1908, was not the first automobile, but the first truly mass-produced automobile, and it brought the American System into the 20th century. From 13,000 in the first year, production jumped to 189,000 in 1913. The company built a new factory at Highland Park on the outskirts of Detroit that both made use of the latest technology of electric lighting and motors and was designed from the first for the smooth flows of material, machinery, and products. Most important, to solve the assembly problems raised by bicycles and now automobiles, Ford's planners adopted the philosophy of "moving the work to the men." Parts and cars now flowed on "assembly lines" that brought a new kind of pace and regularity to the factory. Everything moved on a conveyer belt, running at uniform speed.

The slower men speeded up, the faster ones slowed down. Work was broken down into ever more finite tasks, and each man repeated the same movements over and over again all day. "A cardinal principle of mass production," wrote Henry Ford, "is that hard work, in the old physical sense of laborious burden-bearing, is wasteful. The physical load is lifted off men and placed on machines. The recurrent mental load is shifted from men in production to men in designing." Thus skill and creativity were displaced, not only from people to machines but also from one group of people to another: Engineers and managers increasingly called the shots, not machinists, operators, or laborers.

With the arrival of mass production, the process of making complicated things had been brought under control. Variations in individual parts were reduced with jigs and fixtures; variations in flow through the system were reduced with new factory layouts; variations in individual performance were reduced with the assembly line running at uniform speed. Production, the American System, and now "Fordism" were well on their way to becoming a single, unified system. What remained was to bring the most difficult element under the system's purview: the people. Ford's technical innovations in fixture design, factory layout, and materials flow were augmented by social innovations in managing workers.

The changes in work pace and style were not subtle; indeed they took a direct and immediate toll on those working on the assembly line. In 1913, the employee turnover rate at Ford was 380 percent—meaning that for a factory of 1,000 people, Ford would have to hire 3,800 people over the course of the year just to keep it running!

Ford's solution was to raise pay, and in 1914 he instituted the famous "five-dollar day," more than doubling typical workers' pay of the time. Ford reasoned that the higher pay would encourage workers to stay despite the straining conditions of the assembly line. He was correct, as the anonymous wife of a Ford assembly line worker confirmed: "The chain system you have is a *slave driver! My God!* Mr. Ford. My husband has come home & thrown himself down & won't eat his supper—so done out!...That $5 a day is a blessing—a bigger one than you know but *Oh* they earn it." Ford also realized that workers were also consumers,

ENGLISH FOR COMING AMERICA[

Series A --- Fourth Lesson

PREPARING BREAKFAST

gets	The wife gets the kettl[
takes off	She takes off the lid.
is	The kettle is empty.
puts on	She puts on the lid.
fills	The wife fills the kettle w[
is placed	The kettle is placed on [
burns	The fire burns brightly.
gets	The water gets hot in t[
boils	The water boils.
is taken	The kettle is taken off t[
pours	The wife pours boilin[on the coffee.
puts	She puts the coffee pot [stove.
pours	She pours boiling water [saucepan.
cooks	She cooks the eggs in [
are	The eggs are done.
takes	She takes the eggs out of [
are placed	The eggs are placed on t[
pours out	The wife pours out the c[

Published by ASSOCIATION PRESS, 124 East 28th Street, New York.
Copyright, 1909, by the International Committee of Young Men's Christian Associations.

Show-and-Tell, for grown-ups, instills practical English skills (lower). Immigrant parents delivered their children to the public school "as if it were an act of consecration"— and then struggled to piece together their own linguistic bridge to the new land. Factories and other workplaces held classes (upper); their motives, as job site organizing grew, included the muffling of radical "foreign" influences. The goal became overall "Americanization" for employers like Henry Ford, who insisted that "racial, national, and linguistic differences are to be forgotten."

Buying a new way to shop

Manhattan matrons crowd around artful food displays at Siegel Cooper, one of the new breed of "consumers' palaces" that sprang up from Boston to San Francisco. Modern conveniences—such as electric lights, cash registers, elevators, and interdepartment telephones—sped the palaces' proliferation. So, in the case of ready-to-wear clothing, did an abundance of high-quality textiles, cloth-cutting machines, pressing irons—and immigrant labor. Beyond the reach of the vast emporia, with their "perennial air of festival and excitement," hinterland shoppers could still partake of the consumer cornucopia, through mail-order tomes from Sears, Roebuck and Company (right) or Aaron Montgomery Ward, fierce rivals before 1900. Shortly thereafter, the electric vacuum cleaner (opposite) made its debut, as mass-produced laborsaving devices began to ease household tasks for women of the growing middle class.

For a few, a Gilded Age

Captains of Pittsburgh industry salute the world's first billion-dollar corporation, U.S. Steel, in 1901. Absent from the T-rail formation: just retired Andrew Carnegie, whose annual income of $23 million in 1900 was exceeded only by his ruthlessness toward his own steelworkers, who earned less than $10 for an 84-hour workweek. Carnegie credited an impoverished upbringing for his success; single-minded to the last, he set out in retirement to give away his fortune, and created a lasting model for the business of responsible philanthropy. The Gay Nineties' social Darwinism gave rise to several thousand millionaires, whose unabashed displays of wealth—in an age without income tax—included a $500,000 necklace sported by Mrs. George Jay Gould (above).

Seeking a "sacred right"

Walks of life as varied as the women themselves converge for a march down New York's Fifth Avenue in 1912. Among the 15,000 marchers, society suffragettes made common cause with placard-hoisting immigrant seamstresses seeking the dignity due their trade in the union movement. The following year Quaker leader Alice Paul, taking up the cudgels of an earlier generation of feminists, began a nation-wide lobbying campaign for a constitutional amendment giving women the vote. It finally was enacted as the 19th in 1920, ending a crusade that reformer Elizabeth Cady Stanton had begun in 1848 with a call for women's "sacred right to the elective franchise."

and without them the markets for consumer goods would soon dry up. The extra pay gave workers the income they needed to purchase the products they were themselves producing in the factories.

Higher pay by itself was insufficient, however, because as industry, products, and production methods were changing, so were the people running the machines. Developments in technology intertwined with social changes. In the early 19th century a manager or factory supervisor might have found workers who had grown up on farms with good mechanical skills. Now the workers were as likely as not to be recent immigrants or city dwellers with no familiarity with machinery at all.

Originally, the Ford workforce, like Detroit itself, consisted of earlier immigrants from England, Germany, and other northern European countries. Soon into the new century, however, a wave of immigration swept the country. They still came from Western and northern Europe, but also now from Eastern Europe or the Mediterranean. Only 200,000 came in 1880, but a million arrived in 1905, and millions more kept coming for the next ten years. Companies like Ford were shaping an increasingly global economy and were drawing on a global labor market. The success of American industry drew in more and more workers and sent its tentacles abroad to attract them.

Now workers were likely to have different cultural backgrounds from managers, different language skills, and even different attitudes toward work itself. Sometimes a worker would progressively lose "foreignness," as he or she became assimilated and Americanized. Other workers maintained their separate identities, going home after work to a community of men and women who shared their culture and values. Sometimes people came to America in the first place to escape the desultory effects of industrialization or colonialism in their home countries (particularly in Asia). They might be supporting a family at home or sending wages back to a home country to support a family there.

By 1914 at the Ford Motor Company, only 29 percent of the workers were American-born; two-thirds of them came from southern and Eastern Europe, largely from Russia and Poland. Company literature, distributed in 16 languages, told workers: "Learn to read English." Ford also had an increasing number of black employees, many of whom had migrated north to escape the racism and poverty in the South. U.S. mass production both responded to and depended on large numbers of recently arrived unskilled immigrants with little unity or political power to resist conditions in the new factories.

Companies like Ford extended their "system" into immigrants' homes and communities. Managers, predominantly white and American-born, believed that immigrants needed help in understanding the importance of home, family, leisure, and especially hygiene. The convictions say more about the managers' attitudes toward foreigners than about the people who actually entered the country. The company's Sociological Department (later renamed the Education Department) offered mandatory classes in English. Department representatives investigated workers' homes for standards of thrift, social philosophy, and behavior to determine if they were eligible for the five-dollar day. Workers were easily disqualified. As intrusive and draconian as such policies seem today, they were of a piece with Progressive-era ambitions to use the corporation as a tool for social reform.

It was not just the factory floor or workers' homes that saw a new regulation and devotion to "system." Businesses in general were adopting techniques that began making them into modern enterprises as they entered the 20th century. As companies grew larger, they required new means to coordinate the vast amounts of human effort they enrolled. New techniques originated in the 19th century with the railroads, companies that quickly became the largest commercial enterprises ever seen in America. With "systematic management" and a "line-and-staff" structure for dividing responsibility, the overall organization began to take precedence over the individual. Standards, procedures, and internal communications all ensured that human behavior within large organizations would be as uniform as the interchangeable parts coming off the production lines.

Systematic management evolved in parallel with new technologies of written communication. Carbon paper, vertical filing, pigeonhole desks, typewriters, duplicating machines, and many innovations still in use in today's office originated in the last decades of the 19th century. By 1890, modern offices contained such familiar tools as paper business forms, file cabinets, directories, and telephones. All had been invented in the preceding 20 years, and all were common fixtures in the indoor landscape of office work by 1900. A new and very modern person emerged: the office worker. Between 1900 and 1910, stenographers, typists, and secretaries increased by 189 percent. Bookkeepers, cashiers, office machine operators, and accountants increased by similar proportions. Other, entirely new occupations emerged. Women worked as telephone operators, manually switching communications signals as calls sped from one part of the country to another.

"The operator must now be made as nearly as possible a paragon of perfection," recalled one early operator, "a kind of human machine, the exponent of speed and

Georgia clay toughens the going for a chain gang building a state road. For these Virginians (left) and other African Americans dwelling along the backroads of the American dream, the century brought in newly codified Jim Crow laws, along with the Supreme Court's 1896 Plessy v. Ferguson *decision that rationalized segregation.*

Workpens of childhood

Coal-caked youngsters look up from their labors at noon, the lone pause in a 10-hour workday. The dust-choked chutes where they plucked slate and rocks from rivers of anthracite earned the nickname "nurseries." Though Pennsylvania law made 14 the minimum working age, none of the breaker boys in Lewis Hine's 1911 photo at South Pittston had turned 12. Typically, novices were 8 or 9. But soon, noted an observer, "from the cramped position they have to assume, most of them become more or less deformed and bent-backed like old men…." The story repeated itself, with minor variations, in industries ranging from textiles to agriculture. The flourishing institution of child labor, according to the 1900 census, counted 1,750,000 "gainfully occupied children aged ten to fifteen." Among them, a Charleston sweep (above) spent his days clambering up and down the city's chimneys.

Telephone wires crosshatch Lower Broadway prior to 1900 (and the advent of underground routing). One newspaper daringly forecast a future of phones in "practically every household." In 1900, there was one per 127 Americans. Thomas Edison's offhand phrase, "press the button," encompassed a growing assortment of new inventions that poured into everyday life. Among them, his Ediphone (opposite), the first dictating machine, eased transcriptionists' tasks.

courtesy; a creature spirited enough to move like chain lightning, and with perfect accuracy, docile enough to deny herself the sweet privilege of the last word." Another human icon of 20th-century economic life emerged at the same time: the professional manager. The University of Pennsylvania founded its Wharton School in 1881; the Universities of Chicago and California both founded their business schools in 1898. In 1900, Dartmouth founded its Amos Tuck School of Business Administration and, in 1908, Harvard its graduate School of Business Administration. No longer were large companies run directly by their capitalist owners but rather by trained professionals as loyal to the long-term stability of the system as to the next exciting business opportunity.

On the factory floor, specialized machinery shifted skills and control to engineers and supervisors. Similarly, new technologies for producing and disseminating information extended the purview of managers over ever larger fields of human effort. Once again, standardization and uniformity were the order of the day. Flowing from management down the hierarchy to employees were circular and general orders, employee manuals, forms, and in-house magazines. Flowing up the pyramid, numerous documents described industrial activity in easily comparable categories: monthly and quarterly reports, graphs, Gantt charts (named after

H. L. Gantt, a Taylor disciple), memos, and statistics. Such document technologies alone could not guarantee modern management methods, but they did help implement a systematic philosophy and led to the development of still further technologies for processing information.

Government as well as private enterprise adopted managerial systems to organize human activities and created technologies for managing vast numbers of people. Once again, at the turn of the century technological change was intimately tied to social change. The Constitution of the United States decrees that the population be counted in a census every ten years. Before 1890, new waves of immigrants had so increased the number of Americans that the Census Bureau realized it could not finish the counting in the ten years before it would have to begin a new census. The bureau held a competition and selected a former employee, a young engineer named Herman Hollerith, to develop the necessary automated information-processing equipment.

Drawing on his observations of railroads' punched tickets, Hollerith built tabulating machinery based on punched cards, a veritable switching yard for census data. These machines processed the census of 1890 and of 1900 in record time. Each citizen's information was punched onto a card that recorded age, race, national

Snapshots take off

Wood-and-fabric wonder, the Wright Brothers' type A Flyer astonishes onlookers at a 1909 speed trial. Orville Wright piloted the craft, considered the world's first military airplane, over Virginia in a ten-mile flight from Fort Myer (left) to Alexandria and back. Memorializing events from the mundane to the marvelous, George Eastman's folding pocket Kodak #3 (above) made its appearance in 1903. Photography, said an instruction booklet, "is now feasible for everybody."

origin, marital status, and other variables. The machinery then counted, sorted, and tabulated the cards in rapid succession. "Consider a stack of schedules of thin paper higher than the Washington monument," wrote an exuberant Hollerith. "Imagine the work required in turning over such a pile of schedules page by page, and recording the number of persons on each schedule. This is what was done in one day by the population division of the Census Office." Hollerith's machinery represents an important progenitor of modern information technology—first employed to subdivide and correlate Americans according to their social and economic differences.

Other large organizations quickly realized the potential of Hollerith's machines. The Prudential Life Insurance Company began using them to run actuarial statistics; in the first decade of the new century the Pennsylvania Steel Company began automating its cost accounting, and Marshall Field department stores used Hollerith machinery to track retail sales. A host of other companies soon began using the machinery to track bills, factory orders, production statistics, marketing, and reporting. In 1924, after a series of mergers and acquisitions, Hollerith's company became International Business Machines (IBM), which continues to this day to develop new machinery to process commercial information.

As the 20th century dawned, the nature of work in America was changing. From the stopwatch-timing of Taylor's efficiency experts to the information routing of office workers to the repetitive piecework of assembly line workers to the coordination and control of professional managers, Americans spent their days in new, and sometimes strange, ways. The strike at the Watertown Arsenal revealed to Congress and to the public that these changes were not always beneficial to the people they affected. Newly structured jobs could be exciting, as people experienced the thrill of technology and the satisfaction of many people working together. "The work was not monotonous," recalled a turn-of-the-century telephone operator, "it was fascinating. The telephone was as much a source of wonder to the operator as to the subscriber. I didn't know why things happened, but I knew my touch was magic."

New jobs could also be dulling and monotonous as creativity and decision-making seemed relegated to ever smaller elites, ever further out of sight. Now, as we enter another new century, similar radical changes are upon us. History reminds us that the transformations of work, technology, and technique are always intertwined with changes in people—who they are and how they spend their days.

Model T's in the making roll down the moving assembly line (left), inaugurated by Henry Ford in 1913. "Save ten steps a day for each of 12,000 employees," he explained, "and you will have saved fifty miles of wasted motion and misspent energy." A day's output in 1913: a thousand chassis (above).

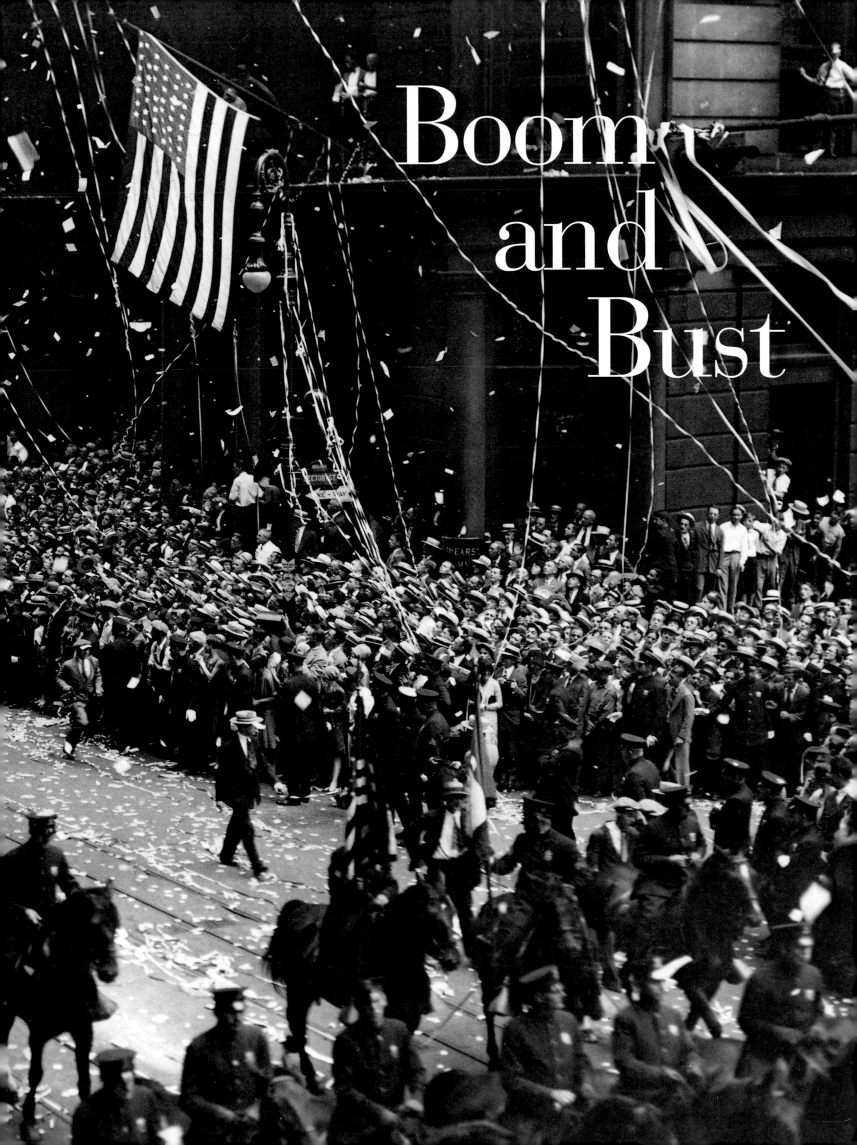

Boom and Bust

BY LESLIE ALLEN

Cascading gusher taps newfound prosperity in Louisiana's De Soto Field (opposite). By 1904, nearly half a century after the first U.S. strike, the nation had produced almost a billion barrels. Soon the automobile would fuel the oil industry's vast expansion —a major factor in 1920s boom times.

PRECEDING PAGES

With a ticker tape parade, New York City salutes the Navy's Richard E. Byrd and his crew after their 42-hour 1927 transatlantic flight.

I t was just a little before noon on September 16, 1920, when a huge explosion ripped through the intersection of New York's Wall and Broad Streets, the postwar world's financial epicenter. Almost instantly, 30 people—bank clerks, stenographers, brokers' helpers on their way to lunch—lay dead, with hundreds more injured. The explosion ruined buildings, hurled a metal projectile through a 34th-floor window of the Bankers' Club, and shattered windows blocks away. At the New York Stock Exchange, heavy silk draperies shielded the trading floor from crashing glass. There, the gong rang. But next day prices resumed their upward momentum.

Several other bombs had exploded around the country since 1919, but this was by far the largest and most lethal. Police linked a horse-drawn wagon at the scene to the crime, as well as a rambling screed, rife with misspellings, found in a neighborhood mailbox. But finally, the trail went cold, as it had with most of the other blasts, seen as probably the handiwork of small anarchist groups.

World War I, the "war to end all wars," had ended, but now peace was proving elusive on the home front. Not just bombs, but race riots and a wave of violent strikes exploded in the wake of the Armistice. Deep disillusionment set in among Americans as details of the European allies' secret wheeling and dealing became common knowledge. And, among a large share of the population, so did fear and loathing at events in revolutionary Russia, a wartime ally. Overnight, the "Bolshevik" replaced the "Hun" as public enemy number one. And if revolution could infect Moscow, why not Milwaukee?

Attorney General A. Mitchell Palmer—himself the target of a 1919 bomb that blew the bomber to bits on Palmer's front lawn—set out to quell the Red Menace. Palmer put an eager young agent named J. Edgar Hoover in charge of the government's new antiradical unit. Enough evidence of communism was mustered to ship out about 600 aliens among some 5,000 arrested. As Palmer brandished pictures of savage-looking, stubble-faced "Bolsheviks," a climate of general intolerance and xenophobia took hold. An Indiana jury took two minutes to acquit a man for killing an alien who shouted, "To hell with the United States." Guilty or not, their foreign origins helped send Italian-born Nicola Sacco and Bartolomeo Vanzetti to the electric chair for the murders of a Massachusetts paymaster and guard in 1920. To nip subversion in the bud, many states made it unlawful to teach in any language except English.

The Red Scare waned, but the sense that evil came from abroad would guide Americans through two decades of isolationism. Recoiling from foreign entanglements, Congress rejected the League of Nations and shored up the U.S. bulwarks with high tariffs and new barriers against immigration. In 1920, the nation found the ideal presidential candidate for the mood of the day: folksy Warren G. Harding, who wore a carnation in his lapel and waged his entire cam-

paign against Democrat James Cox from the front porch of his Ohio home.

The decade's first election swept away all vestiges of Wilsonian idealism; President Wilson himself remained incapacitated, cut down by a stroke in 1919. The electorate in 1920 also changed dramatically. A hefty proportion of voters were now lawbreakers, thanks to the disastrous 18th Amendment—the Volstead Act—which for 13 years would ban the production, traffic, and sale of intoxicating beverages. (Orchestras in big-city hotels and restaurants played funeral dirges the night it took effect.) And there were also nine and a half million potential new voters: The 19th Amendment, passed in 1920, gave women the vote. The handsome Harding was nominated with them in mind, though no candidate wooed many women to the polls.

Harding campaigned on a "return to normalcy," but the 1920s—the decade known as the Roaring Twenties, the Unruly Decade, the Jazz Age defied him. Flaming Youth, flappers, bootleggers, and Lost Generation intellectuals, among others, were its motley foot soldiers. Ballyhoo, alleged critics such as H. L. Mencken, was its marching song; a howling saxophone its voice. *(continued on page 223)*

A long embrace, a whispered promise.…After the last goodbye (opposite), home fires blazed during World War I. At a high school in Buffalo, New York, flying fingers made light work of woolen wear bound for the crew of a Navy cruiser. Six million adult women left the hearth—to work as munitions makers, trolley conductors, government clerks, Navy yeomen for shore duty. Employment gains proved temporary, though, as peacetime ushered prewar routines back into place.

"We're coming over" —training for war

"So prepare, say a pray'r....we're coming over, and we won't come back till it's over over there." Played everywhere, George M. Cohan's bugle-backed "Over There" was a recruiting call for some 24 million Americans who registered for the draft, and a marching song for the 2 million who sailed for war-weary France in 1917 and '18. They were World War I's Doughboys, a name first given to infantrymen along the Rio Grande whose faces were powdered white with adobe dust. But the term also hinted at youth and unformed malleability.

"So prepare...": When war broke out, U.S. military strength stood at some 200,000 men, more than a third of them poorly trained National Guard reservists; about 40,000 of the rest were stationed in the Philipines, Alaska, and other distant possessions. The building of a fighting force was a formidable task that began with the training of new recruits. A civilian army of 200,000 workers erected 32 training cantonments—"soldier-cities" meant for a full division of 27,000 men and 1,000 officers, though most eventually held far more. Americans compared the accomplish-

ment to the recent completion of the Panama Canal, with a notable difference: The canal's building took ten years; the cantonments were built in three months.

Shortages and other problems plagued the new camps. Tents would house the recruits, planners decided—and then discovered that canvas was costlier than wood, and scarcer, because of the demand for canvas cots and haversacks. The planners decided to save money on blankets and heat

---

SIGNAL CORPS RECRUITS SHARPEN RECONNAISSANCE SKILLS IN CAMP (ABOVE).

WOULD-BE PILOTS UNDERGO A BATTERY OF VISUAL-SPATIAL TESTS (OPPOSITE).

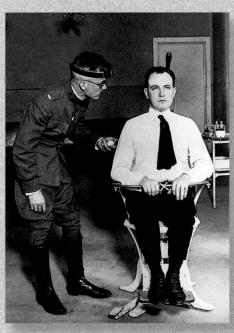

SOLDIERS FLEE AN EXPLODING HYDROGEN BALLOON AT FORT SILL, OKLAHOMA.

by building all the camps in the South. Other regions protested, and prevailed. Awaiting uniforms, men drilled in civvies and reported for calisthenics in their underwear.

Turning raw recruits into battle-ready soldiers took about twice as long as the three to four months originally envisioned. Delays in ordnance were a major reason, especially before war production effectively geared up to meet demand in 1918. Early inductees drilled with broomsticks, and entire machine gun companies never held a machine gun. Few of the Second Division regulars who arrived in France in September 1917 had ever discharged a firearm; some carried bayonets sheathed in newspaper and a few rounds of live ammunition. Disappointed French villagers called them "Boy Scoots." More prescient, Maj. Gen. John J. Pershing observed, "We shall make great soldiers of them," as he watched combat troops wearing campaign hats and choking collars come ashore at Saint-Nazaire.

"It is just as essential that a soldier know how to sing as that he should carry a rifle and know how to shoot it," Gen. Leonard Wood, former Chief of Staff, is reported to have said. Whether recruits knew how to sing or not, collective memory links them to a remarkable legacy of tunes, ranging from "You're in the Army Now" and "The Last Long Mile" to endless variations on the prewar stammering song, "K-K-K-Katy, Beautiful Katy" ("C-C-C-Cootie, Horrible cootie…"). The Committee on Training Camp Activities also brought in movies, pool tables, and other free-time amusements. The new draft law pushed barrooms and bawdy houses away from camps. Eventually, the seemingly endless routine of drilling and FTD ("feeding the dog," or doing nothing) would end, as a thrilling rumor spread through camp:

"Tomorrow we move!"

RECRUITS RELAX IN CANTONMENTS (TOP AND ABOVE).

DEPARTURE OF SEVENTH NEW YORK REGIMENT DRAWS THRONGS OF WELL-WISHERS (OPPOSITE).

To a generation of shocked elders, its dangers coalesced around a symbolic bob-haired, rouged, short-skirted, joyriding young woman who smoked, drank bathtub gin from a flask, and claimed to be "hipped on Freud."

Where did it all come from? The war took the blame—or the credit. New attitudes, people said, were born of the eat-drink-be-merry outlook of soldiers who daily stared down death on Europe's killing fields. Or perhaps it was the contagion of relaxed Continental mores. Wartime directives had shortened skirts to save cloth, loosened corsets to save steel, restricted alcoholic drinks to save grain. World War I was a major factor for another reason, too: It brought prosperity that translated into leisure time, spending power, and new outlooks. The nation's total wealth nearly doubled between 1914 and 1919 and would continue to grow rapidly in the 1920s. Though farmers, African Americans, the urban poor, and many other groups did not share in the good times, jobs were becoming plentiful for millions. In addition, wartime industrial demands brought about major leaps in mass production and efficiency in the nation's factories, which now retooled for the birth of America's consumer society.

We know much about the 1920s, including what the new spending power could purchase, because of a classic study by sociologists Robert and Helen Lynd. In Muncie, Indiana, (which the Lynds camouflaged as "Middletown") a working-class woman boasted an electric washing machine, electric iron, and vacuum sweeper, a big new icebox, and a $1,200 Studebaker, "with a nice California top, semi-enclosed." Only a third of American households had electricity in 1920, but thanks to the spread of electrification, laborsaving appliances were soon easing household drudgery across the land. With a bit of time on her hands, a woman might now put more power in her purse and silk stockings on her legs by taking a job—something millions had done out of need during the war. There were new enticements: cosmetics and true-confessions magazines, and new, "feminine" cigarette brands.

The entire family's horizons broadened. Visits to libraries and museums increased. Gramophones and radios began to sell in the millions. Without leaving their living rooms, people could tune in, day after day, to the deadlocked Democratic convention of 1924, live from Madison Square Garden. Spin a disc: A full jazz orchestra plays just for you. By mid-decade, Americans also ventured out to the movies, typically more than once a week. They imbibed religion and raciness in DeMille's *King of Kings*; chuckled at Chaplin; swooned over Valentino.

The Silver Screen imbued Americans with hero worship, which soon embraced larger-than-life sports stars as Babe Ruth and Jack Dempsey. The impulse to adulate, helped along by the flickering limelight of the new art of public relations, trickled down to obscure European royalty and flagpole sitters. It rose to a crescendo of patriotic pride in the person of solo aviator Charles Lindbergh, "a flash in the still night" piloting his tiny monoplane from New York to Paris in 1927.

Nothing in the 1920s matched the automobile as agent of social change and miracle of mass production. There were already more than 8 million cars on the road in 1920; by 1929, more than 23 million. By the mid-1920s, Henry Ford's assembly line turned out several Model T's a minute, and that was after the Tin Lizzie began losing the popularity contest against upstart rivals like the water-cooled Chevy, or models in Versailles Violet and a wide range of other brand-new hues.

Automobiles were a family priority well before mid-decade: In Muncie, many families had a car but no bathtub. After all, could a bathtub take the family for a Sunday drive or a little holiday at the shady new Kozy Kabins? The Muncie family might simply hope for a new home, with bathtub, in one of the suburban areas that the automobile itself was bringing into being.

There was a dark side to the automobile, in the minds of many. Flaming Youth took to unchaperoned outings to speakeasies, rumble-seat smooching—and worse. The Reverend Wilbur F. Crafts, whose preaching led to the creation of Hollywood's censorship office, demanded that Henry Ford "frame legislation that will stop the use of the motor car for immoral purposes." The task went beyond even Ford's inventiveness. Moral arbiters became more outraged as automakers replaced open cars with closed ones, making them, in effect, mobile rooms. Muncie's juvenile-court judge deemed the closed models "houses of prostitution on wheels." The automobile also played a crucial role in bootlegging. Souped-up eight-cylinder cars with springs sturdy enough to carry 200 one-gallon cans sped out of Appalachia with corn liquor, out of the New Jersey Pine Barrens with applejack, and across the Canadian border with Seagrams whiskey.

Beyond the underground economy, one in nine Americans had a job that depended on the automobile industry. Major industries—petroleum, steel, rubber,

Bigotry rears a hooded head at an Atlanta rally (above)—and across the postwar landscape. Reborn in 1915, the Ku Klux Klan targeted Jews, Catholics, and immigrants, as well as African Americans; its message of racism followed black migrants into the industrial North. An Indiana mob in 1930 gathers to gawk at a double lynching (left).

Dripping through a dotted line

Waging war on Demon Rum, retired Marine Corps Gen. Smedley Butler poses for Philadelphia photographers (opposite). Government propagandists publicized countless such images. And proponents of the "noble experiment" often cited the welfare of children. But despite Prohibition, created by the 18th Amendment, the nation remained awash in drink, much of it from Canada. As one former agent lamented, "You cannot keep liquor from dripping through a dotted line." Speakeasies were not just watering holes; they became hothouses of 1920s culture, places where the newly unshackled flapper could seek self-expression to the wail of a saxophone and trombone. Born at the dawn of what F. Scott Fitzgerald called the Jazz Age, Prohibition was doomed from the start. Thirteen years after it began, the 21st Amendment repealed it in 1933.

glass—tied to Detroit spurred along the 1920s business boom. So did whole new armies of advertising and public relations promoting the nation's faith in business. No one put the credo more succinctly than President Calvin Coolidge, who announced that "the business of America is business."

Veneration of business led to its close association with religion. Bruce Barton's best-selling *The Man Nobody Knows* said this of Jesus: "He picked up twelve men from the bottom ranks of business and forged them into an organization that conquered the world." If business was a religion, religion could be business—show business in the case of white-robed evangelist Aimee Semple McPherson and her made-in-Hollywood Angelus Temple.

Spectacle also reigned during the decade's most important legal proceeding, the 1925 Scopes "monkey trial," named after high school teacher John T. Scopes. He was charged with violating a state law forbidding the teaching of any doctrine that denied the divine creation of human beings. While famed trial lawyer Clarence Darrow and three-time presidential candidate William Jennings Bryan argued over the teaching of evolution in state schools, hellfire revivalists, rawboned farmers, the tabloid press, and hawkers of biology texts jostled for position in the backwater of

Dayton, Tennessee. The human juxtapositions, like the nature of the trial itself, served as a reminder that very real social schisms still polarized Americans, even as the nation as a whole progressed materially and intellectually during the 1920s.

The 1928 Democratic Convention, split over Prohibition and the reinvigorated Ku Klux Klan, reflected some of those same divisions. The party's choice of a "wet," Catholic candidate, New York Governor Al Smith, jarred many voters. But "Coolidge contentment," its mantle passed to the efficiency-minded Herbert Hoover, would have defeated the Democrats anyway. "You can't lick this prosperity thing," humorist Will Rogers noted wryly. "Even the fellow who hasn't got any is all excited over the idea."

As usual, Rogers had the last word. In 1928, the fellow who hadn't got any still amounted to some 60 percent of all Americans—those annual incomes fell below $2,000, the bleak borderland of subsistence. Efficient new factories were pouring forth perennially "new and improved" conveniences. But millions were still too poor to get anywhere near the decade's consumer banquet. For millions of others, new "buy now, pay later" plans masked underlying poverty. Whatever the family finances, most Americans were borrowing *(continued on page 239)*

"Black blizzard," like a glimpse of apocalypse, advances on Hooker, Oklahoma, in June 1937. Through much of the decade, the Great Plains had to reap what was sown in the 1920s, when heedless sodbusting and plowing exposed vulnerable land. Drought completed the damage, and the heartland brought in its bitter harvest of dust. The Dust Bowl spread from Texas to Nebraska.

A nation in Depression

"Brother, can you spare a dime?" It might have served as a nation's refrain, as Americans awoke to a nightmarish new reality in the 1930s. Through the '20s, they had gazed at themselves in a fun-house mirror created by speculation and excessive business expansion. The 1929 stock market crash signaled an end to the frenzy. At the edge of despair in Dorothea Lange's "White Angel Breadline" (opposite), a man awaits sustenance at a San Francisco soup kitchen. Stockbroker? Lawyer? Community pillar? Few were spared the anguish of the Great Depression. Wall Street panicked. Factories closed. Banks failed. Farm families were often doubly, even triply, afflicted. Bystanders during the '20s boom, they now watched helplessly as prices for their crops plummeted—or as the crops withered under cloudless skies and blankets of dust. A dusted-out Texas family (above), along with tens of thousands of other "Okies," took to the road. Tin-and-cardboard hovels sprang up everywhere, becoming cities of the dispossessed known as Hoovervilles; the name itself was an accusing finger pointed at the President, who seemed so rigid and uncaring to millions.

America votes a New Deal

Illinois dairymen (below) upend their milk cans as the bottom falls out of farm prices. Likewise hoping to boost demand by reducing supply, herdsmen slaughtered livestock and farmers let crops rot on the vine. Then came the New Deal, delivered by Franklin Delano Roosevelt, elected to his first term in 1932. He brought relief to some with new farm subsidies and the refinancing of programs, among an alphabet soup of new initiatives—TVA, WPA, NRA—that spelled hope to millions of citizens in despair. Striding confidently toward the future, Civilian Conservation Corps recruits (right) surged into army-style camps for stints of outdoor work that included the planting of millions of trees in the Dust Bowl.

Golden sports in gray days

Record-toppling athletic prowess provided welcome distraction from Depression woes, and, later, storm clouds overseas. Babe Ruth slammed his last homer, number 714, in 1935. But Ted Williams (opposite), who began his professional career the following year, might have bested the Babe if he had not served as a pilot during World War II and the Korean War; military service cost him five seasons. The year 1936 also saw the triumph of runner Jesse Owens (above), who won four gold medals at the Berlin Olympics, a stunning rebuttal to racist Nazi propaganda.

Drink **Coca-Cola** Delicious and Refreshing

"It's the refreshing thing to do"

Youth's delight in "swing music" brings a faster step. *The pause that refreshes* with ice-cold Coca-Cola is a step in the right direction for a fresh start.

* * *

p. s. It's the refreshing thing to do...because Coca-Cola is what refreshment ought to be,...pure, wholesome, delicious, ice-cold.

A NATURAL PARTNER OF GOOD THINGS TO EAT

FOUNTAIN SERVICE DRINK **Coca-Cola**

"Let's get a Coca-Cola"

It's a lucky thirst that meets an ice-cold Coca-Cola...at America's favorite meeting place, the soda fountain. Coca-Cola has the taste thirst goes for. It leaves you with an after-sense of complete refreshment ...making a pause *the pause that refreshes.*

COLD...ICE-COLD...AT BRIGHT AND CHEERFUL FOUNTAINS

Have a Coca-Cola = Howdy, Neighbor

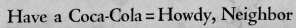

...or greeting friends at home and abroad

One of the first places they head for, when they get back, is the neighborhood soda fountain and all its old associations...among them, Coca-Cola. Many places overseas, too, your American fighting man meets up with that old friend...ice-cold Coca-Cola. It's always like word from home to hear the friendly greeting *Have a "Coke"* in a strange land. Yes, around the globe, Coca-Cola stands for *the pause that refreshes,*—has become a symbol of our way of living.

In news stories, books and magazines, you read how much our fighting men cherish Coca-Cola whenever they get it. Luckily, they find Coca-Cola available in over 35 allied and neutral countries 'round the globe.

Coca-Cola TRADE-MARK

Coca-Cola -the global high-sign

It's natural for popular names to acquire friendly abbreviations. That's why you hear Coca-Cola called "Coke".

COPYRIGHT 1944, THE COCA-COLA COMPANY

DRINK **Coca-Cola**

YOUR HOST OF THE AIRWAVES

The Coca-Cola Company presents
EDGAR BERGEN with **CHARLIE McCARTHY**
CBS 8 p. m. EST every Sunday

And every day...wherever you travel, the familiar red cooler is your
HOST OF THE HIGHWAYS...HOST TO THE WORKER in office and shop...HOST TO THIRSTY MAIN STREET the country over.

COPYRIGHT 1950, THE COCA-COLA COMPANY

Quenching a nation's thirst

Quaint by later, image-driven standards, a half-century of Coca Cola® advertising reflects changes in product, salesmanship, and American society. In 1891, the company pushed a frankly medicinal tonic—"For Headache or Tired Feeling." Free calendars (right) provided inexpensive advertising. Elaborate gimmicks rolled into town (above) in the 1920s, as the advertising industry came into its own. Ads in the 1930s said Coke's "wholesome substances…do most in restoring you to your normal self." Fourteen years of ads for National Geographic *(opposite) maintained a consistent style and sunniness that shone through the Depression—and, later, global conflict, as Coca Cola linked itself to the war effort. Corporate sponsorships and broadcast celebrities, familiar to today's ad-gazers, arrived by 1950.*

to buy automobiles, plug-in appliances, and furniture. Easy credit had its stock market counterpart in margin buying. Shoeshine boys bought $50,000 worth of stock with $500 down; by the time they passed the tip along to their next customers, the share price was up again.

"During most of 1928 and 1929," wrote historian Frederick Lewis Allen, "buying stocks was like betting at a race track at which, fantastically, most of the horses won." While the phantom horses ran, however, the American economy was slowing, and financial problems overseas added to perilous conditions in the banking and credit industries. Days of sliding prices in October 1929 were hiccups in confidence that threatened the whole airy structure. It finally collapsed spectacularly on October 24.

Could it be just a tremor? Business leaders and investors dusted themselves off, shoppers crowded department stores for Christmas buying, and the *New York Times* bypassed Black Thursday as 1929's most newsworthy event (the Navy's Richard Byrd's South Pole overflight took the honor, followed by the St. Valentine's Day gangland massacre in Chicago). There was even a little bull market rally in the spring of 1930.

But the downward spiral of lagging sales and corporate earnings—followed by wage cuts, layoffs, unemployment, and more business losses—accelerated inexorably toward the Great Depression's nadir in 1932. By then, some 5,000 banks had gone under and 86,000 businesses had failed. Gone was $74 billion in investments, three times the cost of World War I. In September 1932, *Fortune* magazine estimated that 34 million Americans, more than a quarter of the population, had no income. *Fortune*'s figures did not include millions of destitute farm families, whose foreclosure notices papered the gateposts of county courthouses.

For the employed, a living wage was often an oxymoron. Desperate competition for jobs allowed employers to bust wages down to a dime an hour for lumberjacks, a nickel an hour for sawmill workers, 80 cents a week for hatmakers in New York sweatshops. Teachers endured "payless paydays" and kept body and soul united by "boarding around" with their students' families. In Chicago, writer Edmund Wilson described an unemployed widow who "fed herself and her fourteen-year-old son on garbage. Before she picked up the meat, she would always take off her glasses so that she couldn't see the maggots."

War brings wrenching partings for the second time in a generation (opposite). On December 7, 1941, Japan launched a surprise attack on Pearl Harbor— and immediately some

125,000 Japanese Americans were targeted by their neighbors and government. Suspicion, harassment, and assault soon led to the infamy of forced relocation to camps. This tagged tot (above), like most others bound for internment, was U.S.-born. Still, love of country never deserted Nisei GIs, and their 442nd Regimental Combat Team earned more citations than any other outfit in the war.

Declaring that "the spirit of charity and mutual self-help" would conquer the Depression, Hoover resisted direct federal aid. The irony was not lost on Americans who had witnessed his rise to the status of world hero for directing relief to millions of starving Europeans after World War I; in Finnish, for instance, a newly minted verb, "to hoover," meant "to help." Now new words entered homegrown parlance: "Hoover blankets," for old newspapers that the homeless slept under; "Hoovervilles," for the tin-and-cardboard shantytowns that housed people who had been evicted and lost their homes to bank foreclosures. Washington, D.C., became one big Hooverville in the summer of 1932, when more than 15,000 unemployed veterans and their families arrived to beg for the bonus Congress had mandated for World War I service. Citing "incipient revolution," Gen. Douglas MacArthur, on Hoover's orders, struck back with cavalry, infantry, tanks, machine guns, and 3,000 tear gas grenades. Across the nation, disgusted Americans began to think of Hoover as the "President-reject."

Beyond the cities, where the misery was so visible because it was so concentrated, armies of jobless men rode freight trains across landscapes of growing bleakness. In the 1920s, the soil-weakening practice of sodbusting in the Great Plains had been accompanied by the optimistic mantra, "Rain follows the plough." But it didn't. By the early 1930s, drought began to devastate the heartland. Fields blew away; dunes drifted cross-country; "black blizzards" of topsoil brought darkness at noon.

More than 250 million acres in Colorado, Kansas, Texas, New Mexico, and Oklahoma were doomed. "And the women came out of their houses to stand beside their men—to feel whether this time the men would break," wrote John Steinbeck in *The Grapes of Wrath*. Sooner or later, of course, they did. The Dust Bowl was the last ordeal for farmers who had known none of the 1920s boom times. Piling pots and mattresses atop broken-down LaSalles and other latter-day prairie schooners, the Okies, as the migrants were labeled, set out for southern California, dreaming, like Steinbeck's Ma Joad, of "the nicest places, little white houses in among the orange trees."

Among the orange trees, dwellers in white houses recoiled at the arrival of 350,000 dusted-out Okies. Black migrants fleeing the impoverished rural South fared much worse, especially in Northern cities, where many were violently scapegoated by white job seekers. Bedraggled migrants, in the millions, contributed to widespread murmuring that revolution was in the air. But if so, Americans had picked a seemingly improbable leader in the blue-blooded Franklin Delano Roosevelt. He won all but six states in November 1932. Election night brought a bumper crop of newborn namesakes, including Franklin Delano Mayblum and Franklin Delano Finkelstein.

Winter rain drenched Washington as Roosevelt delivered the first of his four inaugural speeches on March 4, 1933. He turned fear on its ear by calling it the nation's only true foe—and handed Americans an epiphany. Within a month, household hiding places yielded a billion dollars in hoarded currency to newly reopened banks.

Roosevelt promised Americans a wide-ranging New Deal, but success hinged on quick action to quell panic. During the "first hundred days" of his administration, he barraged Congress. Enacted, his bills and a much longer list of later measures produced an alphabet soup of agencies that made the federal government an activist force in Americans' daily lives. For $30 a month, plus room, board, and health care, 2.9 million "CCC boys" planted trees, dug ditches, and fought fires and erosion with the Civilian Conservation Corps. Artists scaled scaffolding to paint post office murals, writers penned state travel guides, and Burt Lancaster joined

scores of other actors in theater productions financed by the Works Progress Administration (WPA). To Roosevelt himself, the New Deal's "supreme achievement" was the 1935 Social Security Act.

Most Americans adored Roosevelt. But he was "That Man" or "That Fellow" in country-club whispering campaigns and compared to Stalin in corporate boardrooms. He shrugged off the rants of Father Charles E. Coughlin, the Radio Priest, who informed listeners on 60 stations that their President was "a liar" and an "anti-God." Coughlin drew a larger audience than did the "Amos 'n' Andy" show—itself an inspiration to Louisiana demagogue Huey Long, who christened himself "Kingfish," after the head of the fraternal lodge on the black-lampooning show.

Fogbound San Francisco (opposite) welcomes its namesake cruiser, symbol of a tide that began turning in the Allies' favor in June 1942. Following the Japanese defeat at

Midway, victories in both theaters stymied the German-Japanese-Italian Axis. Still, by 1944 the relentless demand for fresh troops kept recruits jumping (above) at the U.S. Army Infantry School in Fort Benning, Georgia.

Women enlist in a war of work

After the Japanese attack on Pearl Harbor on December 7, 1941, women went to war. Emergency legislation gave them the opportunity to serve as clerks, telegraphers, airplane spotters, chauffeurs, and telephone operators, among other jobs, in the hastily created female branches of the armed services. Some 13,000 rushed to enlist on the first day of registration; by war's end, more than 200,000 would serve in the Women's Army Corps (WAC) and the Women Accepted for Volunteer Emergency Service (WAVES).

But it was in the war-production plants that World War II truly became a woman's war. As many as six million women stepped forward to do their part, welding, soldering, operating lathes, and performing other grimy jobs. They turned out thousands of Flying Fortresses, warships, cartridge cases, and countless other items of matériel produced by the "arsenal of democracy." At a Douglas Aircraft plant, which was turning out dive bombers, one out of every three workers was a woman. First treated as objects of contempt—"lipsticks" or "dollies"—by male coworkers, the female recruits soon became every factory manager's dream, renowned for their patience,

eagerness to learn, and, most of all, competence.

Women already employed in domestic service, textile plants, and other low-paying jobs answered the call to arms first, attracted by the high pay and prestige of war-related work. African-American women in particular found a new kind of freedom on the assembly line. A second wave of recruits consisted of teenagers just out of high school. To lure them into the defense plants, the Office of War Information created "Rosie the Riveter." As the world's most winsome grease monkey, she became a symbol in posters, photographs, and song. Norman Rockwell put her on a *Saturday Evening Post* cover. *Life* magazine found real-life Rosie Bonavita and called her "neither drudge nor slave but the heroine of a new order." She could pound 3,345 rivets into a bomber wing in six hours.

But within a year of Pearl Harbor, war planners were forced into a controversial move: the recruitment of homemakers. Aiming for

BOMBER ENGINE HOUSING FRAMES A WORKER AT A CALIFORNIA AIRCRAFT PLANT (OPPOSITE).

FUTURE FLYING FORTRESSES FILL BOEING'S FUSELAGE ASSEMBLY LINE (ABOVE).

A MACHINE GUN UNDERGOES A BREAKDOWN TEST.

almost three million, propagandists emphasized the work's temporary nature and its similarity to domestic routines: "If you've used an electric mixer in your kitchen, you can learn to run a drill press...."

A third of those who responded had children under the age of 14. Soon came reports that shocked the nation: Children were being left untended while their mothers worked. A tireless campaigner for day care, First Lady Eleanor Roosevelt persuaded the Kaiser Company shipyard's owners in Portland, Oregon, to create a child-care center. It would serve as a model for defense plants across the land.

In 1940, women —most of them telephone operators, nurses, teachers, and social workers— made up 24.3 percent of the U.S. workforce; by 1945, the percentage was 34.7. The National War Labor Board established the principle of equal pay for men and women. Spurred by this ruling, Congress in 1946 passed a federal equal-pay law.

When women walked into jobs in war plants and shipyards, they crossed a threshold and would never turn back. Even though there were large-scale layoffs after the war, the percentage of women in the labor force did not drop to its pre-war low but reached 30 percent, heralding the higher percentages of future years.

A POSTER WARNS OF LOOSE LIPS (ABOVE); FAMILIES WHO LOST MEMBERS IN THE WAR DISPLAYED A GOLD-STAR FLAG.

Homeward-bound from the war in Europe, GIs crowd decks of the Queen Elizabeth *(right). Converted from luxury liner to troopship, she was spacious enough for a full Army division. Germany had surrendered in May 1945. But veterans of European combat faced new peril—an invasion of Japan, scheduled for November 1945. On August 14, as word spread of Japan's imminent surrender, joyous servicemen, no longer worried about hitting beaches in Japan, join a conga line that snakes through Lafayette Park, fronting the White House. From there, President Truman announced the surrender. V-J Day and war's end—days after atomic bombs snuffed out Hiroshima and Nagasaki —brought jubilation, tempered by a sense of lost innocence as the nuclear era began.*

Hearing Roosevelt's rich and soothing voice during one of his radio "fireside chats" made most Americans think a welcome friend was with them. His words were not always reassuring: In his 1937 inaugural speech, Roosevelt still saw "one-third of a nation ill-housed, ill-clad, ill-nourished." And while the Depression lingered, newsreels, newspapers, and especially radio brought Americans increasingly horrific reports from overseas. On September 12, 1938, they heard for themselves, through a Berlin shortwave relay, the fathomless hatred in Hitler's voice, live from Nuremberg, threatening the Sudetenland.

In the movies, they laughed, warily, through Chaplin's *The Great Dictator*, and between the feature and the cofeature they saw, in newsreel's grainy footage, the Japanese thrusts in Asia. They heard German soldiers singing, "We're Sailing Against England" and Kate Smith belting out "God Bless America." They heard their old hero Charles Lindbergh, back from self-imposed European exile, broadcasting radio speeches that sounded pro-German to some. Newsman Edward R. Murrow's urgent transatlantic cadence crackled in, along with Roosevelt's steadying voice, until finally, December 7, 1941, arrived with the Japanese attack on Pearl Harbor. The last vestiges of isolationism were overcome.

The monumental war effort would at last unite the nation, something that

neither the First World War—nor the boom and bust that followed it—could do. World War II would also transform the nation in permanent ways. Among them, the war effort would set in motion a vast migration. Between the 15 million-plus Americans who joined the armed forces and the 15 million who went to work in the Arsenal of Democracy, more than 20 percent of the population moved—making American mobility habitual, for better and for worse. As wartime "Help Wanted" signs went up across the land, millions were also able to make a fresh start after years of joblessness, and a truly middle-class nation was born. Long after "Dr. Win-the-War" replaced old "Dr. New Deal," a continuing partnership between a strong government and its citizens secured the gains in peacetime. Most notably, the GI Bill of Rights, providing college and vocational training and loans for home ownership and businesses, smoothed the transition into civilian life for returning veterans.

Suburbs blossomed; Dr. Spock's *Common Sense Book of Baby and Child Care* sold in the millions. Yet as provincial as the new tracts of postwar life might seem, the country's postwar might and prestige—its new dominance and leadership—now bound Americans to the rest of the world. So too did the blinding dawn of the nuclear era, unifying Americans and everyone else in a world of breathtaking fragility.

Gone to the Movies

BY RICHARD SCHICKEL

"Not half a dozen men have ever been able to keep the whole equation of pictures in their heads," F. Scott Fitzgerald wrote in 1940 on the first page of *The Last Tycoon*, the Hollywood novel he did not live to finish. Four decades later, a much more successful screenwriter, William Goldman, implied that Fitzgerald had overestimated the number of those who had solved the mathematics of the movies. "NOBODY KNOWS ANYTHING," he wrote in *Adventures in the Screen Trade*. The caps are his; he wanted us to understand that he wasn't kidding.

And that he was right, or maybe right with an asterisk and a footnote. The movies after all are, and nearly always have been, a profitable business. So from time to time somebody must have known something. That, however, does nothing more than ironize the fact that the medium's history is unpredictable, incoherent, discontinuous—a series of jarring jump cuts; no dissolves, no cross-fades, no smooth and gentle niceties to mark its often brutal transitions.

One day they're doing business one way. Then—bam!—they're doing it another way. And the people who thought they understood how the industry functioned suddenly don't have a clue. These revolutions occur every 12 or 15 or 20 years and they take their toll. "Thank God for the trust funds," said Constance Talmadge, when one of the revolutions, the coming of sound, destroyed her career. But not everyone has trust funds. And even if you do, it's hard to be merely rich when, only yesterday, you were both rich and actively famous, instead of only nostalgically so.

How sweeping these revolutions are! We are pleased to think of them otherwise, because we love historical coherence, we love to see things root, grow, and flourish logically. We look at someone like Gary Cooper among the stars, or John

"I felt ashamed...for even being a member of the species to which such things are addressed," Aldous Huxley wrote after seeing The Jazz Singer. *Obviously, the crowds gathered in front of the theater at its premiere felt otherwise. When the movie opened, only about a hundred movie houses were wired for sound.*

PRECEDING PAGES

D.W. Griffith built an unprecedented set for the Babylonian sequence of his 1916 epic, Intolerance.

253

Ford and Alfred Hitchcock among the directors, see them making their way from the silent to the sound to the CinemaScope era more or less untroubled by the radically revised movie equations, and we think of them as exemplary. But how few their number actually is. From "Broncho Billy" Anderson to Clara Bow, from John Gilbert to Buster Keaton, from Betty Grable to John Payne, most star careers are brutally brief. The same is true of directors. Griffith, Vidor, Sturges, Capra—how many have been stalled, diminished, phased out by their failure to master some new movie math.

All that is true of individual movies as well. We form our attachments to them in our preadolescent and adolescent years, when we're free for the first time to attend the movies on our own. But that state of innocence—when the screen seems so large and bright and we are so small and impressionable—is terribly brief. We grow up, the world hurries on, and the next generation replicates our experience, but with different movies. It takes either a very great movie, or one that somehow seems to immortally capture the spirit of the moment, to survive this endless bustling forward.

"The world is very large," says the critic David Thomson, "and the greatest films so small." How, we may wonder, does even a truly great movie, something like *Citizen Kane*, instruct *Titanic*? Or *Pulp Fiction*? Or take Gary Cooper. How does his career instruct Mel Gibson?

The answer is that it does not. It is a great convenience to think of movie history as driven by great directors or great stars or great movies. But the truth is that only a lucky few catch the tidal rush of megatechnological or megaeconomic change and bob brightly along on its surface. Most of them sink.

The movies have endured five of these sea changes in the course of a history that as a major social, economic, and artistic phenomenon is still less than a hundred years old: The Nickelodeon Era; the Age of the Silent Feature; the so-called Classic Age (the first two decades of sound-film production); the Age of Television, in which they allowed themselves to be defined by a competing medium; and, finally, our own historically heedless moment, when they are ruled almost entirely by the uninformed whims of adolescents caught up in the new and the now, impervious to the fading glories of the past.

Having said that, however, one must also say this: Maybe the kids are right. Maybe the attempt to identify and honor a Great Tradition of the movies is

"That line is a Klondike," said one nickelodeon manager, as he gazed at the crowd gathering outside his theater. Nickelodeons played programs of one-reel "photoplays," and the primal pleasure of movie-going in an atmosphere redolent of "stale tobacco, rank sweat, perfume and dirty drawers while the piano played fast music" was permanently treasured by the likes of critic James Agee.

SAFETY LAST, 1923

feckless, an exercise in the idlest form of nostalgia. It is, perhaps, a premise worth testing by briefly studying those earlier movie ages, determining what, if anything, they accomplished that continues to condition what we see now at the multiplex near us.

The first of the broad historical cycles, the Nickeloden Era, may, oddly enough, have the largest continuing relevance to us. It began in 1903 with the release of the first American story film, *The Great Train Robbery*. It ended in 1915 with the release of the first American spectacle film, *The Birth of a Nation*. When *The Great Train Robbery* was released, there were no theaters in the United States solely devoted to the exhibition of motion pictures. A dozen years later there were between 8,000 and 10,000.

In that first period moviemakers learned that they had to tell a story, and that they needed stars to draw people to those stories. That much about the industry has proved to be unchanging.

Movie narrative was largely the invention of D.W. Griffith, a failed actor and playwright, who found his way to the Biograph Studios in New York in 1908 and over the next five years made more than 400 little one-reel movies on every conceivable subject. In the process of borrowing from the popular fiction and theater of the 19th century, he often crunched whole novels, plays, and epic poems down to one-reel lengths. At his best, he was an inspired realist, making little slices of ordinary life in all its comic, romantic, and melodramatic aspects. He coordinated and codified the basic grammar of film (close-ups, fades, dissolves, crosscutting) into a new visual language, at once efficient, transparent, and thrilling.

Stardom was another, more complicated matter. People almost immediately began noticing the anonymous, poorly paid ($5 a day) players in these little movies and asked theater managers for more pictures featuring them. But the business in those days was dominated by the so-called Patents Trust, a combination of companies that believed the money in movies lay in what we would now term "hardware," the cameras and projectors they controlled through patents. They made their money by licensing this equipment and making an exclusive deal with Kodak for film the moviemakers used. Stars only added what the Patents Trust deemed unacceptable risk and expense to their equation.

But independent filmmakers embraced both stardom and length, beginning with Adolph Zukor, who in 1912 imported from France a four-reel version of

BLOCKHEADS, 1938

THE GOLD RUSH, 1925

"Another fine mess" is about to develop as dim Stan and splenetic Oliver set forth on one of their low-budget, richly comical journeys (upper). In one of his immortal moments, Charlie Chaplin (above) attempts to stave off starvation by eating his shoe. (It was licorice, and it made him very sick.) Silent star Harold Lloyd (opposite) dangles 12 stories up. Below him were mattress-covered platforms.

Queen Elizabeth, starring Sarah Bernhardt. It was not a very good film, but the aging star carried it to handsome profitability, and Zukor immediately began advertising a program of "Famous Players in Famous Plays." Three years later, Charlie Chaplin was making $1,250 a week and Mary Pickford, who had begun with Griffith in 1909, was making $100,000 a year. In 1916 she signed a million-dollar contract with Zukor, a figure Chaplin would match two years later. The star system was fully established in a matter of about three years.

So too were feature films. A year after *Queen Elizabeth*, the Italian-made *Quo Vadis?*—nine reels long—ran for 22 weeks at advanced prices in a legitimate theater on Broadway. It had no stars, but its spectacle was overwhelming. Its splendors challenged Griffith, who answered with *Judith of Bethulia* at four reels, then left Biograph, and spent 1914 making four films that were six or seven reels long—in preparation for *The Birth of a Nation*. Irredeemably racist, undeniably powerful, it ran over two hours, cost more than $100,000, and grossed close to $5 million in its first U.S. run. The film initiated what people called for a while "the feature craze," as if it would soon subside and everyone would return to being sensible.

But the nickelodeons died almost as hastily as they arose, replaced by a new mode of exhibition—the picture palace. S. L. ("Roxy") Rothafel had opened his first in New York in 1913. Over the next decade and a half, hundreds of them opened across the United States, in towns as small as Joliet, Illinois, or Worcester, Massachusetts. They were huge and ornate, evoking everything from oriental splendor to Moorish elegance in their design. As early as 1916 some of them were air-conditioned.

So there it was, an infinitely more expensive way of making movies, a star system—and, by the mid-1920s an oligarchic system of production, distribution, and exhibition. One by one, the smaller producers failed, undone by the costs of doing business in this new way, which established most of the logos that still dominate the movies. Indeed, by the mid-1920s, the producers of *Birth of a Nation* were bankrupt, and Griffith, struggling to remain independent, was virtually so— and in artistic decline as well.

The people who made the films of the high, silent period believed that their movies represented, as Alfred Hitchcock once said, "the purest form of cinema." They felt that they were obliged to communicate thought and feeling solely through pictorial means, "the visual hieroglyphs of the unseen world," as one of

Hollywood musicals of the 1930s transported audiences to a fantasy world where Great Depression troubles were shed by dancing: You could be Fred Astaire and Ginger Rogers, or you could lose yourself in the giddy extravaganzas of Busby Berkeley (opposite), who enlivened a drab era with chorines, "miles of silk, tons of feathers, and gallons of glitter." The entrancing movie musical's life was short, giving way to more realistic, story-driven films like Saturday Night Fever *with John Travolta.*

FOOTLIGHT PARADE, 1933

The Godfather's *grandfather,*
Edward G. Robinson's dapper
Little Caesar, *stops lead in the*
1930 gangster film (left), one of
60 made between 1930 and
1932. Robinson was of a new
breed of stars—snarling tough,
yet somehow vulnerable—who
spoke in the harsh tones of a
newly urbanized American in
the early days of talkies—and of
the Depression. James Cagney,
who, in a startling scene, pushed
a grapefruit into the face of moll
Mae Clarke (opposite, center),
died by the gun in The Public
Enemy. *Barbara Stanwyck and*
Fred MacMurray (opposite,
upper) pioneered more private
but equally deadly criminality
in Billy Wilder's Double
Indemnity, *one of the great*
film noirs, a decade later. In
1974, Jack Nicholson's private
eye (opposite, lower) traced the
tragic links between a vast pub-
lic corruption and an equally
terrible personal one in another
great film noir Chinatown,
written by Robert Towne,
directed by Roman Polanski.

LITTLE CAESAR, 1930

the early theoreticians of the medium put it. This suggests a high seriousness of purpose—the brutal force of *Greed* or the cynical power of *The Wedding March,* to name just two of Erich von Stroheim's masterpieces. Or the intense expressionism of King Vidor's *The Crowd* or the ravishing beauty of F. W. Murnau's *Sunrise.* All of these films flirt entrancingly with the ineffable.

And yet they don't quite catch the spirit of the age. There was something much giddier about it. One thinks of the silent clowns: Keaton's stony melancholy in the face of a malevolent universe; Lloyd's eager, thrilling, yet curiously touching wrangles with modernity; Chaplin's sometimes sublime sentimentality. Or the long, lovely arc of Douglas Fairbanks's superbly orchestrated athletic sequences. Or Pickford's spunky, utterly persuasive sweetness. Or Valentino's eye-rolling eroticism, so often comical now, and yet somehow expressing a kind of sweet, romantic panic, too. Or the gravitas of Chaney's marginalized, vulnerable cripples. And even then we are not done: Clara Bow's flapper, Garbo's doomed but bravely enduring adulteress, Tom Mix's gaudy cowboy, John Barrymore's magnificent rogue (or better still his chilling Dr. Jekyll and Mr. Hyde). They are all part of the antirealistic essence of the silent picture, that sense that the movies were a kind of dreamland, playland, cloud-cuckoo land, where almost anything could happen, precisely because their every frame advertised their remoteness from reality.

DOUBLE INDEMNITY, 1944

THE PUBLIC ENEMY, 1930

CHINATOWN, 1974

Because the movies could not speak, everything else was permitted them—improbable romance, impossible derring-do, and a sort of innocent raciness. "We were movie-mad," the late, great historian of the silent film, George Pratt, once remarked, because the movies were so mad. By 1929, some 95 million people went to the movies every week. By 1946, the estimated weekly U.S. movie attendance was 100 million, or more than 5 billion tickets a year. Today, the annual U.S. movie attendance is about 1.5 billion—and that includes people who stay home and watch their movies on cassettes.

At the height of their popularity, movies once again embarked on another era of radical change. They learned to talk. 1926: Barrymore's *Don Juan* has a music and effects track. 1927: Al Jolson's *The Jazz Singer* has him singing and uttering

The Duke, John Wayne (left), was the greatest of all heroes of Westerns—the angry, honorable stranger who used fierce moral force to tame the wilderness. Like his predecessor, William S. Hart (opposite, top), Wayne came to total identification with the largely mythic pioneering values he represented. But unlike Hart, he had no firsthand experience of those values when

he was growing up. During his long career, Wayne played more soldiers than Westerners, just as his successor, Clint Eastwood (opposite, lower) played more cops than cowboys. But they were both tall, taciturn men, confident and reassuring in their silences. No actors have spent more years in the box office top ten than Wayne and Eastwood.

RED RIVER, 1948

THE GUN FIGHTER, 1917

UNFORGIVEN, 1992

a few lines of dialogue. 1928: *The Lights of New York,* the first 100 percent talking movie. 1929: *Applause,* the first good talkie, with Helen Morgan playing a doomed musical comedy star.

From 1927 to 1929 sound and silence co-existed, with many of the great works of silent cinema coming to the screen in that period (*Wings, The General, Flesh and the Devil, The Crowd, The Wedding March, The Last Command, The Wind*). Garbo held out against talk until 1930, Chaplin until 1940. But these were quixotic gestures. For once again the revolution was total. It's hard to think of a major star of the silent era who survived the transition with his or her career totally intact. The movies became a fundamentally different medium when they began to talk.

Were the movies of the sound era more realistic than those of the silent period? What we can certainly say is that the movies became tougher and brisker in tone, reflecting the hard realities of an urbanized nation enduring the hard times of the Great Depression. More important, Hollywood entered on the long period of genre filmmaking that sound opened up to them. That meant musicals: the grandeur of Busby Berkeley's goofy, spectacular geometries; the intimate quarrelsomeness of Astaire and Rogers. It was also the great age of horror films, because music and sound—the creaking door, the howling wind—were so important to achieving their full creepiness. At the same time came the gangster films: Edward G. Robinson of *Little Caesar*, James Cagney of *The Public Enemy*, Paul Muni of *Scarface*. They were players of a new type—not conventionally handsome, snarling class resentment, suiting the more naturalistic demands of the revolutionized screen.

They had their female equivalents: Jean Harlow in *Red-Headed Woman,* Joan Crawford in *Possessed*—working girls (as they were called) daring to aspire romantically above their station. There were furtive romances, too, like Irene Dunne's *Back Street* and Ann Vickers and Barbara Stanwyck's *Forbidden,* in which smart women subsumed their own ambitions to those of the married lovers whose calls they patiently waited for.

Above all else, the 1930s gave us the great age of romantic comedy. The wrangles between Clark Gable and Claudette Colbert in *It Happened One Night,* or Cary Grant and Katharine Hepburn in *Bringing Up Baby,* or Grant and Irene Dunne in *The Awful Truth* all involved love affairs that crossed class lines.

Typically, one lover is rich, careless, and haughty, while the other is poor, striving, and capable of teaching the other how to dunk doughnuts. These films—as a group, the best American movies of their times—shared with all the other new genres the quality of their dialogue. Critic Stanley Kauffman has characterized it as "tight-packed wisecrackese which sounds like life but is really the…equivalent of blank verse. For it is not realism, but real speech distilled and heightened….an American convention, an abstraction." It also finally made people forget about the picturesque glories of the silent film.

Hollywood was truly an industry now, having achieved a perfect vertical integration of its operations: It owned the means of production, distribution, and exhibition of almost all of its product—usually including both features on the double bill, the newsreel, the short subjects, the animated cartoon. To this mix the poverty-row companies might contribute the odd second feature to the small-town theaters, and here and there an independent producer like David O. Selznick might make something like *Gone With the Wind* for release by one of the majors. There was even room, from time to time, for a rebel statement like *Citizen Kane.*

The studios had something for everyone, arriving at predictable intervals, at every price range (from the first-runs downtown to the last suburban sub-run, where late into the 1940s you could still see a movie for a quarter). The system seemed to run itself, with the major stars bound to long-term studio contracts and basically obliged to do anything the bosses told them to do. Darryl F. Zanuck, head of production at Twentieth Century-Fox, claimed he could make up his entire year's production schedule—so many musicals, so many comedies, so many action-adventures—in a single afternoon.

This system continued through World War II and for several years thereafter, with attendance from 1945 through 1948 staying close to its 90-million-tickets-a-week heights. The content of the movies changed somewhat in the 1940s. Adventure films naturally tended to be about wartime derring-do; romantic comedies were abandoned (although the great Preston Sturges took up some of the slack with his portraits of slightly addled American dreamers); musicals and other lighter fare searched for and found a usably inspiring past in turn-of-the-century America. (*Meet Me in St. Louis* is a good example.) During the war, and peaking immediately thereafter, a new and wonderfully stylized genre, film noir, with its weak men and its spiderishly evil women drawing their victims *(continued on page 270)*

"We sell tickets to theaters, not movies," said exhibition mogul Marcus Loew. Theaters like his Loew's Paradise in New York (above) replaced the nickelodeons in the 1920s. Old-timers mutter about the modern multiplex, which duplicates nickel movie squalor but not its economy. Ushers in New York's Roxy (left) used hands to signal available seats.

E. T.: THE EXTRA-TERRESTRIAL, 1982

Picking the Classics

A classic, according to the American Film Institute, is a feature-length movie that achieved critical recognition, won major awards, demonstrated popularity over time, had historical significance, and made a cultural impact. In 1998 AFI created a list of 400 such films, sent a ballot to film industry leaders and asked them to choose 100 of them, which it then described as the greatest American films of all time. The results omitted Buster Keaton, Greta Garbo, Astaire and Rogers, Ernst Lubitsh, and Preston Sturges—and started a thousand arguments. No one quarreled with AFI's top choice, Citizen Kane *(opposite). Or with* The Godfather, *which came in third, or* Casablanca *and* Gone With the Wind *(overleaf), which came in second and fourth. "There were some among us," writes Richard Schickel, "who would have raised* E.T.: The Extra-Terrestrial *(above) higher and passed altogether on the antique political correctness of* Guess Who's Coming to Dinner? *(right) ....There was something stirring about the discussion....There was a general agreement that the hubbub had been salutary—and surprising. Who would have thought that the movies—once a true mass medium, now a niche market dominated by adolescents—could still stir such high passions?"*

GUESS WHO'S COMING TO DINNER, 1969

The Classic List—
"Kane" to "Dandy"

Here are "The 100 Best American Movies of All Time," as compiled by the American Film Institute on the basis of votes by 1,500 people connected with films, including screenwriters, directors, and critics.

1. Citizen Kane, *1941*
2. Casablanca, *1942*
3. The Godfather, *1972*
4. Gone With the Wind, *1939*
5. Lawrence of Arabia, *1962*
6. The Wizard of Oz, *1939*
7. The Graduate, *1967*
8. On the Waterfront, *1954*
9. Schindler's List, *1993*
10. Singin' in the Rain, *1952*
11. It's a Wonderful Life, *1946*
12. Sunset Boulevard, *1950*
13. Bridge on the River Kwai, *1957*
14. Some Like It Hot, *1959*
15. Star Wars, *1977*
16. All About Eve, *1950*
17. The African Queen, *1951*
18. Psycho, *1960*
19. Chinatown, *1974*
20. One Flew Over the Cuckoo's Nest, *1975*
21. Grapes of Wrath, *1940*
22. 2001: A Space Odyssey, *1968*
23. The Maltese Falcon, *1941*
24. Raging Bull, *1980*
25. E.T.: The Extra-Terrestrial, *1982*
26. Dr. Strangelove, *1964*
27. Bonnie and Clyde, *1967*
28. Apocalypse Now, *1979*
29. Mr. Smith Goes to Washington, *1939*
30. Treasure of the Sierra Madre, *1948*
31. Annie Hall, *1977*
32. The Godfather Part II, *1974*
33. High Noon, *1952*
34. To Kill a Mockingbird, *1962*
35. It Happened One Night, *1934*
36. Midnight Cowboy, *1969*
37. The Best Years of Our Lives, *1946*
38. Double Indemnity, *1944*
39. Doctor Zhivago, *1965*
40. North by Northwest, *1959*
41. West Side Story, *1961*
42. Rear Window, *1954*
43. King Kong, *1933*
44. The Birth of a Nation, *1915*
45. A Streetcar Named Desire, *1951*
46. A Clockwork Orange, *1971*
47. Taxi Driver, *1976*
48. Jaws, *1975*
49. Snow White and the Seven Dwarfs, *1937*
50. Butch Cassidy and the Sundance Kid, *1969*
51. The Philadelphia Story, *1940*
52. From Here to Eternity, *1953*
53. Amadeus, *1984*
54. All Quiet on the Western Front, *1930*
55. The Sound of Music, *1965*
56. M*A*S*H, *1970*
57. The Third Man, *1949*
58. Fantasia, *1940*
59. Rebel Without a Cause, *1955*
60. Raiders of the Lost Ark, *1981*
61. Vertigo, *1958*
62. Tootsie, *1982*
63. Stagecoach, *1939*
64. Close Encounters of the Third Kind, *1977*
65. The Silence of the Lambs, *1991*
66. Network, *1976*
67. The Manchurian Candidate, *1962*
68. An American in Paris, *1951*
69. Shane, *1953*
70. The French Connection, *1971*
71. Forrest Gump, *1994*
72. Ben-Hur, *1959*
73. Wuthering Heights, *1939*
74. The Gold Rush, *1925*
75. Dances With Wolves, *1990*
76. City Lights, *1931*
77. American Graffiti, *1973*
78. Rocky, *1976*
79. The Deer Hunter, *1978*
80. The Wild Bunch, *1969*
81. Modern Times, *1936*
82. Giant, *1956*
83. Platoon, *1986*
84. Fargo, *1996*
85. Duck Soup, *1933*
86. Mutiny on the Bounty, *1935*
87. Frankenstein, *1931*
88. Easy Rider, *1969*
89. Patton, *1970*
90. The Jazz Singer, *1927*
91. My Fair Lady, *1964*
92. A Place in the Sun, *1951*
93. The Apartment, *1961*
94. Goodfellas, *1990*
95. Pulp Fiction, *1994*
96. The Searchers, *1956*
97. Bringing Up Baby, *1938*
98. Unforgiven, *1992*
99. Guess Who's Coming to Dinner, *1969*
100. Yankee Doodle Dandy, *1942*

See no evil: Maureen O'Sullivan's costume as Tarzan's Jane was scanty in 1934's Tarzan and His Mate *(above). Then came the Motion Picture Production Code's serious enforcement, and in 1942's* Tarzan's New York Adventure *Jane is more modestly attired. (No one seemed to worry about Johnny Weissmuller's loincloth.) The code was replaced by the somewhat more liberal-minded licentious ratings system of 1968. So no censors kept Dustin Hoffman and Mia Farrow out of bed in* John and Mary *in 1969. It had been a long time since Mia's mother had to worry about what she wore in a Tarzan movie.*

into their webs, introduced something disturbing about the battle of the sexes. (*Double Indemnity* is the great example.) At the same time, the studios began making social-problem pictures that took up issues from alcoholism (*The Lost Weekend*) to anti-Semitism (*Gentlemen's Agreement*) to racism (*Lost Boundaries, Pinky, Home of the Brave*). They were judged to be a sign that the industry was finally growing up, shouldering the social burdens of a mature capitalist enterprise.

It was a great system, flexible, tested in minor adversity and major triumph. As of 1948, no one could see any reason for it not to go on forever. And then, in a single year, one-third of the movie audience disappeared. Attendance dropped to 60 million a week. And that was just the beginning. A decade later, attendance was less than half of what it had been. A decade after that it was about one-sixth of what it had been in 1948.

Television had arrived. TV could do all the old movie genres right in your own living room, for free. TV didn't do the genres as well as the movies had, but they were done well enough, and a lot more conveniently.

A crucial anecdote: Sometime in 1953 the director Elia Kazan and the writer Budd Schulberg arrived at Zanuck's office to finish the deal for *On the Waterfront*. It was exactly the kind of film with which everyone had done well. It had a serious subject, melodramatically yet romantically spun, with a cast headed by Marlon Brando, hot at the box office and leader of the new "method" of acting—subjective, wearing his moral and emotional ambiguities on the sleeve of his torn T-shirt. Zanuck told his visitors he would not be making the film. He had seen the future, and it was *The Robe*—in CinemaScope and color, a spectacle of the sort TV could not offer. Henceforth, he said, all Twentieth Century-Fox products would be in the new process. He waxed rhapsodic about the studio's next film, *Prince Valiant*.

Waterfront was made elsewhere, winning Oscars and profits, but it was a sign-post on a road hastily abandoned by Hollywood. Over the next decade, genre filmmaking essentially ceased (except for science fiction and Westerns, both of which enjoyed golden ages in the 1950s). Hollywood essentially devoted itself to spectacle. Some of these films—*The Bridge on the River Kwai, Lawrence of Arabia, The Sound of Music*—did very well. But some of them (*Mutiny on the Bounty* and *Cleopatra*) did something no single film had ever done before: They threatened their studios with ruin.

The wide-screen age was the least instructive in Hollywood history. The number of pictures produced fell to less than half the number made in the late 1940s. The stars who could carry a film to profitability grew fewer. But, freed of studio indenture and producing independently, they grew richer. Aside from the little oddball, black-and-white throwbacks—such as *Baby Doll, The Sweet Smell of Success, Some Like It Hot*—the movies were ponderous with the bland pieties of the 1950s. They seemed like old men's movies, and they were. Many of the old moguls still clung to power, and they kept employing old Hollywood hands to write and direct their movies.

As the 1950s dragged into the 1960s and the flops piled up, critics such as Pauline Kael began to suggest that the system was "rotting," with the studios "so enervated that they're sinking under their own weight." At one point, she proposed that the leading directors form some sort of cooperative and finance their films outside the studio system.

That turned out to be unnecessary. For Warren Beatty somehow got one of the old moguls, Jack Warner, to finance *Bonnie and Clyde*. Directed by Arthur Penn, this brilliantly transgressive gangster film analogized the bloody doings of its protagonists to what was going on in Vietnam in the year it was released (1967). Along with *The Graduate* and *Easy Rider*, made around the same time, they nudged the door ajar for a new generation of filmmakers. Among them were Peter Bogdanovich, Woody Allen, Francis Ford Coppola, Robert Altman, Martin Scorsese, Steven Spielberg, and George Lucas. The films this group made in the 1970s were *M*A*S*H, The Last Picture Show, Mean Streets, Taxi Driver, The Godfather, Annie Hall, American Graffiti, Jaws,* and *Star Wars.* That says nothing of 1960s films scarcely less good,

The Rocky Horror Picture Show, *a send-up of science fiction and horror movies, flopped in conventional release in 1975, but as a midnight movie it remains a rite of passage for younger adolescents.* Rocky Horror's *transgression in the galaxy Transylvania (below) wears a goofy grin. It may or may not get young fans ready for the harsher violence of films like* Pulp Fiction.

made by their co-religionists of the new cinema: *Midnight Cowboy, 2001: A Space Odyssey, The Wild Bunch, Five Easy Pieces, Chinatown, The French Connection, Badlands,* and so on and on.

A lot of these movies were genre pictures. But they were hip genre films, spinning the old tropes in new directions, commenting knowingly on a tradition rather than wearily adding to it. All of them had a freshness—something in the rhythm of their cutting, a boldness in their language and playing—that separated them from the lumbering of traditional Hollywood moviemaking.

Once again, however belatedly, it appeared that Hollywood had identified a surefire formula for success: Identify the emerging "auteurs," give them the modest (at first) sums of money they needed to do their work, sit back, and let the money roll in.

It didn't quite work out that way. Urged on by their agents—increasingly important as packagers of projects—some of the new filmmakers succumbed to their own grandiosity, some addled themselves with drugs and messy sexual entanglements, and some discovered that the limits of their talents were narrower than they imagined. Only a few, such as Scorsese, Spielberg, and Lucas, digested their inevitable setbacks and kept going and growing. Though they were few, they gave Hollywood the hits it needed. Attendance in the 1970s inched back up to its present level of slightly less than 30 million admissions per week. That alone, however, would not have been enough to rescue the American movie.

What saved it was a combination of two films, Spielberg's *Jaws* and Lucas's *Star Wars.* The former had been a troubled production that went wildly over budget largely because the mechanical shark, essential to its thrills, didn't work. It was saved in the editing, which turned the creature into a largely unseen menace, and in its release. Until the summer of 1975, pictures had gone to market pretty much as they had since the 1920s: limited release in the first-run theaters in the major markets, slowly expanding into the sub-runs until, over two or three months everybody who wanted to see the movie did. It was a quiet, cost-effective way of doing business, and it had the advantage, sometimes, of letting the public find a picture in its own good time.

Jaws, however, opened in 500 theaters on the same summer day. It was a pattern that had occasionally been tried before, with bad pictures trying to scoop up what money they could before the reviews caught up with them. No one had tried

At the end of The Wizard of Oz's *Yellow Brick Road (opposite), there stood a fraudulent Wiz—booming idle threats into an amplifying system. At the end of* Star Wars' *long ago, far away galaxy, Darth Vader (below) lurked. And there was nothing fake about his evil. Thus were the stakes raised in kid films between 1939 and 1977. But George Lucas's epic reinvention of sci-fi (and the Saturday afternoon serial) wore its mythic weight as lightly as its predecessor.*

Carried away by special effects

Special effects were an inherent part of movie magic from the beginning. We've come a long way from 1907's Rescued from an Eagle's Nest *(left). Herky-jerky as it was, the avian kidnapping probably wowed its audience as surely as* Twister *(right) or* Volcano *(far right) has modern moviegoers. In the last decade, thanks largely to digital technology, special effects have loomed as large as the alien spaceship over the White House in* Independence Day *(above). In George Lucas's* Star Wars *prequel,* The Phantom Menace, *90 percent of the shots are enhanced by the wizardry of his technicians.*

In the 1950s, drive-in movies represented nearly one-third of the movie screens in the United States. It was a terrible way to see a movie, but did anyone go to a drive-in for the movie? Virtually extinct now, for a time they were a place you could both see The Ten Commandments *and test your commitment to one or two of them.*

it with a well-made, well-publicized picture that people wanted to see. The results were phenomenal—and they changed, within a matter of years, the way movies were presented.

Most big studio pictures today open in anywhere from 1,500 to 2,500 theaters. Their fate depends entirely on their first-weekend grosses, which are eagerly reported in the press and on TV the following Monday. All such movies must appeal to the movies' only reliable remaining mass audience, which is male and under twenty. They control roughly sixty percent of the market. Boys largely determine where a couple will go for a Saturday night date—and boys are basically interested in just two kinds of movies: action-adventure or sci-fi movies driven by special effects and gross-out comedies. In the last two decades they have driven all other movies to the fringe.

Two years after *Jaws*, another troubled movie whose director had lost confidence, sealed this new way of doing business. That was *Star Wars*. It was a huge hit domestically. But it became even more of a success internationally, teaching Hollywood that special effects pictures—short on dialogue, long on loud, unambiguous action—could be translated easily into other languages.

By the early 1980s the studios were making more money from the quaintly named "ancillary" markets—foreign sales, licensing to home video and television— than they were at the domestic box office, particularly with these juvenile spectacles. There is a fringe of independent movies, and occasionally something like *Shakespeare in Love* bucks the trend. But not often. No one aspires any more to the kind of something-for-everyone slate of films that were the goal of the studios in their greatest day. No one aspires to anything but a $20 million gross on Monday.

George Lucas now wants to make movies with pixels, not actors. Pixels don't talk back or get the sulks. That he probably cannot have. We want and need our stars. But he also wants to make movies that are not placed on film in the time-honored fashion but are encoded in digital tape and sent to theaters by satellites. And that he can probably have.

Will this change "the whole equation" of movies again? It seems likely, since so much of it involves the way movies are distributed and marketed. Maybe they will be fewer still, and more expensive still, and playing to an ever narrowing market. But about that we cannot be sure. If we have learned anything about the movies, it is that their past is a prologue to nothing and predicts nothing—other than the unpredictability and suddenness of change.

America the Beautiful

"In the United States there is more space where nobody is than where anybody is.

This is what makes America what it is."

—GERTRUDE STEIN

BY WILLIAM LEAST HEAT-MOON

As the 20th century burst its seams, Americans embraced more fully than ever before the notion that being in nature lifted the soul and soothed the jangled nerves of urban dwellers. The middle class blossomed. Its members earned vacations, purchased cars, and drove to their dreams—such as fly fishing vacations on Washington's Skykomish River.

PRECEDING PAGES

Visitors of the 1950s view the majesty of Yosemite National Park. Cars began climbing its rocky roads in 1913.

Things were not much different for us in 1949 than they were for many other American families. My father, having hauled us around in the same Chevrolet through World War II, was ready for a new car, and Detroit was again capable of offering one. Six years earlier, manufacturers made a mere 139 automobiles in the United States, and the following season only a few more came down the assembly line. But after V-J Day, as gas rationing came to an end, the plants returned to making vehicles for civilians. Postwar prosperity eradicated not simply the privations of war but also the lingering ones of the Great Depression, and a new era began that would change America—topographically, socially, economically—more than any other period since the arrival of European settlers. At the heart of much of that change was the highway.

To celebrate the end of the long, lean, and worry-fraught 1930s and 1940s, my father bought a Pontiac Chieftain sedan—his first new auto, although he was at the edge of middle age: He wanted it to get to work in downtown Kansas City, Missouri, yes, but even more to take onto the open road because he believed almost devotedly a slogan of the time, "See America First."

His preferred method of taking a vacation, those two weeks away from the law office, was to pick out a federal highway passing through our town, the one nearly at the exact center of the forty-eight states, and follow the two-lane to its terminus. Over four summers, always in August, we first took U.S. 40 toward the Jersey shore; the next year U.S. 50 to San Francisco; then it was U.S. 71 to International Falls, Minnesota; and on the subsequent vacation, 71 to Baton Rouge at the edge of Cajun country. The boardwalk, the embarcadero, Huey Long's statehouse, and a lake full of northern pike became for me, by the time I was 14, not remote places but memories only a few days down the highway from home. Maryland and California were not like foreign countries across an ocean. They lay along the road, just as did our neighbors on Flora Avenue.

Six cylinders and 1,200 miles of reinforced concrete patched with asphalt gave me a sense of the United States and the varieties of being American that no social studies class could ever do. I believed in this country far beyond the required morning Pledge of Allegiance or even the propaganda movies of the war, because I encountered the land itself and the faces and voices that went with it. Highways gave me native accents, regional cookery, local hopes and angers, ancient bigotries, the scent of a farmer's loam after dewfall, the smell of a Gulf shrimp boat. As different as the miles were, they still lay connected, and the street in front of my house was a continuous strip reaching all of them. Highways made me belong to a nation for which more than 400,000 defenders had recently died.

If there was one book that showed me America, it was my 1950 road atlas. After I'd ridden the Chieftain sedan down some of those mapped and numbered lines of red or blue, the main routes and the back roads, the atlas became a kind of snapshot album. I could prop up in bed on a winter night and take a journey through certain parts of the country and see again stretches of territory that highway numbers or town names elicited: Manti, Utah, with its old stone temple improbably big in such a small place; Frederick, Maryland, with Barbara Fritchie's home; the buckwheat cakes in Plainfield, Indiana; the dusty hat I bought at the five-and-dime in Vicksburg, Mississippi.

In those days, as we were leaving an older economy and social order dominated by rural life, we were still calling the Sears, Roebuck annual catalog "the wish book." But my book of longings was a Rand McNally with its apparently endless miles of highways, county by-routes, parkways, and even a new kind of road called a turnpike running four-lanes wide over and through the mountains of Pennsylvania, out of the very country of the most famous American travel vehicle ever— the Conestoga wagon. President Eisenhower was about to point out the turnpike as the model for a vast national system of super roadways to be called interstates, which would let us go coast to coast, border to border, without ever having a red light stop us. We could hardly wait for such a marvel to open up the horizon in front of the long, streamlined hood of our car.

Without considering the consequences of such presumably unfettered travel, we began, year by year, to put an increasing premium *(continued on page 292)*

Destinations like the Wawona Tunnel Tree in Yosemite (left) and Glacier National Park (below) became important reasons for owning a car. Automobiles propelled tourism into a major industry. By the late 1990s, Yosemite counted 4.1 million visitations a year. More than 7,000 vehicles now creep along its roads during peak periods.

Get out
and get under

For many enthusiasts, the prestige and thrill of wheeling anywhere were as compelling as the pleasure of arriving somewhere. Which was just as well. Early cars were mechanically finicky. Motor tourists, like these aboard the White Steamer (left), spent perhaps $100 a month to maintain their car, which cost $2,500. Many early car owners became amateur mechanics.

In 1906, Hammacher, Schlemmer and Company sold this tool kit for cars. It weighed 18 pounds and contained files, cold chisels, pliers, and other essential tools for the road.

285

To the top
with dust and pluck

Driven by curiosity and auto ardor, early tourists bucked ragged roads to reach mountain overlooks (left) and to stage stunts, like parking on Overhanging Rock at Yosemite's Glacier Point (above). Cars carried more people to parks, increasing their fame and popularity. Even John Muir, founder of the Sierra Club, approved of automobiles. But as their numbers increased, cars brought treeside traffic jams and pollution. Cars have outgrown their welcome at many national parks—especially at Yosemite, where vehicles of every kind face growing restrictions.

287

Home, home on the road

By the 1920s, there was one passenger car for every thirteen Americans. By 1930, the number had increased to two cars for every eleven citizens. Roadside eateries sprang up, some of them competing for business by becoming attractions themselves (left). Roadside tent and trailer camps lured families to get out of town and on the road. To sing a parody on Burma-Shave signs:

> Twenties tourists
> Washed their hair
> Neath trees 'n' tarp
> And open air.

In the West, car campers who visited national parks were called "sagebrushers." Car ownership was democratizing the great outdoors, opening national parks and other treasured spaces to people from what used to be called all walks of life.

Driving to the drive-in

Teenagers and cars just naturally merged. Lucky ones got their own, like this '39 Ford belonging to a Roosevelt High Schooler. Teens courted in cars and customized them by lavishly repainting, chopping, and channeling them. And they ate in drive-ins. Ray Kroc met the two McDonald brothers at their California drive-in and began franchising in 1955. Opening the first McDonald's (upper) in Des Plaines, a Chicago suburb, he continued the fast service and low-price menu (above).

on speed, as we came to value rate of passage rather than the nature of it; the road came to be only a means to a destination. If it was good to be able to move across Pennsylvania fast, then logically it would also be desirable to get in and out of those places that for so long had slowed travelers: hotels with the weary lugging of grips up to the sixth floor and cafés where each order came out one at a time, cooked to suit a request: "Sunny-side up." Or, "Serve the noodle pie cold, if you please." Or, "Fried tomatoes with the kedgeree."

Across the land, if something was faster than what preceded it, if it took less of our time to use it, then it was better. So, in our neighborhood, when the Dari Delite (its soft-serve of the same quality as its orthography) opened directly across the street from old Duncan's Drugstore, we gave up the infinite variety of a genuine soda fountain for the limitations of fast-serve. We forgot the legendary concoctions of a knowledgeable soda jerk—Hiawatha floats, Jersey fizzes, Delmonico frappés, Rex phosphates, an Ollie Moore (syrups of lemon, raspberry, and orange mixed with sweet cream and a raw egg, shaken, strained, poured over ice, shot with seltzer). The old collection I take this "receipt" from, *The American Soda Book*, says, "There is as much difference between the soda of different stores as between the roast beef of different restaurants." A proud statement and true. We could comfortably, lazily drive right up to the Dari Delite window, and we could get in and out quickly, partly because there was only one kind of ice cream, only three kinds of soft drinks, ditto on the syrups; even a simple, fresh-squeezed limeade wasn't there. Then we could cart the stuff off to a drive-in movie, our feet never touching the ground.

As the 1960s arrived, family vacations were changing how we saw and interpreted America. Each year we seemed to give up a little more of being travelers to become mere tourists to whom arrival is all. What lay between us and Yellowstone or the Everglades turned into miles to be grudgingly got through. Small-town America—cities even more so—became not possibilities for exploration or adventure but purgatories to be endured. Because our demigeneration believed so much in destination, Yazoo City could become less real than Yosemite, Des Moines less alive than Disneyland. At first we didn't see that the plastic history of theme parks was akin to the roofs of the new grabba-burger stands, and we thought a Jeep ride through a big Texas "ranch" to glimpse a zebra or giraffe was a better experience than an evening idle through the Arkansas hills in hopes we might spot a red fox.

Today, that changed means of travel seems logical to me. Americans are descendants of earlier travelers who, commonly, did not leave home to see the territory and meet the natives but to avoid strangers and get to a place—a particular place—and, once there, take it up and remake it according to one's various expectations. Nomadic hunters walking or boating across the Bering Strait and the Pilgrims sailing the Atlantic went not as travelers but as settlers set on arriving; the people passing through the Cumberland Gap or along the Oregon Trail weren't moving to see the sights but to reach a destination. The American past, the most wheeled history on Earth, is not so much about travel as it is about getting there—not that we've ever been all that attached to a place once we do set down.

Of the blueprints and tools we've used to lay out and construct this nation, none, it seems to me, is any more important than maps and highways, and from the beginning we've shown our predilection to move as quickly and comfortably as possible, speed nearly always dominating comfort (consider your seat the next time you fly commercially).

B y the time President Eisenhower's grand interstate scheme began to look complete in the 1970s, many travelers were realizing that the freeway, like anything else, takes away as much as it gives; after all, things always, eventually, move toward balance. If you wish a metaphor for what happened as we autobahned ourselves, consider those series of six little red signs once adorning the two-lanes: PEDRO / WALKED / BACK HOME, BY GOLLY / HIS BRISTLY CHIN / WAS HOT-TO-MOLLY / BURMA-SHAVE. Although advertising a product for men, whole families might read the placards aloud and could find themselves watching the countryside closely for the next one: SLOW DOWN, PA / SAKES ALIVE / MA MISSED SIGNS / FOUR / AND FIVE / BURMA-SHAVE. Those narrow boards drew out travelers, lured them for a few moments to participate in their own passage. But the four-lanes were too big, too fast for such reading, and in those states that gave up scenic control of their highways, sky-

As cars evolved (opposite) from boxy to sleek, America's highway system improved, and vacationers ventured farther and farther. To accommodate them, entrepreneurs built tourist cabins, often offering little more than a bed and a roof. Vacationers' postcards, sent back home to say, "We're here," also were advertisements for alluring destinations (above). And they came in an eye-catching variety—from leather to sand-covered to birch bark.

293

sundering mega-billboards, readable a mile away, began sprouting up overnight like mushrooms. Their witless messages advertised booze and tobacco, and later, even vasectomy reversals—messages a generation of children, yet to reach their nostalgic years, may find difficult to remember as things that made them feel a part of America.

Independent cafés could rarely afford to move to set up along an interstate, and so vanished hundreds of Missus Somebody's own blue-ribbon-at-the-county-fair recipe for corncob soup or Confederate pudding. Gone were places with names like Jimmy Wells Catfish Parlor and with it his secret batter and the hard-earned magic in his old cast-iron skillets. Menus no longer revealed a particular locale with its history, and they no longer showed a region and its culture. They had become, from one Swif-Stop to the next Fast-Way, lists of ditto food, and the only way you could tell where you were was to ask where you were. To be sure, some of the roadfood of earlier times was of the gag-and-grimace variety, for inconsistency was a certainty of two-lane travel. But, as in other things, the absence of quality gave not just meaning but memorableness to the good meal that did turn up. Passion and excitement depend upon their scantiness—else how should we know them?

Experienced wayfarers learned to laugh off the poor dinner, aware that, were it bad enough, at least they would have a story to tell when they returned home. I realized friends listened more intently to a tale of the wretched oyster stew in the U-Drop Inn one night than to any account of how beautiful the Rockies were the next morning. Part of the point of travel is to make home look sweet; otherwise we all would become itinerants with no one staying around to serve us stew, good or bad. What's more, the quest for toothsome roadfood, like those little red signs, drew us more deeply into the country, made us a part of a place for a few moments. It was even rewarding just to learn the tricks of travel: Hunting for a good grinder, the sandwich with a dozen regional names? Don't ask the pump man at the filling station. Ask the librarian, a bookstore owner, the jeweler, a bank teller. The old tourist traps lured in only the lazy.

In the early days, fresh from the war, politicians and road contractors told us the interstate system was necessary for our national defense in order to move munitions and weapons if the need arose. For a number of years we believed that too—until it became apparent the four-lanes were there to move not rifles but radios, not bombs but baubles. The superhighways existed primarily for teamsters whom we, perhaps driven by a new nostalgia for real highway adventure, turned into instant folk figures, mixes of Casey Jones, Mike Fink, and Bronco Billy.

As we watched the interstates dice up city neighborhoods and then move into the country and, like giant incubuses, suck the mercantile life out of a village or small town as they pulled commerce to intersections only yesterday cornfields, we could pass down main streets of vacant buildings, and one more of the reasons for slow travel all but disappeared. Village centers turned into stacks of broken-open bones, the marrow eaten out, and we at last realized that a lunch stop of Qwik-Nuggets in Bangor would more likely put us next to someone from Ohio or Delaware than a Down-Easter.

Economies of scale and expediency had come to define much American travel. Plates of foodlike-substance assembled in New Jersey arrived in cartons requiring only a microwave before they reached our palates—all of that stuff served up in places of reiterated shoddy architecture, where the roofs and signs might have been made from our leftovers, a temporary if strung out realm of waxed cups and Styrofoam. And, at night, that bedspread and painting above the motel bed in Battle Creek—weren't they the same ones we'd seen a day earlier in Kokomo? Husbands muttered to wives about once sleeping in a motor court where each room was a concrete teepee—corny but funny and unforgettable. And what about that cup of joe from the roadside stand in the shape of a two-story coffeepot?

The result was a nation of travelers who drove fast and long throughout the day only to arrive, for all they could tell, where they had started from; the only thing the open road had given them was a tired back and bloodshot eyes. Something had gone awry in the grand interstate scheme. By the late 1970s, vacationers began asking themselves, "What's the point of such miles? We might as well fly to the beach resort." And they were right. It was faster and easier to treat the land between home and destination as flyover country and cease using the interstates, except as long and often congested runways from which we never took off.

Passengers were few in the 1930s, despite the launching of several airlines from the late 1920s to early 1930s—Pan Am, TWA, Delta, American, and United. This American Clipper (opposite; top) carried 44 passengers in cushy seats next to large windows in the 1930s, when a nearly 17-hour flight from San Francisco to New York cost around $160. In 1940, female passengers could refresh themselves in a "flying boudoir." As competition among the airlines escalated, the number of passengers increased, from only a few thousand in 1930 to more than 16 million in 1949 and more than 600 million a year in the late 1990s.

About then, a few Americans began trying to turn themselves back into travelers rather than tourists, to become explorers in search of the genius of a place, searchers for the quiddity of Garfield County or Hell Roaring Creek or the Rosebud Reservation. And as they headed down some of those abundant miles of American two-lane, they began uncovering here and there living fossils: a village still possessed of its mercantile heart, a diner grinding its own coffee beans, a clam shack so good the kids stopped saying "slimy," a neighborhood tavern with real neighbors who could tell about living there, a 19th-century inn where one could sleep inside history, a pub brewing its own ales.

Before we could have realistically expected it, a new line of guidebooks began appearing—to bed-and-breakfasts, genuine inns, real ice cream stands, flea markets, fried-chicken emporiums. Many of the guides had *Forgotten* or *Hidden* in the title, and some of them were from mom-and-pop publishers, people who lived in two-lane America and had seen the changes but were not in accord with them. Any critic who interprets this vast change as only an urge for nostalgia hasn't yet traveled far or deeply enough, for what has been happening since about 1980 is

significantly reshaping us. A number of Americans, driven mad by the interstates, awakened and, knowing the trail frontiers were gone, began seeking highway adventures in a well-settled land, a thoroughly roaded place no longer wilderness but still similarly full of the challenge and unpredictability that sharpen one's senses, whittle one's perception into keenness, and carve a deep and lasting mark in the memory.

To escape the expressways was to distinguish Penn Yan from Mandan, to know the difference between Mount Vernon, Illinois, and the one on the Potomac, to differentiate the speech of coastal Carolina from that of the Piedmont, to understand in Rockport, Massachusetts, you might find creamed lobster but in Rock Port, Missouri, it would be ham baked in milk.

Ike's interstates don't much disturb me any longer, because their 46,000 miles not only opened up three million miles of two-lanes, they also taught us how to travel in ways that allow us to enter the American landscape, to inhabit our heritage of history and place. I think that may be why, the week after next, I'll be headed for Tennessee. There's this place I remember not far out of Tullahoma.

In Everybody's Living Room

BY JOHN LEONARD

In the quarter-century since a National Geographic book looked at the talking furniture in the American living room, our options may have multiplied unto a lurid swarm, but we still feel cheated. Twenty-five years ago was before "Hill Street Blues," Oprah Winfrey, Rupert Murdoch, "Seinfeld," Pat Robertson, Howard Stern, and Mortal Kombat, not to mention cable television, hate radio, video cassettes, smart-bomb minicams, a personal computer in every closet, and a Web site for every Chicken Little or Jar Jar Binks. We used to sit in blue druidic light, watching the shadows cast on the wall by three networks and a single public television station. Now we're more likely to be plugged into multiple outlets, crouched at our very own software as if it were a harpsichord, slugabed in a "home entertainment center" Romper Room, tethered to an all-news war porn channel, flatlined by an adman/music-video consumer grid, sampling on a CD carousel a customized sequence of cowbilly deathmetal technopop, surfing a digitized Xanadu, feeling as remote as our controls.

It's amazing, really. Everything that Ed Sullivan until 1971 had to do all by himself—comedy and magic, animal acts and acrobats, ventriloquists and marching bands, Brigitte Bardot, David Ben-Gurion, Willie Mays, and the Singing Nun—now seems to have a channel of its very own, from pop tarts to pro wrestling to Bravo to C-SPAN, besides all-news, all-sports, all-weather, all-food, all-kids, all-cartoons, all-nostalgia, all-travel, all-stock market, all sci-fi, for women only, canned laughter, canned history, courtroom TV, and pay-per-view.

Even more amazing is that we complain about all of them. That we blame television not only for Jerry Springer, Ricki Lake, and Geraldo Rivera but also for O. J. Simpson, Monica Lewinsky, and the Littleton massacre. Headline-hungry politicians and the moralizing coalitions to which they pander blame the box for

While members of the speaking cast gather at the microphone, sound effects men produce real gunfire for "Gangbusters," a cops-and-robbers radio show. It opened to a rat-tat-tat-tat of a tommy gun, the tread of convicts in lockstep, and the wailing siren of a police car. The opening theme inspired a phrase to describe a full-decibel entrance: "coming on like gangbusters."

most of the sex and violence in our Republic, just as once upon a time they blamed vaudeville, talkies, unions, comics, communists, Elvis, and progressive schools. Why not wrathful gods, recessive genes, or the designated hitter?

This amazes because TV has had more to tell us about common decency, social justice, and civil discourse than big-screen Hollywood and big-time magazine journalism and most New York book publishers, certainly in the past 25 years. Seeking to please or distract as many people as possible, to assemble and divert multitudes, television is famously inclusive, with a huge stake in consensus. Of course, brokering social and political gridlock, it tends to soften lines and edges to make a prettier picture. But it is also weirdly democratic, multicultural, utopian, quixotic, and more welcoming of difference and diversity than much of its distracted audience. It's been overwhelmingly pro-gun control, anti-capital punishment, and antiwar (as in "M*A*S*H" and "China Beach"). It's been suspicious of big business, sympathetic to the homeless and the ecosystem, alert to child abuse, spouse-battering, alcoholism, sexual discrimination, rape, and medical malpractice. TV began worrying about AIDS as far back as 1983, in "St. Elsewhere," a decade before Tom Hanks showed up on the big screen in *Philadelphia*.

Crucially, television, where ad cult meets melting pot and mulligan stew to stipulate a color-blind consumer, may be the only American institution outside of the public school system and the armed forces still to believe in integration of the races, at least on camera. We'd actually be a kinder, gentler, healthier nation if we embraced the scruples and imitated the behaviors recommended by most TV entertainment programs—more of a community than an agglomeration of market segments and seething sects. The same can't be said for most of what we see in video games or on the Internet.

How this has been possible is problematic—given the fact that the same people who own television (both network and cable) also own or have owned just about everything else, from satellite systems, long-distance telephone lines, nuclear-reactor turbines, aircraft engines, diesel and electric trains, appliance and insurance companies, and financial and medical services, to film studios, home video production facilities, music companies, publishing houses, theme parks, and ice hockey teams, to wireless communication and security systems, refrigeration and waste disposal, nuclear reactors for submarines and aircraft carriers, and nuclear-power plants. Plus movie studios, newspapers, a couple of record companies, and a book publisher, *TV Guide,* and the *Weekly Standard.*

Radio fans started early. Kids sent in sponsors' box tops to get such rewards as membership in Radio Orphan Annie's Secret Society or a Captain Midnight decoder. Two popular radio characters, Fred Allen and Jack Benny faked a feud: Benny's wife, Mary Livingstone (at right below), clutches Allen, who menaces Benny, held back by Fred's wife, Portland Hoffa.

*A one-day composite of some
of the most popular radio shows
of 1939 and 1940. Times listed
are actual.*

9:00	Don McNeill's Breakfast Club
10:00	Marriage Clinic
10:30	Just Plain Bill
10:45	Houseboat Hannah
11:00	Betty Moore: Home Decorating
11:15	Lorenzo Jones
11:30	Big Sister
11:45	Road of Life
12:00	Mary Margaret McBride
12:15	Her Honor, Nancy James
12:30	Helen Trent
12:45	Our Gal Sunday
1:00	The Goldbergs
1:15	Life Can Be Beautiful
1:30	Right to Happiness
1:45	Betty and Bob
2:00	AMA Health Dramas
2:30	American School of the Air
2:45	Betty Crocker: Cooking Hints
3:00	Orphans of Divorce
3:15	Ma Perkins
3:30	Pepper Young's Family
3:45	Ted Malone: Between the Bookends
4:00	Backstage Wife
4:15	Stella Dallas
4:30	Vic and Sade
4:45	Girl Alone
5:00	Dick Tracy
5:15	Terry and the Pirates
5:30	Jack Armstrong, the All-American Boy
5:45	Little Orphan Annie
6:00	Edwin C. Hill: News
6:15	Hedda Hopper
6:30	Bill Stern: Sports
6:45	Lowell Thomas
7:00	Amos 'n' Andy
7:15	Jimmy Fidler
7:30	Eddie Cantor Program
8:00	Charlie McCarthy Show
8:30	Burns and Allen
9:00	Texaco Star Theatre
9:30	Death Valley Days
10:00	Bob Hope Show

The television owners commune with their mystical parts by the medium of advertising agencies. This hypno-therapeutic business, as essayist Barbara Ehrenreich once explained, is to sell us cars by promising adventure, to sell us beer by promising friendship, and sell stock to those of us who are speculators by promising a Midas-size quarterly dividend after the usual downsizing. They are so busy synergizing everything—from book-to-movie-to-TV series and then on to music video, to magazine puff piece, and on to the fried-food franchise sale of associated toys and trading cards—that soon there won't be a pro athlete, a park bench, or even a childhood fairy tale without a logo, a patent, or a copyright. They cannot therefore be expected to encourage the suits who work for them to devote a lot of time to bad-news programs about declining cities, race war, foreign-policy adventurism, indeterminate sexuality, corporate predation, or anything else that sentimental progressives can be counted on to care about.

Still, television keeps asking us as citizens to acknowledge that the capacity to imagine the disadvantaged and the dispossessed leads to the discovery that we might have obligations to them. Even if hotshot writers, creators, and executive producers like David E. Kelley ("Picket Fences," "Chicago Hope," "Ally McBeal," "The Practice"), Tom Fontana ("St. Elsewhere," "Homicide," "Oz"), Dick Wolf ("Law & Order," "New York Undercover"), Barney Rosenzweig ("Cagney & Lacey," "Trials of Rosie O'Neill"), John Sacret Young ("China Beach," "VR.5"), and John Falsey and Joshua Brand ("Northern Exposure," "I'll Fly Away") are only doing it to please the high school English teacher who once held out such high hopes for the bright boy, it nevertheless amounts to something almost radical.

Moreover, what we see, if we want to, is actually better than it used to be—and not only because it includes, besides every English-language movie ever made, everything that was ever on television before—syndicated reruns of almost any series that lasted more than two seasons. We have museums of the moving image on TNT, TBS, USA, A & E, and "Nick at Nite." And we have "M*A*S*H" forever. But the original programming is itself superior: better written, better acted, better produced, and better directed. Much as we loved Lucy, what we did to our children before "Sesame Street" was Howdy Doody and Captain Video.

When John Cameron Swayze died several years ago, we ought to have been reminded of how bad TV news used to be as his Camel News Caravan went "hopscotching the world for headlines."

TV's ageless Golden Age

Shows in television's golden 1950s won TV audiences that dwarf latter-day records. Lucille Ball's "I Love Lucy" (right: Lucy, Vivian Vance, Desi Arnaz, William Frawley), which ran from 1951 to 1957, captured 71 percent of the audience in her first season and 92 percent in 1953, when she gave ballyhooed birth to Little Ricky—in real life and on prerecorded film. "Seinfeld," by comparison, got 33 percent in 1995-96. Milton Berle (opposite, lower left) in "Texaco Star Theater" in 1950-51 got 81 percent and reigned for eight years as "Mr. Television." Skits on Jackie Gleason's variety show evolved into 39 episodes of "The Honeymooners" in 1955 (below left: Gleason, Art Carney, Audrey Meadows, and Joyce Randolph). On cable nostalgia channels and World Wide Web fan pages, "Lucy" and "The Honeymooners" live on. "What's My Line?" lasted from 1950 to 1967; panelists (below, Dorothy Kilgallen, Steve Allen, Arlene Francis, Bennet Cerf, with moderator John Daly) guessed guests' jobs. Stoic Ed Sullivan's Sunday night show (1948 to 1971) in 1956 introduced middle-class America to Elvis Presley and in 1964 to the Beatles (opposite, far right). In the third Elvis appearance Sullivan showed him only from the waist up.

I LOVE LUCY

WHAT'S MY LINE?

THE HONEYMOONERS

TEXACO STAR THEATER

THE ED SULLIVAN SHOW

Television has not been around that long, as historian Erik Barnouw reminded National Geographic readers a quarter-century ago. The Radio Corporation of America added TV to radio in 1935, but television's commercial debut did not come until 1939 at the New York World's Fair. As Barnouw wrote, a test pickup from the unfinished fair grounds featured an "Amos 'n' Andy" telecast with actors in blackface. Then, on April 30, at the formal opening of the fair, Franklin D. Roosevelt became the first President in office to appear on television. RCA sets with five- and nine-inch picture tubes went on display at the fair at prices ranging from $199.50 to $600. "Crowds stared at the flickering scenes," Barnouw wrote, seeing "plays, snatches of opera, kitchen demonstrations; comedians, singers, jugglers, puppets."

World War II interrupted TV's short life, and not until 1953, with about 15 million television sets glowing throughout America, did networks begin to take shape. In that same year, *TV Guide* was born, as was Lucille Ball's baby on "I Love Lucy," one of the sensational hits of television's so-called Golden Age.

Even the Golden Age was full of Kmart Ibsens like Paddy Chayevsky, greeting card Kafkas like Rod Serling, along with bargain-basement Italian neorealism and kitchen-sink Sigmund Freud, where everybody explained too much in expository gusts yet all were simultaneously inarticulate, as if a want of eloquence were a proof of sincerity and an excess of sincerity guaranteed nobility of sentiment, like a bunch of clean old Tolstoy peasants. And how clean were they, really?

So clean that you almost never saw a black face, not even on a railroad porter. So clean that when Chayevsky based his drama, *The Catered Affair*, on his own family, the family had to be Irish instead of Jewish, just as the Jewish butcher in *Marty* had to be Italian. So clean that when Serling wanted to tell the story of Emmett Till, the black teenager lynched for whistling at a Mississippi white woman, "U.S. Steel Hour" turned the story into a pawnbroker's murder in New England. So clean that the Mars candy bar company would not allow "Circus Boy" to have a single reference to competitive sweets like cookies or ice cream; the "Alcoa Hour" was so solicitous of a good opinion about aluminum that it would not let Reginald Rose set a grim teleplay in a trailer park; you couldn't have a character cough or portray the crime of arson on shows sponsored by a cigarette company back in those days when tobacco could be advertised on television; and, most famously, the American Gas Company, as a sponsor of "Playhouse 90," insisted on removing any mention of "gas chambers" from a production of a play about the Nuremberg trial of Nazi war criminals.

When NBC and CBS launched commercial television in 1941, "home-makers" (left) starred in one of the first regularly broadcast NBC shows. A news camera of the 1950s, on the roof of a not-so-mobile studio, focuses on New York City's Easter Parade. Cables tether the van to NBC facilities in a nearby building.

The improvements since the Golden Age shouldn't surprise us. The novelist Theodore Sturgeon once observed that 90 percent of science-fiction is rubbish, but that's all right because 90 percent of everything is rubbish. With so much more production needed to feed so many goatish channels at the end of the millennium, this 10 percent is huge. I am not just talking about the remedial seriousness of public television series like "Frontline" and "P.O.V.," Bill Moyers on South Africa or Frederick Wiseman on public housing, Ofra Bikel on the satanic-ritual abuse hysteria, or Marlon Riggs on "Tongues Untied." Nor C-Span's pair of citizen bands, its basilisk eye on Congress and its weekend book-chat programs. Nor Discovery Channel's remarkable miniseries on the CIA. Nor David Halberstam's History Channel account of the 1950s. Nor Neal Gabler's A&E meditation on Jews, Hollywood, and the American Dream. Nor John Frankenheimer's films for HBO and TNT on Attica, Andersonville, and George Wallace. Nor the almost unnoticed development of premium-cable news documentary units, like "America Undercover" on HBO (covering such topics as death row, breast cancer, and homophobia) and "Reel Life" on Cinemax (an umbrella series of short, independent documentary films mostly from abroad: war crimes against Muslim women in Bosnia, children in China, what captured Hamas and Hezbollah suicide bombers have to say for themselves under Israeli interrogation).

Feature films looking for a home—such as Adrian Lyne's *Lolita* and Anjelica Huston's *Bastard Out of Carolina*—found a sanctuary on Showtime cable. American viewers also could see aberrant genius Ingmar Bergman's *Scenes from a Marriage*, originally a six-episode miniseries for Swedish television. They also saw Marcel Ophuls's *Sorrow and the Pity*, conceived for French television; Werner Fassbinder's *Berlin Alexanderplatz*, commissioned by German TV; and from England, Dennis Potter's *Singing Detective* and Paul Scott's *Jewel in the Crown*. There were also U.S. brand names like Kurt Vonnegut and David Mamet on cable; Norman Mailer, who wrote a teleplay for *The Executioner's Song;* and Gore Vidal, who gave us *Lincoln* with Mary Tyler Moore as Mary Todd.

Looking back at the past 25 years, we see that writers who used to make a living writing short stories for upscale slick magazines have gone to Burbank to work for television. So have directors who would rather not make Hollywood movies that depend on the repeat business of 12-year-old boys. Premium cable channels encouraged them to say something about race and class and rain forests. In the century's last decade, Robert Altman and Garry Trudeau ran for President in *Tanner.* Socialists took over England in *A Very British Coup.* James Woods

At the 1952 Democratic National Convention, candidate Adlai Stevenson denounced the television-era merchandising of candidates "like breakfast cereal." But in 1956 delegates who renominated him got tips on TV etiquette (above). When John F. Kennedy debated Richard M. Nixon in 1960 (right), most viewers thought Kennedy had won; radio listeners weren't so sure. Television got high ratings tracking the Watergate scandal that led to Nixon's resignation (right). Negative TV advertising became an issue in 1988 when the campaign of George Bush attacked his opponent, Massachusetts' Gov. Michael Dukakis (far right), as soft on crime.

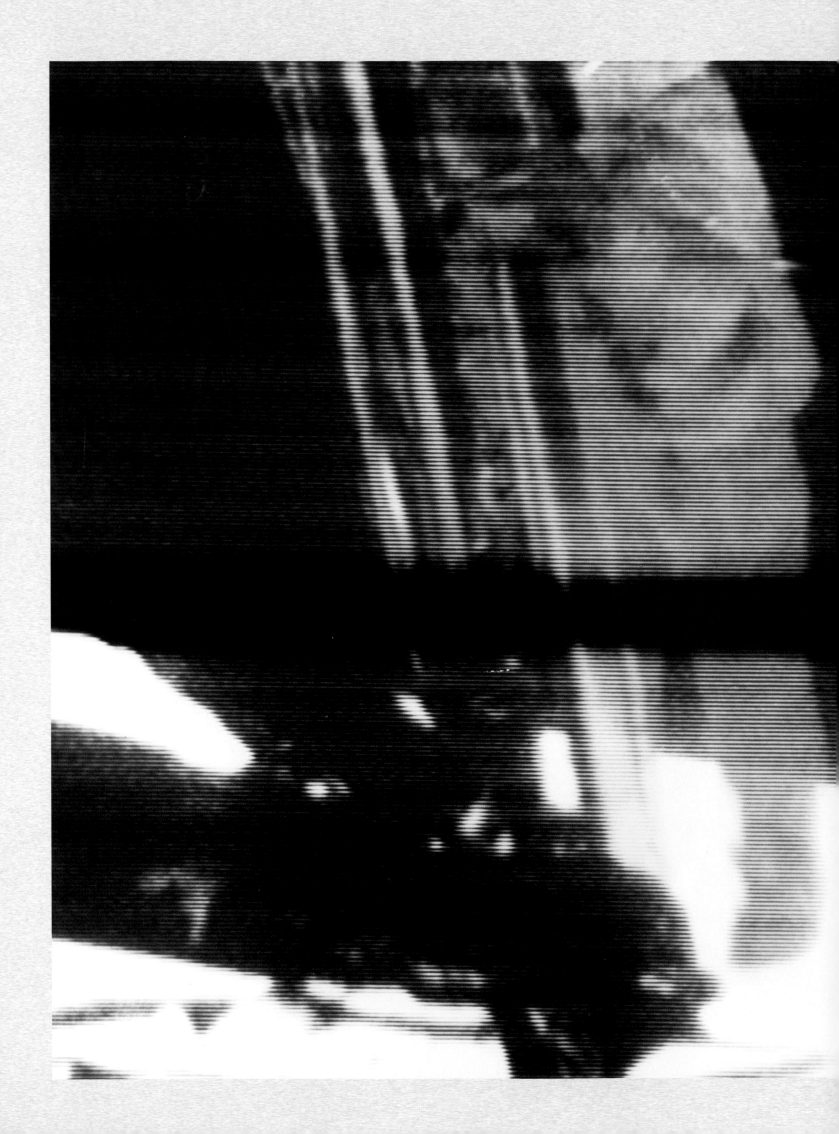

*Fighting police in the streets of
Chicago in 1968, young protesters chanted those words.
They were right. Television
cameras covering the Democratic National Convention
shifted to covering the rioting.*

*And the world saw that anti-
Vietnam War protesting had
turned violent. Images of the
war—like this one from
1966—brought combat into
living rooms and inspired televised protests. When Astronaut
Neil Armstrong stepped from
his spacecraft to the moon on
July 20, 1969 (left), the streaky
image was seen by some 600
million people; adding in those
who heard it on radio, the moon
landing reached about one out
of every four people on Earth.
The Soviet Union blacked out
the TV images from the moon.*

founded Alcoholics Anonymous in *My Name Is Bill W.* Holly Hunter got into the Supreme Court *Roe* v. *Wade.* Theodore Bikel played Dr. Henry Kissinger in *The Final Days of Richard Nixon. Common Threads* celebrated every name on the AIDS quilt.

Plus the terrific look at America's civil rights struggle, *Eyes on the Prize,* and Elaine Stritch in a postmortem on Mary McCarthy and Lillian Hellman. We saw *Sense and Sensibility,* Sidney Poitier as Thurgood Marshall in *Separate But Equal,* Robin Williams in Saul Bellow's *Seize the Day,* and Diana Rigg, warming up for the Medea she would later bring to Broadway, in *Mother Love.*

Bill Moyers was the host of a special on Irangate and the scandal of our intelligence agencies, *High Crimes & Misdemeanors.* In *Sessions,* Billy Crystal used Elliott Gould to bite psychoanalysis in its pineal gland. Larry Gelbart gave us *Barbarians at the Gate,* his send-up of vulture capitalism. Julie Dash's *Daughters of the Dust* was a painterly meditation on Gullah culture off the Carolina coast. *The Boys of St. Vincent* told about the sexual abuse of Canadian orphans by Roman Catholic priests. In *The Sopranos* David Chase succeeded in improving on at least one out of three Godfathers.

We saw Helen Mirren in *Prime Suspect,* Bette Midler in *Gypsy.* And we saw the works of Evelyn Waugh, Graham Greene, Philip Roth, John Updike, Dorothy Allison, Arthur Miller, Anne Tyler, Vladimir Nabokov, Gloria Naylor, Gabriel Garcia Marquez, George Eliot, and Stephen Sondheim—not to neglect those hoots without which any popular culture would be tedious, such as Liz Taylor in *Sweet Bird of Youth* and the Redgrave sisters in the remake of *Whatever Happened to Baby Jane.*

Even such a list ignores what we actually watch, out of lassitude, habit, or incapacitation. We leave home expecting, for a lot of money, to be exalted by food, a play, or a movie, and almost never are. But staying put on certain nights to watch TV—the way on other nights we'd order in—we're ambushed into sentience. Suddenly, Napoleon shows up on "Northern Exposure" like a popsicle, while Chris reads Proust. Or "Law & Order" mixes up a World Trade Center bombing and the Branch Davidian firestorm, to suggest that not all terrorism is fundamentally Islamic. Or "Picket Fences" moves on from elephant abuse to gay-bashing and euthanasia. Or on "Homicide" someone is killing the angels of Baltimore. Or on "Ally McBeal" the shrink-wrapped Tracy Ullman insists that Calista Flockhart get herself a theme song. Or Alan

Alda on "M*A*S*H" suffers a nervous breakdown. Or Jane Curtin on "Kate & Allie" suddenly discovers what it feels like to be homeless. Or Tim Reid on "Frank's Place" must take a paper-bag test to see if his skin color's light enough for membership in a New Orleans men's club. Or Dixie Carter opens her mouth in "Designing Women" to deliver an impassioned aria on Clarence Thomas and Anita Hill. And Roseanne opens her mouth to kiss Mariel Hemingway.

I might also mention my two favorite episodes of "The X-Files." In one, a turbanned cult of vegetarians is blamed for kidnapping and terrorizing farm-town teenagers who turn out to have been doped with alien DNA disguised as bovine growth hormone. In the other, a serial-killing translator of medieval Italian poetry meets lonely women in chat rooms on the Internet, parks with them in big American cars in bereft municipal spaces, secretes a membrane of gastric juice that smothers even

better than a baggie, and then feeds on their fatty tissue: vampire liposuction!

To be sure, there are far too many serial killers on television. Also berserk Latino drug lords, rogue spooks with purloined nukes, and Arab terrorists with plague germs. There are likewise far too many cable-yak show pundits who have been reliably wrong on everything from the collapse of the police states of Eastern Europe to the behavior of the American electorate.

Although you have to admire how public television managed to fend off a guns-and-God Republican Congress inclined to think that all public TV programs promoted an ulterior agenda of multiculti/feminazi/gay pride/socialized medicine/ performance art: Public TV just bought off the right-wing critics by sandbagging poor Bill Moyers with a new series ("On Values") from Peggy Noonan, ex-speechwriter for Presidents Reagan and Bush; joining conservative political commentator Fred Barnes and liberal Morton Kondracke ("Reverse Angle"); giving President Bush speechwriter Tony Snow a show, "New Militant Center"; and putting Ronald Reagan's former Secretary of Education William Bennett on Ben Wattenberg's "Think Tank."

Then there is the disappearance from prime time of all of those private detectives—"The Rockford Files," "Mannix"—and defense attorneys like Perry Mason,

The Cable News Network newsroom, its CNN logo known throughout the world, traces its roots to a near-bankrupt station in Atlanta, Georgia. In 1980 local entrepreneur Ted Turner used the station as his base for the first network broadcasting nonstop news. CNN's coverage of the Persian Gulf War produced indelible images— here, Baghdad's night sky ablaze—and demonstrated television's ability to show war in real time.

Once they contained peanut butter sandwiches. Now, enshrined in the Smithsonian's National Museum of American History, they proclaim the way promotional tie-ins keep dead TV shows from really dying. Advertising, wrote communications guru Marshall McLuhan, "stretches out toward the ultimate electronic goal of a collective consciousness," including lunch boxes. And they're collectibles. "Dukes of Hazzard," for example, is worth about $35.

who once upon a time could be counted on to presume our innocence and leave the law entirely in the hands of prosecutors. It has been a truism ever since Todd Gitlin published *Inside Prime Time* in 1983 that Steven Bochco's "Hill Street Blues" was the first "post-liberal" TV police show. On such mean streets, where even characters we cared about had a habit of dying, the city no longer seemed to work, nor the justice system, nor what Gitlin called "the middle-class therapeutic ethos." At the contested site of this social meltdown, the best the stoic Lieutenant Furillo could hope for were negotiated truces. Even Detective Henry Goldblume started packing a gun. And now just look how far we've come—with Bochco, who lives and breathes cop shows the way the Greek poets lived and breathed vehement dithyrambs, leading the way. As if a despairing conscience had been laundered in the cynical rinse of "L.A. Law," we get terrific television that is also impotent rage. As the 1990s cop show sees it, the big picture is chaos theory. In the brute face of urban pathologies, crime is increasingly random and brainless, beyond greed or social science to the depraved indifference of gangbangers, cocaine cartels, and TV versions of Hannibal Lecters.

Peace of mind is a losing cause and so is a civil society. All that stands between the solid citizen and savage tribes is a thin blue line, a secret society. Besieged in their bunker by pettifogging lawyers, dishonest judges, grandstanding pols, glory hound feds, vampire media, and knee-jerk civil libertarians, the cops can't count on anybody except their own safe sect. Thus they wage a holy war on crime that takes no prisoners: warrantless searches, street-side shakedowns; wiretaps; abuse of plea bargains and immunity waivers; an impatience with Miranda warnings and a contempt for every other nicety that is supposed to distinguish our legal system from, say, Myanmar's. Sam Waterston's Jack McCoy, on "Law & Order," will do anything to win a case, and even when he loses, it's because defense attorneys beat him on a technicality.

When "Homicide" found itself taking the law into its own hands, it went off the air. But most egregious in the rush to judgment is Bochco's own "NYPD Blue." Night after Tuesday night, sometimes Simone, even Martinez and Medavoy—and always Sipowicz—will trample on the weedy rights of suspects, smack a snitch, or coerce a confession from an uppity perp. Maybe one reason why so many of us watch hospital shows instead is that the sick, by medical definition, are all of them innocent—unless, of course, they don't have health insurance.

That said, a medium capable of such dramatic series as "St. Elsewhere," "Lou Grant," "Cagney & Lacey," "China Beach,"   *(continued on page 325)*

STAR TREK

THE WALTONS

DALLAS

ER

Fantasy as reality

"There is a fifth dimension…we call the Twilight Zone," Rod Serling (opposite) intoned, leading television into a fictional realm that either soared beyond reality, as in "Star Trek," or stayed in a televised near reality, such as "The Waltons," a family that began fictionally in 1933 (but really in 1972) and continued until 1943 (ending in 1981 real time). There is a real museum for the fictional Waltons in Schuyler, Virginia. "The Twilight Zone," which ran from 1959 to 1964, exists today as a spectral presence in syndication around the world. "Star Trek" fostered fans who call themselves Trekkies and eschew their real lives. "Dallas," which lasted from 1978 to 1991 and was seen in 91 countries, made slickly nasty J.R. Ewing (played by Larry Hagman) so real that "Who Shot J.R?" reverberated throughout the world in 1980. (J.R.'s wife's sister did it.) "ER," admitting viewers into County General Memorial Hospital, treats them with arcane medical procedures and feverish romances.

THE COSBY SHOW

Funny answers to what's funny

Television comedies search constantly for America's funny bone. "M*A*S*H" from 1972 to 1983, was not so much about the Korean War as about men and women fending off horror with humor; "All in the Family" made Archie Bunker rude and bigoted but believably genuine, saying out loud, from 1971 to 1979, what some Americans were too polite to say; his armchair went to the Smithsonian. Bill Cosby made entertainment history in 1965 playing, in "I Spy," a black man on equal terms with a white partner; in "The Cosby Show" his black family got laughs reflecting middle-class, color-blind values. "Seinfeld," a turn-on for Seinfeld-age viewers (he was born in 1955), somehow generated laughs by being about nothing. "The Simpsons" took the comedians out of TV comedy, replacing them with cartoons.

SEINFELD

In the press box at Boston's Fenway Park (right), television sees the action better than the fans in the stands. After Super Bowl XXXI, cameras surround Reggie White of the Green Bay Packers carrying away the winner's trophy. TV's first commercials—touting a soap and a cereal—appeared in 1939 during a baseball game. Now Super Bowl commercials cost about $50,000 a second.

"Northern Exposure," "Homicide," "Hill Street Blues," "The Practice," and "The X-Files" need not apologize to anybody in Hollywood or on Broadway or on the *New York Times* best-seller list.

Of course, something happens to us when we watch TV. The networks couldn't sell their millions of pairs of eyes to the advertising agencies (at an amazing $50,000 for every second of a Super Bowl, for example), nor would those agencies buy more than $150 billion worth of ad space and commercial time a year if speech and sight did not somehow modify behavior. But what happens is usually fuzzy and will not be greatly clarified by lab studies of habits and behaviors isolated from the larger feedback loops and echo chambers of a culture full of gaudy contradictions. It is as preposterous to believe that all entertainment is hypodermic, directly injecting bad ideas into the innocent bloodstream of the passive masses, as it is to pretend that all behavior is mimetic, and our only models are Eliot Ness or Dirty Harry. (What about Mr. Rogers or Jessica Fletcher?)

Every sitcom of the 1950s celebrated the two-parent nuclear family—and the U.S. divorce rate began to take off. The most popular program in the 1980s was "The Cosby Show," and race relations had seldom been worse. Until 1996, every TV movie and every episode of a dramatic series that ever contemplated the death penalty opposed execution. Yet there were 45 executions in 1996, and more than 3,000 prisoners were under a death sentence.

Why, after so much "M*A*S*H" every week for 11 years in prime time and every night in reruns ever since, aren't all of us tree-hugging wise guy pacifists? Because we each bring to the dream box our separate embattled selves, a constructed identity that is, on the one hand, the space in the middle where everything else about us intersects and overlaps (race, gender, faith, socioeconomic status, sexual orientation, family obligations, professional associations, friends, enemies, health), and, on the other hand, what the postmodern theorists call "a radically overdetermined site for the contestation of core cultural notions"—that is, whatever gets dumped on us. And even this poor composite is provisional. It depends: You got lucky or a raise, whereas last night I sang a sorrow song.

Finally, it would be nice if a single social scientist bestirred himself to wonder why our politics and culture got so mean while television was asking us, night after night, to be nicer to women, children, minorities, immigrants, poor people, sick people, old people, odd people, and strangers.

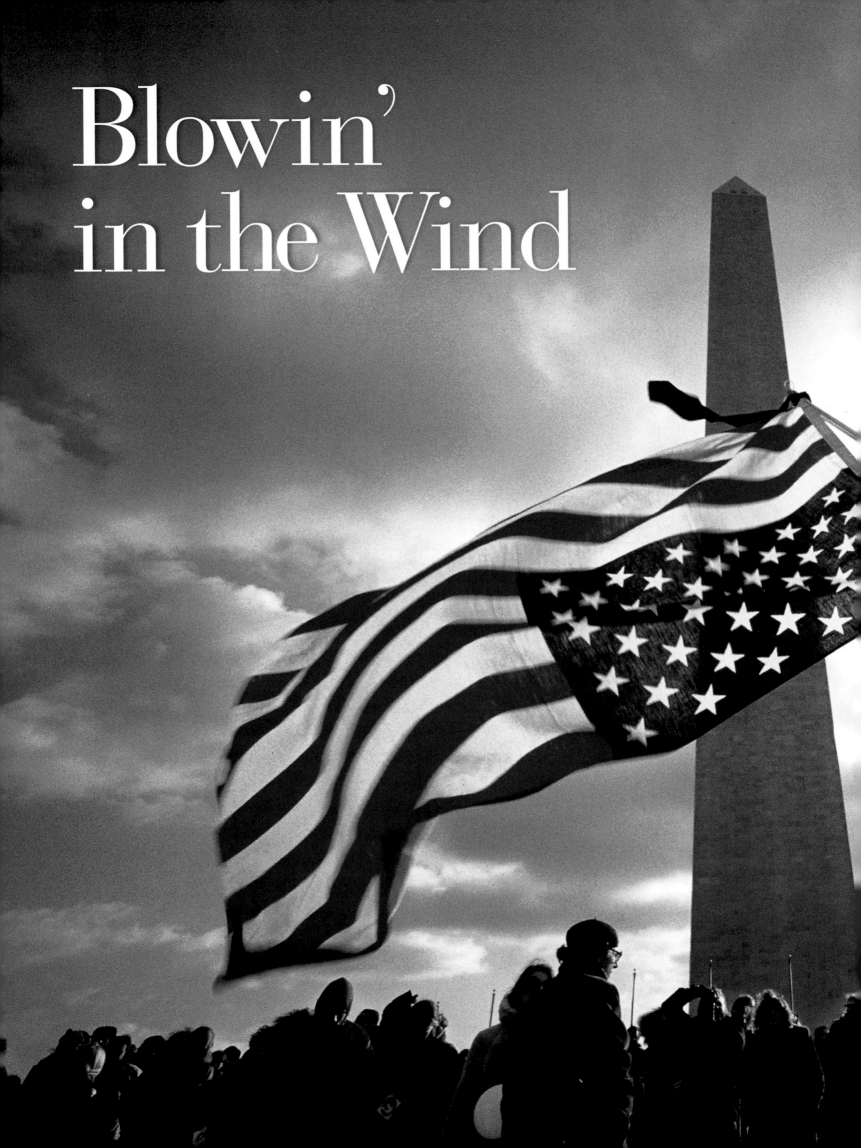

Blowin' in the Wind

"One has to conquer the fear of death, if he is going to do anything constructive in life, and take a stand against evil."

—MARTIN LUTHER KING, JR.

BY CHARLES KAISER

The 1960s are remembered by many as a decade of mass movements—in favor of civil rights, against the Vietnam War, for "free love." But more than anything else, these years vibrated with the power of the individual. Thirty years later, it is almost impossible to imagine a President whose election alone could elevate the national mood, a civil rights leader who spoke to (and for) almost every enlightened American, or an eccentric guitar player who could provide a moral blueprint for most of his generation. But John Kennedy, Martin Luther King, Jr., and Bob Dylan did all of those things, and they were not alone. John Lennon wasn't exaggerating when he remarked, "I came out of the…sticks to take over the world, it seemed to me."

In January 1968, thousands of Viet Cong and North Vietnamese troops launched the Tet Offensive (named after the lunar New Year) throughout South Vietnam. Tet stunned American officials who had recently claimed that the end of the Vietnam War—or at least the "light at the end of the tunnel"—was in sight. A few weeks after Tet, a network anchorman commandeered an hour of prime-time television to challenge a President to reverse his position on a crucial question of war and peace—and then carried much of the country with him. That kind of leadership from a television journalist was equally unimaginable by the end of the century. But Walter Cronkite of CBS News did that.

The charisma of these men—as well as a handful of women—was only one of the reasons that so much about America changed so quickly in this era. The combined power of culture and politics had rarely been so potent a force. For a fleeting moment, millions of members of the new generation, along with quite a few from the old, felt a synergy between artists and politicians: Bob Dylan and John Kennedy, rock-and-roll and the antiwar movement, Aretha Franklin and Martin Luther King, Jr., even Janis Joplin and the women's movement.

The Vietnam War was another powerful agent of change. This war affected the country differently from all of its predecessors. Vietnam was the corrosive that dissolved America's confidence in all kinds of conventional wisdom. The war's opponents challenged the dual legacies of Senator Joseph McCarthy and a disastrous European summit meeting that history had labeled "Munich." In the 1950s McCarthy had spurred a national hysteria over communist infiltration with wild charges that the

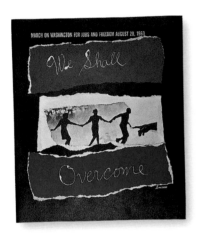

U.S. Communist Party had penetrated every segment of American society. In combination with the accusation that President Harry Truman had "lost China" to the Chinese communists, national Democrats were terrified of the charge of being "soft on communism."

That fear merged with a dread of repeating the "appeasement" of British Prime Minister Neville Chamberlain, who had failed to stand up to Adolf Hitler at Munich in 1938. Many people, including Lyndon Johnson, the President who led America into a wider war in Vietnam, preached that a failure to confront the communists there would have exactly the same consequences as Munich. He believed that in the absence of American resolve, Thailand, Indonesia, and the rest of Southeast Asia would fall under the communist yoke as surely as Europe had been temporarily conquered by the Nazis during the last great war.

These parallels were gradually discredited, especially after Tet, when Walter Cronkite's declaration that outright victory was extremely unlikely was echoed by NBC News, the *New York Times*, and even the editorial page of the *Wall Street Journal*. And once Americans realized that their government could be wrong about such a crucial matter of national policy, their skepticism spread to established notions about almost everything else—from extramarital sex to the use of illegal drugs like marijuana and LSD.

Young men and women—79 million of them born between 1943 and 1960, the largest generation America had yet produced—challenged dozens of traditional assumptions, and their power was multiplied by a uniquely efficient method of communication. All of them could speak to each other simultaneously through the songs of their bards on the radio.

The impetus for most of these transformations had powerful roots in the previous decade. "America changed," said historian Joan Nestle, "because of work-

Hundreds of thousands throng Washington in 1963 to hear Martin Luther King, Jr., shout: "I have a dream that one day, even the state of Mississippi...will be transformed into an oasis of freedom and justice." And his audience roars back: "AMEN!" His call for a march on Washington inspired one of the countless posters (opposite) of the era.

Struggle in the streets

In the spring of 1963, firemen in Birmingham, Alabama, attack black demonstrators with high-pressure hoses that tear the clothes off some victims' backs. The assaults with fire hoses and police dogs were ordered by public safety commissioner Bull Connor, who became a symbol of Southern resistance to black civil rights. Three years after Birmingham, Stokely Carmichael, with a call for "black power," stiffened black resistance to white supremacists. James Meredith, the first African American enrolled at the University of Mississippi in 1962, was shot— but not gravely wounded—during his 1966 March through Mississippi. Marxist activist Angela Davis was acquitted of all charges that she had assisted in an attempted court- room escape that killed four people.

ing black Southerners who decided they were going to take on America's apartheid." The black civil rights fighters of the 1950s were the first modern Americans who challenged the centuries-old notion that practically all power belonged in the hands of Protestant white men.

In the 1950s, Rosa Parks had been a perfect example of an ordinary person almost casually assuming an extraordinary role. A 42-year-old tailor's assistant in Montgomery, Alabama, Mrs. Parks had been an active member of the National Association for the Advancement of Colored People since 1943. On December 1, 1955, with "no previous resolution until it happened," she refused to give up her seat on a city bus to spare a white man the indignity of sitting in the same row as a black woman. Her impulsive act of conscience sparked a black boycott of the bus system that lasted 382 days, until the city's resistance collapsed and a 27-year-old minister named Martin Luther King, Jr., became the first African-American passenger to sit in one of the first ten rows of a Montgomery bus.

Four years later, four black students from North Carolina Agricultural & Technical College started the sit-in movement, by taking seats at the "whites only" Woolworth's lunch counter in Greensboro, North Carolina. When no one served them, they refused to leave. This tactic, designed to desegregate public accommodations, quickly spread across the South. Fifteen days after the protest began, Martin Luther King, Jr., came to Durham, North Carolina, to address more than a thousand supporters of the sit-ins. "What is new in your fight," he declared, "is the fact that it was initiated, fed, and sustained by students....When you have found by the help of God a correct course, a morally sound objective, you do not equivocate, you do not retreat—you struggle to win a victory." The struggle was for true personal freedom, for "freedom is necessary for one's self-

San Francisco (opposite) and the University of California at Berkeley (above) were early centers of protest against the Vietnam War. Police and troops invaded many campuses. In 1970, National Guardsmen, called to quell protesters at Kent State in Ohio, killed four students and wounded nine. And during a protest at Jackson State College in Mississippi, police killed two students.

In a tableau of the antiwar movement, a protester puts carnations into the rifle barrels of military police troops during the "siege of the Pentagon," produced by activist Jerry Rubin in October 1967. While this group proffered flowers, others taunted troops with ugly epithets. Robert Kennedy, who took up the antiwar banner in the 1968 presidential campaign, was assassinated (opposite).

hood, for one's intrinsic worth." Here were the roots of the moral certainty that many members of the Vietnam generation would discover through their opposition to the war. As Thomas Powers observed in *The War at Home,* "the single most important influence on white students" in the early sixties was "the example of black students in the South."

At the same time, African Americans were spreading their influence through the culture with unprecedented power, as rock-and-roll began to make its way onto AM radio stations across the country. This music—whether performed by Little Richard or Elvis Presley—owed its largest artistic debt to black Americans and their forebears from Africa.

Building on the energy of those songs and the idealism of those black civil rights workers, the first half of the 1960s was about hope and idealism. In 1961, John Kennedy challenged Americans to do something for their country, instead of themselves, and two years later, Martin Luther King, Jr., told hundreds of thousands in front of the Lincoln Memorial to "transform the jangling discords of our nation into a beautiful symphony of brotherhood." Simultaneously, Bob Dylan proclaimed, "The Times They Are A-Changin'," and hundreds of imitators on college campuses across the country repeated his choruses. "When people sang and danced, picketed, protested and defied authority," novelist Jeremy Larner wrote, "it really seemed we might find a way to live happily."

In 1962, radical whites who belonged to Students for a Democratic Society offered nothing less than a blueprint for a new "participatory democracy." At a national convention in Port Huron, Michigan, leaders of the SDS drafted a statement written primarily by Tom Hayden, a student at the University of Michigan. Although written two years before anyone was describing a "counterculture," the SDS's Port Huron statement came closer to outlining its philosophy than any other written document.

"We regard men as infinitely precious and possessed of unfulfilled capacities for reason, freedom, and love," it said. "…The goal of men and society should be human independence: a concern not with image or popularity but with finding a meaning in life that is personally authentic….We would replace power rooted in possession, privilege, or circumstance by

power and uniqueness rooted in love, reflectiveness, reason and creativity." Here we see the first hints of a strain of antimaterialism, which would be an important (though quickly forgotten) theme of this entire era. In a characteristic declaration, Martin Luther King, Jr., said, "I am convinced that if we are to get on the right side of the world revolution, we as a nation must undergo a radical revolution of values. We must rapidly begin the shift from a 'thing-oriented' society to a 'person-oriented' society."

This period of naive hopefulness was shattered forever by the bullets that struck John F. Kennedy in Dallas on November 22, 1963. Looking back, Vietnam and Watergate appear to be the largest reasons for a general decline in the nation's confidence in its government. But the doubts about officialdom definitely began in the months immediately after Kennedy's assassination. It was during those months that millions of Americans, including Lyndon Johnson, refused to accept fully the government's official verdict, as rendered by the Johnson-appointed Warren Commission, that Lee Harvey Oswald acted alone in killing the President. Although the bulk of the available evidence continues to support that controversial conclusion, the evidence has never been enough to obliterate those early doubts.

The kind of shock that America experienced after Kennedy's assassination is almost unimaginable today. America had not witnessed the murder of a President since the shooting of William McKinley in 1901. In the six decades since that assassination, the possibility of such a catastrophe had completely disappeared from the nation's consciousness. It was at this precise moment that the historical memory of America mutated from black-and-white into color—as color television sets replaced black-and-white, and wars and celebrations in full color displaced the memory of John Kennedy's black-and-white funeral.

For the young people of America, the emotional void created by Kennedy's death was filled almost immediately in a most unlikely way. It began in America on December 26, 1963, with the release of two minutes and twenty-four seconds of music that by February 1 had become the number-one-selling single in the country. Even before their first appearance on the "Ed Sullivan Show" (page 309), the Beatles had conquered young America. The utterly sentimental lyrics of "I Want To Hold Your Hand" just happened to be a perfect fit for the sensibilities of the new generation. Kennedy, following an elderly general into the White House, had illuminated the power of the individual, showing how one man could change the way a whole country felt about itself, particularly if that man was young and charismatic.

Advertised as "a great new game in the American tradition," a Johnson dartboard (opposite) aims at a President who had won a landslide victory over Republican Barry Goldwater in 1964 and won plaudits as a civil rights champion. But as he escalated the Vietnam War, he became a target of darts and protest. His successor, Richard Nixon, another antiwar target, promised "peace with honor" but faced impeachment over Watergate. He decorates a T-shirt—the personal billboard of the era.

John Lennon, Paul McCartney, George Harrison, and Ringo Starr illuminated the power of collaboration, and their message was even more surprising. These Liverpudlians proved that four kids from a decaying British port—rock-and-roll musicians without money or connections (just good looks, a canny manager, and colossal talent)—could change the way the whole world felt about itself, practically overnight.

For most people under 30, the Beatles and Bob Dylan were the two great unifying forces of a generation. And no one recognized the importance of these British invaders more quickly than Dylan did. "We were driving through Colorado," Dylan remembered. "We had the radio on, and eight of the Top Ten songs were Beatles songs. In Colorado! 'I Want to Hold Your Hand,' all those early ones. They were doing things nobody was doing. Their chords were outrageous, and their harmonies made it all valid. But I kept it to myself that I really dug them. Everybody else thought they were for the teenyboppers, that they were gonna pass right away. But it was obvious to me that they had staying power. I knew they were pointing the direction where music had to go."

Dylan's contribution to the counterculture was obvious, because his earliest songs were explicitly political in a way that the Beatles almost never were. At the beginning of the decade he wrote antiwar songs like "A Hard Rain's A-Gonna Fall" and "Masters of War," both before there was an antiwar movement. His "Blowin' in the Wind" became almost as important to the civil rights movement as "We Shall Overcome"—which Martin Luther King first heard Pete Seeger sing.

The Beatles mostly shied away from explicit political statements, but they did nothing less than change the way men and women related to each other. The writings of Jack Kerouac, Allen Ginsberg, and the rest of the "Beats" had anticipated the counterculture in the 1950s, and Ginsberg was quick to embrace Dylan and the Beatles as his disciples. Ginsberg pointed out that simply by spending time together as "a community group," the Beatles provided "an example to youth around the world—that guys could be friends," a radical notion in the macho America of the early 1960s.

Their music embodied the rebellious spirit of the era, and by the time they released their masterpiece, "Sgt. Peppers Lonely Hearts Club Band," in 1967, the Beatles were indisputably the most famous people on the planet.

The music of such rock women as Janis Joplin, Grace Slick, and even Aretha Franklin would be equally important to the women's movement. Their status as virtual equals of men like Jerry Garcia and Jimi Hendrix *(continued on page 346)*

Candlelight illumines an antiwar protest centered on the White House. In May 1970 more than 100,000 demonstrators besieged Washington—and the President in the White House, Richard Nixon, who had just widened the Vietnam War by sending U.S. troops into Cambodia. Early on the morning of May 9, Nixon impulsively went to the Lincoln Memorial and began talking to young protesters huddled there. "I know that most of you think I'm an SOB," he told them, "but I want you to know that I understand just how you feel." By then, Congress was turning against the war. In June Nixon pulled the troops out of Cambodia.

The Wall: in touch with memory

When the Vietnam Veterans Memorial Fund first proposed a permanent monument in Washington, one of the guidelines said that it should be "reflective and contemplative in character." The winning design by Maya Ying Lin is literally reflective: Visitors see themselves in the highly polished black granite as they walk down and then up the hill in front of the names of more than 58,000 Americans who died or are still listed as missing in action in Vietnam.

For those who lived through the war—on the battlefield or back home—visiting the Wall is like reliving the war itself. Starting at either end, at first you feel larger than the memorial, just as America felt utterly superior to this conflict when the U.S. role in the war began to expand. But as you walk toward the middle, the wall gradually looms above you, and you begin to feel overwhelmed by the whole experience, just as America did by 1968, in the middle of its involvement in the conflict. Then, as the monument makes a sharp turn, the wall gradually recedes into the

ground, just as American entanglement in the war eventually disappeared.

The design infuriated many Vietnam veterans when it was first announced on May 1, 1981. The brainchild of a 21-year old student at Yale University, the design was derided by many as "a black slab of death." But no one (except perhaps Lin herself) imagined just how successful it would be until it became a living object next to Constitution Gardens, not far from the Lincoln Memorial, in October 1982. It quickly won the enthusiastic approval of both veterans of the war and veterans of antiwar demonstrators. There is

AMONG THE MANY OBJECTS LEFT AT THE WALL: HUNDREDS OF BUTTONS THAT LINK MEMORIES OF THE LIVING AND THE DEAD.

A MAN (OPPOSITE) CLINGS IN SORROW TO THE WALL.

Carved & painted by a 12 year
old boy, who died a 21 year
old man March 23rd 1969
IAN J. FRANKS
Love, Mom Dad Ron Andy
+ Our Families you Never meT.

an almost mystical power in the way you see your face mirrored in the rows of names and in the middle of the reflected images of surrounding Washington monuments.

Regardless of what anyone may have believed about the war while it was being waged, the memorial has the remarkable ability to provide what America needed most after the agony of its involvement: a sense of closure. "When we touch the Wall," said a poem left at the memorial, "we know that you are there."

Soon after the Wall was dedicated, visitors began leaving objects at the Wall—flags and roses, kids' treasures (above), teddy bears, garlands of dog tags, packs of cigarettes, cans of beer, letters, and birthday cards for birthdays that would never come again. The tradition continued when the Vietnam Women's Memorial was built near the Wall in 1993. Among the first were eight gold bracelets, each carrying the name of one of the eight women remembered on the Wall.

Many of the objects enshrine moments in the lives of people who kept on living after a name on the Wall died. One such offering was a pair of fetal sonograms. They were in one side of a double picture frame. In the other frame was this message: "Happy Father's Day, Dad. Here are the first images of your first grandchild. I don't know if it's a boy or a girl. If the baby is a boy he'll be named after you. Dad—this child will know you just how I have grown to know & love you—even though the last time I saw you I was only 4 mos old. I ♥ U Daddy. Your daughter, Jeannette."

None of the offerings, numbering in the tens of thousands, are thrown away. They have been gathered by the National Park Service, custodian of the monument, and placed in a building housing the Vietnam Veterans Memorial Collection.

MANY TEDDY BEARS HAVE BEEN FOUND AT THE WALL. ONE, A FEMALE WEARING LIPSTICK, WAS LEFT AT THE VIETNAM WOMEN'S MEMORIAL.

MISSING IN ACTION BRACELETS (OPPOSITE) ACKNOWLEDGE THAT NAMES ONCE CARRIED ON WRISTS ARE REMEMBERED ON THE WALL.

provided powerful subliminal evidence of sexual equality for teenagers everywhere. At least in the case of Joplin, this equality went well beyond the easy matter of equal fame. When Joplin wailed, "Come on, take another little piece of my heart," she wasn't merely just as famous as any male rock-and-roll star—she was also just as tough. As Ellen Willis put it, "Joplin's metamorphosis from the ugly duckling of Port Arthur to the peacock of Haight-Ashbury" meant that "a woman who was not conventionally pretty, who had acne and an intermittent weight problem…" could "invent her own beauty out of sheer energy, soul, sweetness, arrogance, and a sense of humor," changing the very "notions of attractiveness."

Radical organizations like Students for a Democratic Society advocated the overthrow of traditional forms of government and disrupted campuses from the University of California at Berkeley in 1964 to Columbia University in New York City in 1968 and again in 1972. But these radicals only constituted a tiny minority of the burgeoning new generation. Many more people found a new sense of power by working within the system, by trying to overthrow Lyndon Johnson in 1968 in the primaries, rather than in the streets.

Inspired first by Allard Lowenstein, the kind of full-time left-wing activist who had practically disappeared from the American scene by the end of the century, an

army of young people followed Eugene McCarthy to New Hampshire to challenge the war and its Commander in Chief in 1968. McCarthy was a diffident man, who never imagined that he might actually deprive Johnson of renomination when he started his campaign; his only serious goal was to change the nation's policies in Vietnam. But all the energies of the 1960s came together in March, and Johnson narrowly escaped defeat in the crucial New Hampshire primary. Stimulated by McCarthy's example, Bobby Kennedy jumped into the race, and on March 31 Johnson astounded the nation when he pulled himself out of the competition.

This is how he described his feelings about that moment to historian Doris Kearns Goodwin: "I felt that I was being chased on all sides by a giant stampede.... I was being forced over the edge by rioting blacks, demonstrating students, marching welfare mothers, squawking professors, and hysterical reporters. And then the final straw. The thing I feared from the first day of my Presidency was actually coming true. Robert Kennedy had openly announced his intention to reclaim the throne in the memory of his brother. And the American people, swayed by the magic of the name, were dancing in the streets."

For everyone who believed that fundamental change was possible and necessary, Lyndon Johnson's announcement produced the kind of pure political joy that most

If you're not one of us, you're one of them

The youthful us-not-them spirit of the '60s gradually spread into the American heartland the following decade, with such experiments in living as the commune. One was the Farm, an agricultural commune near Summertown, Tennessee, where a woman and a man take turns riding and plowing as they cultivate a turnip field (right); harvest inspires outdoor dancing (opposite). Most such experiments were short-lived.

But the hairstyles, clothing, and drug-taking habits of the earliest hippies gradually were adopted by young people throughout Middle America. Psychedelic buses like this one (above) carried many espousing the alternative lifestyle around. One such trip gained fame when Tom Wolfe published his chronicle of a wild bus tour in The Electric Kool-Aid Acid Test.

people believed had disappeared forever after that Dallas motorcade tragedy less than five years earlier.

This time the celebration would last only four days, before dissolving into another paroxysm of violence.

The Thursday after the Sunday of Johnson's speech, Martin Luther King, Jr., was assassinated on a motel balcony in Memphis, Tennessee. Black Americans responded by burning up their own neighborhoods in 130 cities across the country. In Washington, the fires and the looting spread to within blocks of the White House. Federal troops mounted machine guns on the grounds of the Capitol and marshaled in a tunnel connecting the Treasury Building and the White House, poised to repel mobs that might attack the President himself. Thousands of troops patrolled Washington's riot-torn streets. For a while the President's men worried that they might actually run out of soldiers to quell the spreading disturbances. The riots claimed 39 lives, and nearly 20,000 were arrested.

Bobby Kennedy redoubled his energies on the campaign trail—until he too was cut down by an assassin, exactly two months after King was killed. The day before Kennedy was murdered, Andy Warhol was gravely wounded by Valerie Solanis, the founder of SCUM, the Society for Cutting Up Men. As Warhol recovered from his operation, he recalled that he heard, on a television going somewhere, "the words 'Kennedy' and 'assassin' and 'shot' over and over again. Robert Kennedy had been shot, but what was so weird was that I had no understanding that this was a *second* Kennedy assassination—I just thought that maybe after you die, they rerun things for you, like President Kennedy's assassination."

The world was completely out of joint, and television brought every gory detail into the living room. Author John Updike wondered out loud whether God might have withdrawn his blessing on America. The riots in the streets outside the Democratic National Convention 12 weeks later only confirmed the general impression that America was falling apart. It was hardly surprising that in November America chose Richard Nixon, who promised to restore "law and order" and a much more old-fashioned kind of America.

Nixon's paranoiac distrust toward his radical enemies exploded with the publication of the "Pentagon Papers" by the *New York Times* in 1971. The U.S. Supreme

Taking their cue from the civil rights movement, women began fighting for their own liberation. The first public action was a protest outside the Miss America pageant in Atlantic City, New Jersey, in 1968. The sprightly Smith College Class of '21 (opposite) showed its colors, greeting the Class of '71. The Supreme Court guaranteed a woman's right to an abortion in its 1973 Roe v. Wade *decision which inspired pro (above) and anti demonstrations.*

Court refused to suppress this secret history of the Vietnam War, which revealed that the government had deceived the public from the start about its intentions and its prospects in Vietnam. Nixon reacted by becoming more determined than ever to suppress all kinds of dissent. A secret group financed by the White House broke into the offices of the Democratic National Committee a year after the Pentagon Papers were published, and Nixon's subsequent effort to cover up the crime turned into the scandal known as Watergate. Two years later, he was forced to resign his Presidency, and what the nation still remembers as the 1960s were finally over.

In a variation on 1960s demonstrations, advocates for more research about Acquired Immune Deficiency Syndrome took their campaign to Washington. Friends grieve (below)

The possibility of a real political revolution turned out to have been a mirage, but the changes that occurred in the country's social fabric were real. The spirit of change embodied by the 1960s remained alive and well long after Nixon's election. Betty Friedan's 1963 book, *The Feminine Mystique*, scorned suburbia as a "prison for housewives," and three years later she founded the National Organization for Women, aimed at putting women "in a truly equal partnership with men." The first Earth Day, in 1970, signaled a new interest in the environment. The year before, a riot led by drag queens outside a New York City bar announced the birth of the Gay Liberation Movement. The year 1969 also witnessed the largest antiwar demonstrations to date in the nation's capital, and America finally began a long, slow withdrawal from Vietnam.

In 1973, the Supreme Court handed the women's movement its single most important legal victory—*Roe* v. *Wade*, a seven-to-two decision that guaranteed a woman's right to an abortion. The example of black Americans, with sit-ins and protests, had started it all, inspiring women, gay people, Native Americans, and, eventually, members of every other disenfranchised group to stake their rightful claim to what was still the American Dream.

The 1960s came second only to the Great Depression as a 20th-century era of turmoil. The changes that the 1960s had wrought were profound and lasting, although the country was still debating their purpose and their value at the end of the century. Inequality was still endemic as America entered the new millennium. And the gap between its richest and poorest citizens was greater than ever. But a new generation was growing up in a freer America—with more opportunities for more different kinds of people than any previous generation had ever experienced.

over a panel in the AIDS Memorial Quilt, whose 8,288 panels—each representing an AIDS victim—covered the Mall (opposite) in Washington in October 1988. By 1999, the quilt had been displayed all over the country and included more than 41,000 panels. Veteran activist Cleve Jones conceived the quilt project in 1985, after more than 1,000 San Francisco residents had died from AIDS.

353

Clicking
Toward Y2K

"The information superhighway is about the global movement of weightless bits at the speed of light."

—NICHOLAS NEGROPONTE

BY HOWARD RHEINGOLD

"Y2K." The turn of the third millennium was given a popular name years before the event because of a phenomenon that has now taken its place in technology mythology–the "millennium" bug, the misprogramming and befuddling of many data processing devices on January 1, 2000. In the larger sense, this nomenclature is perfectly appropriate, and should extend for the rest of the 21st century—a century centrally concerned with the way humanity is enmeshed in technology.

We've been dependent on a mostly invisible mesh of micro-technologies for decades. We depend upon chips and lasers and microprocessors to keep our planes in the air, purvey our groceries, and ensure supplies of the necessities of life. Sewage plants, skyscraper elevators, emergency services, traffic lights, bank accounts, hospitals, offices, farms, subways, automobiles all depend on microchips, software, and global networks. We live inside a machine of our own devising, and life is, for the most part, better for it.

We've become dependent on our own creations because our machines have been so useful to us. They amplify our power. They save our children from dying. They help to feed us. Our machines have proved so beneficial that we've created cities amenable to being run like machines. We've used our machines to design a high-tech civilization that operates at a pace and scale that would be impossible without sophisticated mechanical assistance.

Our tools accomplish magic for us. They also change us. The first century of the coming millennium will see fundamental changes in what it means to be human, because of what we have learned to do with machines. The nature of those changes is profoundly influenced by the most complex of our many tools: machines for manipulating and communicating symbols.

ENIAC, the Electronic Numerical Integrator and Computer, commisioned by the U.S. Army to calculate trajectories of new artillery, was completed in 1945 at the University of Pennsylvania. It was used instead in top secret work on weapons computing.

PRECEDING PAGES
Reaching out to touch what is not there, children react to virtual reality. Headsets convert images on a screen into a three-dimensional wonderland.

The lives of billions of people are inextricably interconnected with an underground, undersea, desktop, palmtop, satellite-linked network of symbol-manipulating technologies. Microchips, bar codes and their laser readers, personal computers, television screens, CD players. And on the computer screen photographs, music videos, encyclopedias, a World Wide Web, corporate logos. People who never touch a computer in their lives depend upon interlinked and cybernated sanitation, transportation, communication, and life-support infrastructures.

One of the most challenging characteristics of the digital revolution has been a pace of change far greater than that of previous technological revolutions, including the industrial revolution. Over the past three decades, I've watched microchip technology trigger three separate revolutions in symbol-manipulating tools: the computer graphics revolution that started at the end of the 1970s, the personal computer revolution of the 1970s and 1980s, and the emergence of the Internet as a mass medium in the 1990s. Anybody over 30 can remember living in a world that was distinctly and irrecoverably different before these techno-cultural revolutions changed the way we live, work, communicate, govern, and entertain ourselves.

It is impossible to understand these revolutions without understanding what has come to be known as "Moore's Law," after the person who first articulated it—Gordon Moore, one of the founders of Intel. The law originated with an observation that Moore made in 1964. According to Intel's official account, Moore noticed that when he analyzed the growth in memory chip performance, he discovered that each new chip "contained roughly twice as much capacity as its predecessor, and each chip was released within 18-24 months of the previous chip." He reasoned that if this trend continued, "computing power would rise exponentially over relatively brief periods of time."

Moore's Law describes a trend that is still remarkably accurate. By Intel estimates, in 26 years the number of transistors on a chip has increased from 2,300 on the 4004 processor in 1971 to 7.5 million on the Pentium II processor. Intel's first transistors sold for $1.50 in 1959. Today you can buy the equivalent of about 16 million transistors for about $6. The magic of modern technology growth, predicted by Moore's Law, makes it possible for an infant today to have a toy with more processing power than the Department of Defense had in 1950.

CBS reporter Charles Collingwood (foreground, above) teams up with Univac I, a pioneer computer, to project the results of the 1952 presidential election. Univac's electoral-college vote prediction (top) was off by less than 1 percent; its popular-vote projection was off about 3 percent. By the 1980s, computers had permeated all aspects of life and had speeded up stock trading (opposite). The Black Monday stock market crash of 1987 was caused in part by insufficient computing power in the trading system.

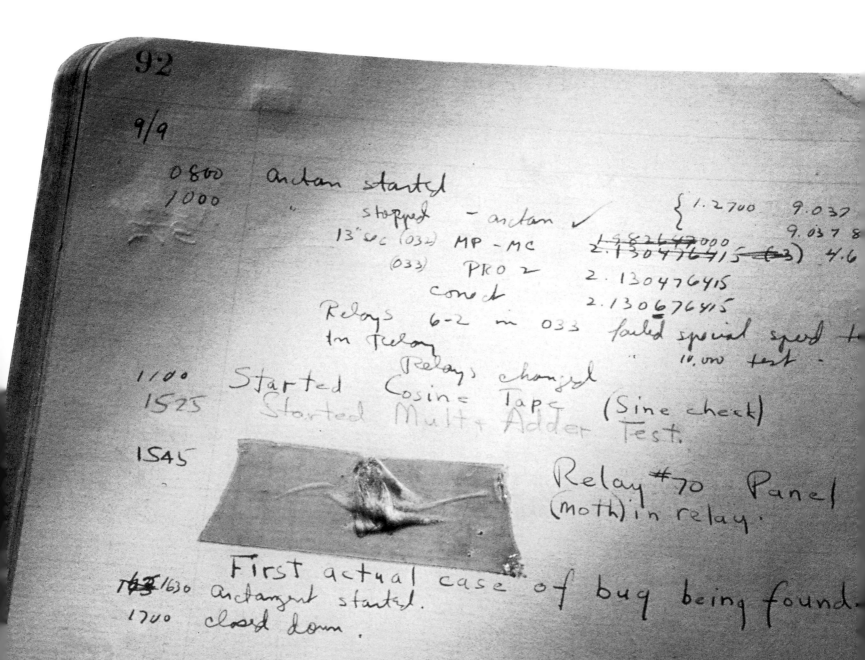

Affordable micro-devices that included millions of components made today's media possible. It was up to a small number of visionaries, however, to make mind-amplifiers from those microchips. And without the support of the U.S. military—the backers of the electronic digital computer, miniaturized electronic components, computer graphics, and the Internet—neither the miraculous microchips nor the visionaries could have created the foundations of today's digital civilization.

The computer is, at its foundation, nothing but a set of fast on and off switches. The rational tool kit known as Boolean logic (named after a 19th-century British mathematician and logician) uses a system based on two values, "true" and "false." It can map to any other two-value system, such as "on" and "off" or "zero" and "one." A network of mechanical or electrical on-off switches can emulate any logical operation possible with a Boolean system. These logical operations are the fundamental building blocks of software. By combining the right "and gates," "not gates," and "or gates," electrical engineers can build the capacity for mathematical and symbolic operations into the circuit structure of computing devices.

The hardware itself is only the rock-bottom foundation. Useful chunks of these hardware-based logical operations are given their own names and become the alphabet for building complex software tools—"higher level languages" that enable humans to interact with the computer. Symbolic languages are made out of building blocks that are themselves symbolic languages. The result is that software capabilities quickly evolve even beyond the power of their hardware base. Every time you see an icon on the screen and move your mouse to click on it, you initiate an action that requires millions of tiny on-off switches and dozens of hierarchies of abstractions to weave logical patterns in your computer's central processing unit (CPU).

The more on-off operations your CPU can process every microsecond, the more powerful the operations your computer can perform, which means that Moore's Law drives not only the economics of microchip technology but also the evolution of newer technologies—and they drive ever newer technologies. Hardware is the "platform" upon which software designers build "virtual machines" that accomplish further wizardry, beyond the capacity of software alone.

None of this happened automatically. Visionaries saw possibilities, engineers took raw potential and turned it into applications, the Department of Defense funded them, entrepreneurs turned military research into commercial products, and millions of people took the new tools into their hands and minds and created things with them. Then the tools we created started influencing our thoughts, relationships, and institutions.

The groundbreaking electronic digital computer, ENIAC, was commissioned for the U.S. Army to perform ballistics calculations; it crunched its first numbers in 1945. The electronic digital computers of the earliest generations were used primarily for scientific calculations related to weaponry. Development of miniature electronic components was necessitated by the desire to put nuclear weapons in the nose cones of guided missiles. After the transistor was invented at Bell Labs in the late 1940s, the Pentagon continued to play a strong role in pushing the development of miniaturization. Military-inspired research had been converging through the 1960s. Computer graphics, which made possible the graphic user interface for today's personal computers, grew from the need to defend against missile attack.

We wouldn't have educational software and online support groups and medical information systems and all the other goodies computer technology brings to our lives if it weren't for ballistics—the science of hurling heavy objects at other human beings. By the 1950s, bombs capable of destroying entire cities were aloft continuously, hours away from their targets. To defend against air attack, a network of radar stations and U.S. Air Force bases, from the Distant Early Warning radar stations in the Arctic to the underground command post of the North American Air Defense Command in Colorado, had to stay in constant communication. The amount of information that had to be collected quickly from a variety of sources and displayed for humans to make decisions under intense time pressure was becoming overwhelming. So display screens for making sense of this data began to use the maturing technology of television tubes.

In the early and mid-1950s, the Massachusetts Institute of Technology and IBM created what would be the largest computers ever built, the IBM AN/FSQ-7s, as the control centers of a new continental air defense system for the United States. SAGE (Semi-Automatic Ground Environment) was the Air Force's answer to the new problem of potential nuclear-bomb attack. The computers weighed 250 tons, took up 20,000 feet of floor space, and were delivered in 18 large vans. MIT set up a top secret facility, Lincoln Laboratory, in Lexington, Massachusetts, to design SAGE.

Computer graphics grew out of the government-sponsored research into better display systems for nuclear defense. But, unquestionably, the entire world of computer-generated graphics owes a great deal to a young man who was a graduate student in the early 1960s—just in time to demonstrate how a computer could

be used as a magical, image-making device. His name was Ivan Sutherland. Both the fields of computer graphics and virtual reality grew from his efforts as a young engineer at MIT, Lincoln Laboratory, and the Advanced Research Projects Agency of the U.S. Defense Department (ARPA, now called DARPA).

While working with a group at Lincoln Lab, Sutherland, a student of Claude Shannon, the father of information theory, created a computer program as his MIT thesis. The computer program, called Sketchpad, demonstrated not only ways computers could be used to control the shape and movement of graphic objects on a display screen but also ways that computer graphics displays could do things no other representational tool could do, such as controlling the operations of computers. You could display complex diagrams on a screen, from specifications programmed into the computer—and you could use a device we now know as a light pen to alter directly the graphics on the screen and thereby alter the underlying program.

Sutherland had created something that even the most ambitious researcher had not even hypothesized. "If I had known how hard it was to do," Sutherland once said of Sketchpad, "I probably wouldn't have done it."

Another computer prophet saw the implications of Sketchpad and other heretofore-esoteric wonders of personal computing. He was an irreverent, unorthodox, counterculture fellow by the name of Ted Nelson, who had long been in the

Steve Jobs and Steve Wozniak, of the Homebrew Computer Club, designed the Apple I computer in 1976. It had no keyboard or case. The owner of this one (above) added them. The Apple II, introduced in 1977, had a built-in keyboard and power supply. All this miniaturization was made possible by the invention of the transistor (1947), the integrated circuit (1958), and the microchip (1971).

habit of self-publishing quirky, cranky, amazingly accurate commentaries on the future of computing. In the late 1970s, in *The Home Computer Revolution*, Nelson entitled a chapter "The Most Important Computer Program Ever Written," and he had this to say about Sutherland's pioneering program: "You could draw a picture on the screen with the lightpen—and then file the picture away in the computer's memory. You could, indeed, save numerous pictures this way.... For example, you could make a picture of a rabbit and a picture of a rocket, and then put little rabbits all over a large rocket. Or little rockets all over a large rabbit."

The screen on which the picture appeared, Nelson continued, "did not necessarily show all the details; the important thing was that the details were *in* the computer; when you magnified a picture sufficiently, they would come into view." Using Sketchpad, "You could magnify and shrink a picture to a spectacular degree. You could fill a rocket picture with rabbit pictures, then shrink that until all that

was visible was a tiny rocket; then you could make copies of that, and dot them all over a large copy of the rabbit picture. So that when you expanded the big rabbit till only a small part showed (so it would be the size of a house, if the screen were large enough), then the foot-long rockets on the screen would each have rabbits the size of a dime."

And "if you changed the master picture—say, by putting a third ear on the big rabbit—all the copies would change correspondingly. Thus Sketchpad let you try things out before deciding. Instead of making you position a line in one specific way, it was set up to allow you to try a number of different positions and arrangements, with the ease of moving cut-outs around on a table."

Sketchpad "allowed room for human vagueness and judgment," Nelson noted. The user no longer had to divide elements into "sharp categories" or follow strict computer rules. The program "let you slide things around to your heart's content.

Home, chip home: Virtually every object serving this home (above) has at least one microprocessor—from furnace and air conditioner to stove and washing machine. By one estimate, each day, before eating lunch, the average American touches 70 products containing embedded microchips.

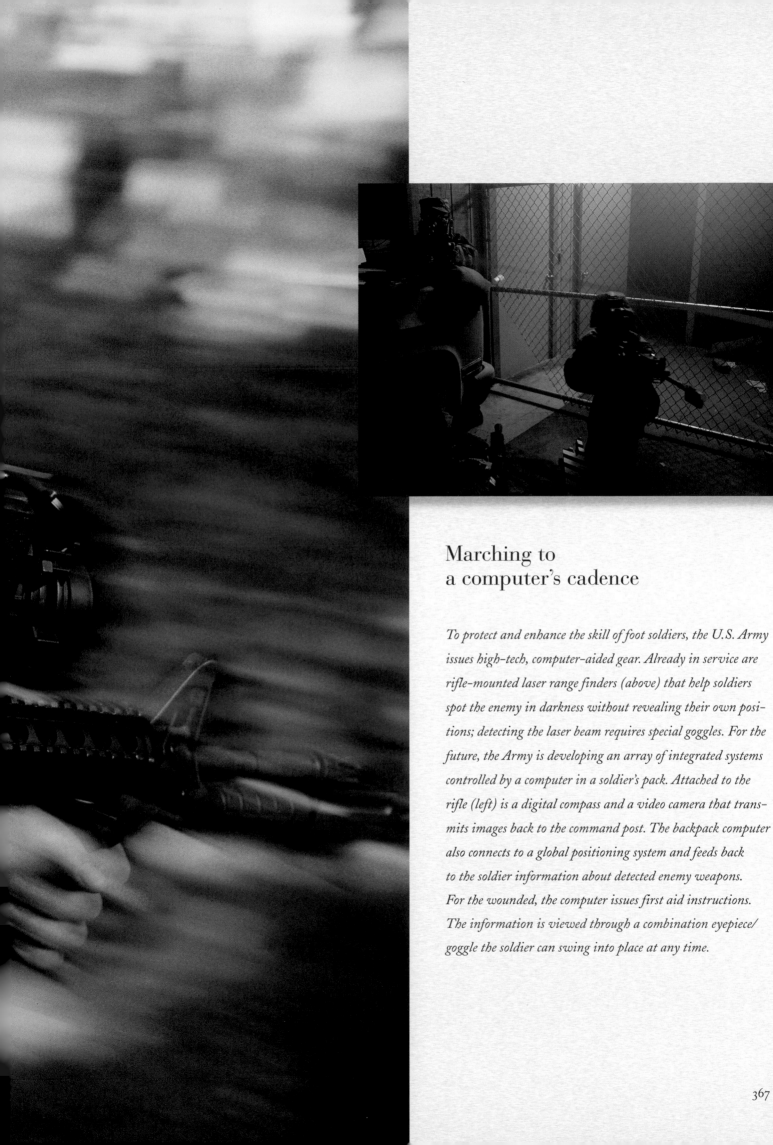

Marching to a computer's cadence

To protect and enhance the skill of foot soldiers, the U.S. Army issues high-tech, computer-aided gear. Already in service are rifle-mounted laser range finders (above) that help soldiers spot the enemy in darkness without revealing their own positions; detecting the laser beam requires special goggles. For the future, the Army is developing an array of integrated systems controlled by a computer in a soldier's pack. Attached to the rifle (left) is a digital compass and a video camera that transmits images back to the command post. The backpack computer also connects to a global positioning system and feeds back to the soldier information about detected enemy weapons. For the wounded, the computer issues first aid instructions. The information is viewed through a combination eyepiece/goggle the soldier can swing into place at any time.

You could rearrange till you got what you wanted, no matter for what reason you wanted it."

The importance of Sketchpad came not from being first—there had been light pens and screens for graphics before its arrival. What was important was its simplicity. "Indeed," as Nelson remarked, "it lacked any complications normally tangled with what people actually do. It was, in short, an innocent program, showing how easy human work could be if a computer were set up to be really helpful."

Sketchpad was the grandparent of computer graphics, and it was also the immediate boost for an innovation known as "interactive computing," a step that made today's personal computers possible.

The early generations of computers, found in research laboratories and at such commercial computer manufacturers as Sperry Rand and IBM, were not "interactive." That is, programmers and operators did not directly put instructions into the machine, nor did they see their results immediately. Computer programs, usually translated into the form of punched paper cards, were submitted to computer operators, who then ran the programs in a batch and later returned the printouts to the people who had submitted the programs. In the 1960s, however, a new paradigm was made possible with the advent of display devices like CRTs (cathode ray tubes, which resemble television screens) and small but powerful transistorized "minicomputers."

Interactive computing did not come about as the result of normal technological commercial development. It was cultivated and nurtured by a new research-funding agency known as ARPA.

On October 4, 1957, the Soviet Union launched its famous 184-pound sphere, Sputnik I, which began orbiting the earth as the world's first artificial satellite. Sputnik demonstrated that the Soviets could propel bomb-size objects anywhere in the world. And that the U.S.S.R. had beaten the United States in what was called the space race. The U.S. Department of Defense, which had been accustomed to being the world leader in military-related technologies, immediately took steps to make sure the Russians would never surprise America again. ARPA was created specifically to leapfrog existing technologies and fund far-out ideas. A small office within ARPA, the Information Processing Techniques Office (IPTO), became the incubator for most of what we recognize today as important information-processing technologies, from computer graphics to computer networks.

Independent counsel Ken Starr chose the Internet for distributing his report on President Clinton in 1998, making it available to everyone. Washington Post staffers gather round a screen to read it (below). Publishing on the Internet has become easy—and Web sites hawking sexy scenes (left) ignite debates over pornography and free speech. While the debate rages, pornography continues to lead in e-commerce profitability.

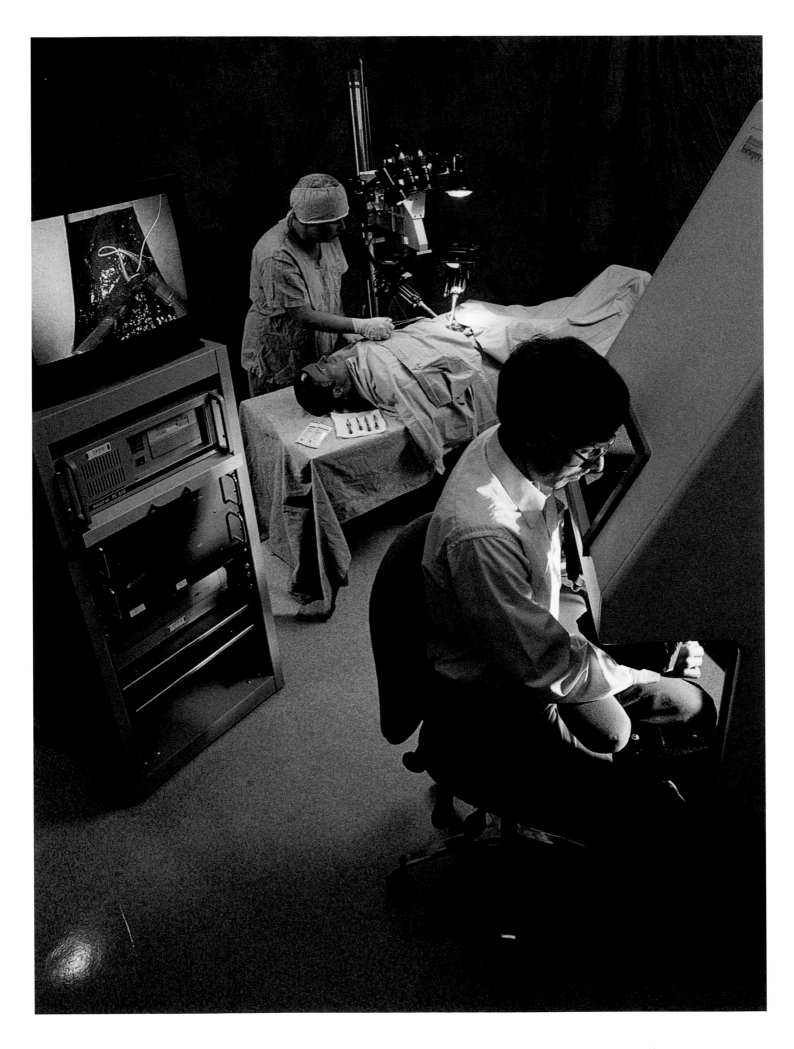

IPTO's first leader, J. C. R. Licklider, turned out to be the visionary leader of the movement to create interactive computing. He was a researcher in psychoacoustics, using mathematical models to try to understand human hearing. Through his work at Lincoln Lab, he had become aware of the new kinds of mini-computers that enabled people like himself—researchers who were not themselves computer scientists—to interact more directly with computers. Licklider sponsored Ivan Sutherland and dozens of other bright computer scientists around the country.

And he appointed Sutherland, who was 26 years old at the time, to succeed him as IPTO director. Licklider's long-term vision was a dramatic one, which he called "man-computer symbiosis."

In 1960, he wrote about his vision: "The fig tree is pollinated only by the insect *Blastophaga grossorum*. The larva of the insect lives in the ovary of the fig tree, and there it gets its food. The tree and the insect are thus heavily interdependent: the tree cannot reproduce without the insect; the insect cannot eat without the tree; together, they constitute not only a viable but a productive and thriving partnership. This cooperative 'living together in intimate association, or even close union, of two dissimilar organisms' is called symbiosis."

Man-computer symbiosis, he continued, "is a subclass of man-machine systems. There are many man-machine systems. At present, however, there are no man-computer symbioses…. The hope is that, in not too many years, human brains and computing machines will be coupled together very tightly, and that the resulting partnership will think as no human being has ever thought and process data in a way not approached by the information-handling machines we know today."

Licklider and Sutherland's successor at IPTO, a young man by the name of Bob Taylor, funded another kind of visionary out in California—a fellow who had been thinking for a surprisingly long time about how to use computers to amplify the power of the human mind. His name was Doug Engelbart, and almost all the essential elements of today's personal computing devices came from his laboratory in the 1960s: the mouse, clickable links on a screen, windows of information on a screen, mixed video- and computer-generated information, collaborative work over a network, hypertext. It took 30 years to recognize what Engelbart had known all along: Computers that aid human intellectual activity were not created by the computer industry or by othrodox computer science. Both of those fields had

Reaching out on the World Wide Web

An American soldier in Bosnia talks with his wife and makes faces at his three-week-old daughter 5,000 miles away in North Carolina, thanks to a computerized video conferencing program using off-the-shelf products found in computer stores everywhere. The program demonstrates the World Wide Web's role as a communications hub. Champions of the Web foster a goal called convergence, and reaching it has flared into one of the great technology battles of the 1990s. Companies that succeed in installing an Internet highway with a bandwidth capable of simultaneously and instantly carrying digitized signals from a multitude of sources—telephones, faxes, modems, television, radio, interactive multimedia—likely will dominate the communications industry of the future.

373

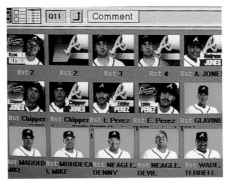

The Atlanta Braves baseball stadium relies on high-tech accessories to please fans. A 22-by-16-foot video screen offers arrivals live interviews with players (above). Technicians who control specially designed audio and video systems (left) select each batter's mug shot and game statistics (far left) to show on the scoreboard. A computerized system monitors moisture and either drains the field—up to 102,000 gallons an hour—or waters the turf.

ignored or scorned Engelbart in the 1950s, when he tried to convince people that computers and televisions could help people think and collaborate.

When Engelbart started crusading for the design of a new kind of computer that was capable of supporting cooperative and intellectual work, computers were used for scientific and military calculations, as well as in the business world for data processing, mostly payrolls for huge corporations. The idea that you could use a computer to think with was simply not part of the landscape of possibility. So Engelbart enlisted allies and invented the kind of machines he had envisioned. Together with a laboratory of young wizards, who are now the technology directors of the central companies in the Internet industry, Engelbart created a now legendary demonstration in San Francisco in December 1968. Sitting on stage with a keyboard, screen, mouse, and earphone-microphone device, he called up documents from the computer's memory and orchestrated a stunning demonstration of computer navigation.

Engelbart's laboratory was the first "Network Information Center" for another ARPA project, the ARPAnet, an experiment in computer communications that grew into today's Internet. Many of Engelbart's students, together with many of the ARPA programmers—creators of computer graphics, interactive computing, and the ARPAnet—joined former IPTO director Bob Taylor when Xerox created the Palo Alto Research Center (PARC). In the 1970s, Taylor's team, building on the fundamental work of Sutherland, Licklider, and Engelbart, created the Alto, the first personal computer and graphic user interface (GUI). In 1979, a young Steve Jobs saw an Alto demonstrated at PARC and took the idea of a GUI back to his own fledgling company, Apple Computer.

Jobs and his engineering-genius partner, Steve Wozniak, were a younger generation than the university-based researchers at ARPA and PARC, and they came along at a time when Moore's Law made the first computer-on-a-chip possible. They started out not as entrepreneurs but as enthusiasts. Jobs and Wozniak and other pioneers at Palo Alto's Homebrew Computer Club worked on computers simply because it was fun to do. Again, the transition to a new industry—and a new way of doing business, a new way of thinking for millions of people—was not accomplished by the computer industry or the computer science establishment. It was the accomplishment of two visionaries who happened to be young and wanted to get their hands on their own personal computing machines.

The ARPAnet was driven by social communication—people using e-mail, news groups, electronic bulletin boards, chat rooms and MUDs (Multi-User

Focusing on a model subject, camera and computer scan and catalog 266 distinctive character-istics of the iris, the colored part of the eye. In 1999, a Texas bank made the first commercial use of iris scanners in the United States. Its customers do not have to carry ATM cards or remember their PINs. The eye offers more dependable identification than a fingerprint.

Dimensions in which a player "incarnates"—creates a character—and interacts with other players in the environment). The ARPAnet began to emerge from decades in research laboratories and universities, and in the mid-1990s the Internet linked hundreds of millions into a popular culture that had been a more elite culture involving hundreds of thousands for 20 years. The interactive computing and computer graphics research of the 1950s made possible the intellectual augmentation research of the 1960s. That in turn led to the personal computer research and development of the 1970s, which was brought to the masses by the personal computer revolution of the 1980s and interconnected into a global network in the 1990s via the Internet and the Web.

The personal computer and the Internet were created by people who had a clear vision of a new use for a tool that had been created for different reasons. However, the vision of computers and networks as mind amplifiers and online communities—Licklider's "symbiotic" relationship between humans and machines—has been followed by more recent, perhaps more deeply disturbing visions of the future role of computing machinery.

For example, inventor Raymond Kurzweil wrote in his book *The Age of Spiritual Machines* that a 1998 personal computer "can perform about 150 million instructions per second for about $1,000. By doubling every twelve months, we get…300 billion instructions per second in 2009….With $1,000 personal computers providing about 1 trillion calculations per second (particularly of the neural-connection type of calculation) in 2009, the more powerful supercomputers will provide about 20 million billion calculations per second, which is about equal to the estimated processing power of the human brain…."

The human brain has a weakness that computers do not have: The brain works at a relatively slow speed. For this reason, Kurzweil believes, "DNA-based evolution will eventually have to be abandoned. DNA-based evolution is good at tinkering with and extending its designs, but it is unable to scrap an entire design and start over…." He sees computer technology as an invention that allows us to get past the limitations of our own brains.

We are approaching the theoretical point that past visionaries have anticipated, when the thought-like capabilities of our silicon creations might rival our own homegrown cognitive powers. Will tomorrow's computers be our partners, our masters, or our evolutionary successors? Did Licklider or Kurzweil have the more accurate vision of the future? Y2K was only the first systemic reminder that we've created something in our own image, and it is coming of age.

We Americans 2000

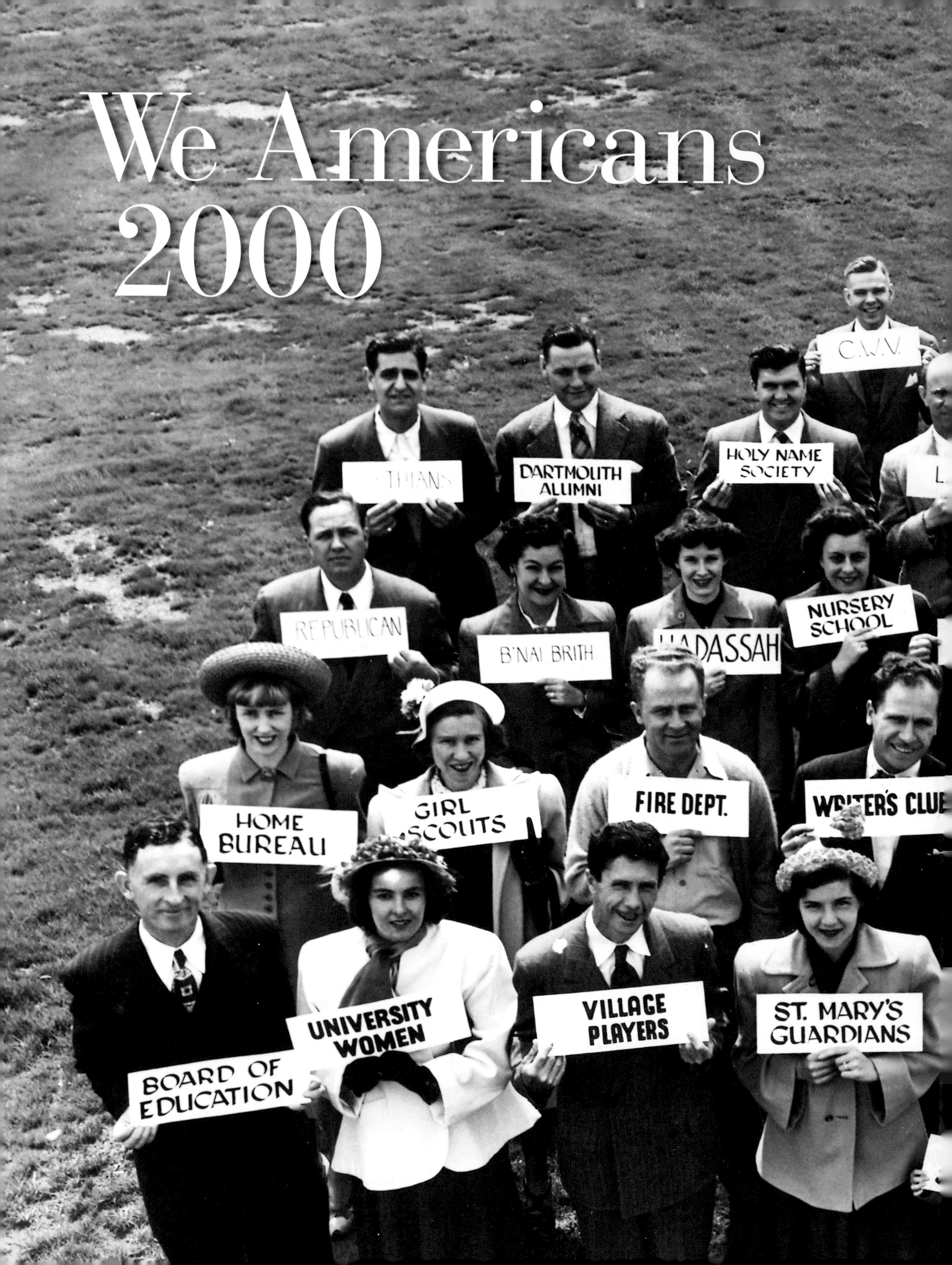

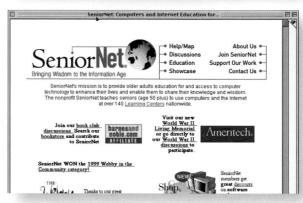

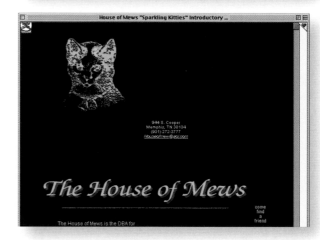

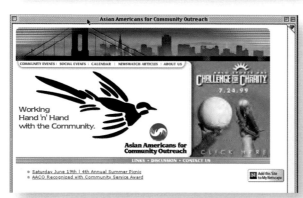

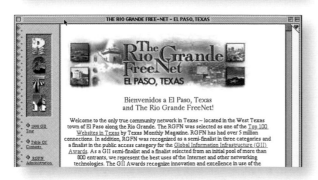

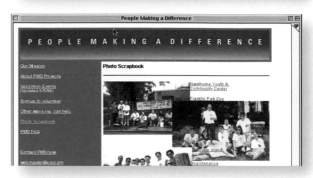

"O, let America be America again—

The land that never has been yet—

And yet must be."

— LANGSTON HUGHES

BY ISABEL WILKERSON

In February 1916, the *Chicago Defender,* an eight-page broadsheet originating within the narrow ribbon of Chicago's South Side, remarked upon what seemed to be the isolated departure of several hundred black families from Selma, Alabama. It was a single paragraph on a front page dominated by news of threats to the 13th Amendment and of a new building going up at a small college in Florida. It was an event little noticed by the mainstream press or society at large.

Over the succeeding months, a swelling number of black arrivals would alight from the Illinois Central Railroad with their worldly possessions stuffed into cardboard suitcases tied with string. Some were in overalls and hats of straw, walking into the Northern, big-city morning, fresh from the small towns and cotton fields of the South. It was the middle of World War I, and some held in their hands the classified ads and addresses of factories that had recruited them to work in munitions plants, meat packing houses, and other big businesses lacking workers due to the suspension of immigration from Europe.

In its day and within an isolated part of the population, the weekly *Defender* was the closest thing to a Web site for black Americans during what would become one of the largest migrations ever to occur in this country. The *Defender* made its way from the streets of Chicago's South Side onto the baggage cars of the Illinois Central under the arms of black Pullman porters and into sharecropper shacks and barbershops throughout the South. In the more dangerous precincts, it was folded into bundles of other merchandise and sold and passed among neighbors in secrecy, since it openly must rebuke the feudal caste system of the South. In black households, the *Defender* was read like the Bible. Propagandistic and virulently anti-South, it held out to the beleaguered black

World Wide Web pages (opposite) offer a variety of connections to an Internet community. In 40 percent of America's households, at least one member has access to the Internet.

PRECEDING PAGES
Clubby 1950s residents of Levittown show their connections. The Long Island community, named after the entrepreneur who conceived it, led post–World War II America into suburbia—and reflected the racism of the time: This Levittown was for whites only.

masses of the South the promise of liberty in the great urban North.

In the pages of the *Defender* came the first stirrings of what historians now call the Great Migration, a population shift goaded by war, hope, and desperation. With the war underway in Europe, Northern labor agents went South in search of a source of inexpensive labor—just as sneaker manufacturers would turn to developing countries like Malaysia as the century drew to a close. Venturing into hostile terrain, the labor agents faced violence and punitive fees imposed by resentful Southern planters.

The agents watered the seeds of agitation already taking root in the hearts of Southern blacks. They dangled the prospect of jobs that could triple and quadruple a black laborer's wages— and gave out free train tickets besides.

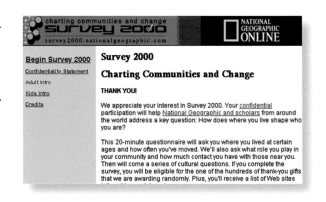

The migration had already begun but few had noticed until February 1916. Between editorials denouncing Jim Crow laws and society pages cataloguing the balls and cotillions of the small community of well-heeled blacks in Chicago, the *Defender* made its passing reference to the start of a demographic sea change that would alter the face of the urban North.

Over the decades that followed, the private, personal, often measured, occasionally rash decisions of a multitude, together in one leaderless movement, would help redistribute an entire population. From 1915 to 1970, some six million black Americans left the South in one of the largest U.S. migrations in history. Their individual decisions led to the dispersal of the black population from South to North and West, from rural to urban. The migration drained the South of much of its cheap labor and undercut the remnants of the slave hierarchy that the American South was built upon. It forced Southern whites to search their souls and confront their dependence on cheap black labor, nudging them toward mechanization to reduce their vulnerability.

The migration strained the resources of ill-prepared cities. Ghettoes formed as the migrants were forced into cramped urban islands with real but invisible boundaries. And just as the largest wave of black migrants was arriving during

Is community an antique idea in a nation full of people on the move? The National Geographic Society's Survey 2000, using the Geographic home page (left) as a survey site, examines that question and others. The study is the largest such Internet survey ever conducted. About 66,000 people 16 or older logged on and clicked through the survey, answering questions about when and where they moved, what roles they play in their communities, and how geography has shaped their tastes in food, music, and literature. (Some 14,300 children answered questions aimed at them.) Nearly the same number of women as men took the adult survey; 73% of the adults and 67% of the kids were American. A profile of Survey 2000 Americans:

RACE

White	92.5%
Black	1.5%
Other	4.5%
(1.5% did not give race)	

EDUCATION

Less than high school	1.1%
High School graduate	32.2%
Associate's degree	7.9%
Bachelor's degree	33.7%
Graduate degree	25.1%

Our Community Attitudes

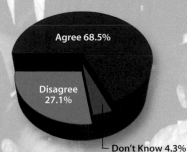

Agree 68.5%
Disagree 27.1%
Don't Know 4.3%

I feel close to other people in my community

People in Alaska and Hawaii showed the highest percentage of positive response to this statement.

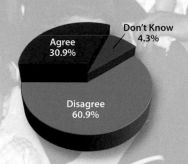

Don't Know 4.3%
Agree 30.9%
Disagree 60.9%

My daily activities do not create anything worthwhile for my community

Alienation, so often spoken of in U.S. society, does not afflict the majority of survey respondents.

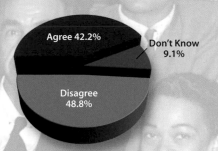

Agree 42.2%
Don't Know 9.1%
Disagree 48.8%

People who do a favor expect nothing in return

Sociologists studying the data hope to learn whether attitudes such as this are linked to mobility: Does moving undercut a sense of altruism?

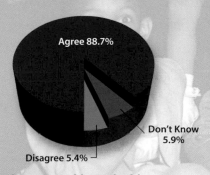

Agree 88.7%
Don't Know 5.9%
Disagree 5.4%

I have something valuable to give to the world

This drew the highest positive response. Its reverse—"I have nothing…"—got only 4.5% agreement.

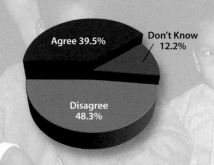

Agree 39.5%
Don't Know 12.2%
Disagree 48.3%

The world is becoming a better place for everyone

The "world," to most people, is the home community. But it can encompass an entire region or nation.

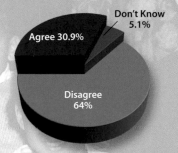

Don't Know 5.1%
Agree 30.9%
Disagree 64%

I cannot make sense of what's going on in the world

Survey 2000 sought the respondents' views of the world in terms of complexity and optimism.

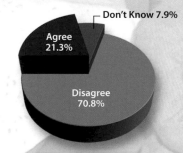

Don't Know 7.9%
Agree 21.3%
Disagree 70.8%

Society has stopped making progress

On progress, one person wrote in: "If we… spend some of our competitive energy cooperating for common progress, we may survive."

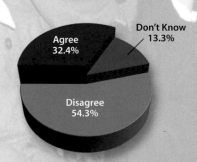

Agree 32.4%
Don't Know 13.3%
Disagree 54.3%

I find it easy to predict what will happen next in society

Among the written-in predictions: "No more paper money" and English as the world's principal language.

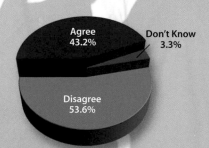

Agree 43.2%
Don't Know 3.3%
Disagree 53.6%

People do not care about other people's problems

The survey found that longtime Internet users, though socially and politically active "digital citizens," feel more connected to the "on-line community" than to the community they live in.

and immediately after World War II, a new migration was underway: Whites were moving out of the cities and into the tract homes and split-levels of the newly drawn suburbs to raise the baby boom generation.

The black migration changed the character of race relations and the nature of protest. When the migration began, panicked white Southerners searched for ways to keep black workers from leaving. For a time, some raised wages to induce them to stay. Others used coercion and violence to keep them from leaving. In Macon, Georgia, and Brookhaven, Mississippi, for example, black men and women caught trying to leave were arrested on railroad platforms. In some towns, trains were prevented from stopping at the station when large black contingents were holding northbound tickets. The noose-tightening made some all the more determined to leave. And the spirit of protest in the air emboldened those who stayed to fight for civil rights, knowing they had a place to go if they absolutely had to. The protest movements of the final third of the century—for women, for peace, for gay rights—owe much to the black struggle for civil rights, and thus to the quietly rebellious steps of participants in the Great Migration.

The movement altered the national culture in ways that no one foresaw at the time and that often go unrecognized even today. It transported an isolated regional culture into the national mainstream, as the migrants brought with them their speech patterns and folk music—the blues. Their songs of hardship and survival, made grittier by life in the big city, were set on vinyl in studios in Chicago and distributed all over the world. Picked up by teenagers like Mick Jagger and Eric Clapton, the music became the progenitor of rock-and-roll. Muddy Waters and B.B. King, for example, were both participants in the Great Migration during World War II.

The early stages of the migration were studied by a handful of struggling scholars working without the technology we take for granted today. They used pads and paper and, where they could find them, the telephone and telegraph. It was a hodgepodge attempt to sort out a demographic shift whose scope they could not have imagined, one that would ultimately span half a century. Its ramifications—especially the current state of our big cities—still haunt the national discourse on race and diversity.

Not until 1917 did intellectuals, most of them black and working outside the mainstream in publications geared toward a black readership, began taking note and looking into the phenomenon. W.E.B. DuBois, then the editor of *Crisis,* the journal of the National Association of Colored People, and Charles S. Johnson, a sociology graduate student at the University of Chicago, were among the first scholars to sit down with black migrants and search out the reasons and motivations for what was being called the "exodus to the Promised Land."

Nearly every scholar and commentator described the migration in the past tense, as if the movement was done with. But no one bothered to tell black Southerners that the migration was over. They kept coming. Because much of the migration analysis in the mainstream press focused on the problems caused by the arrivals, rather than the motivations and dreams of the participants, few Americans other than the migrants themselves knew about their plans and intentions. In 1920, before the bulk of the migrants had left and before many were even born, Emmett J. Scott, author of *Negro Migration During the War*, wrote with an air of finality, "A most striking feature of the northern migration was its individualism….The motives prompting the thousands of negroes were not always the same, not even in the case of close neighbors." After those words were published, five million more black men and women left the South—ten times the number who had fled during the World War I era that Scott examined. The migration continued for five more decades and did not end until the civil rights movement produced desegregation reforms in the South.

We now have the luxury of looking back at the Great Migration with the clarity of hindsight. We know what the most visionary scholars of the day could not have known. We can now say that the migration peaked during the Second World War with 1.5 million black departures from the South in the 1940s alone. We know that the migration continued until 1970 and that, with an improved Southern economy and an apparent détente in race relations, many black Americans have returned to the South in the past 20 years in a smaller but culturally significant reverse migration.

One of the largest movements of human beings ever seen in this country occurred with few people anticipating it, understanding it, or even being aware of it until it was well underway and beyond anyone's influence or control. Scholars and policymakers could not see into the human heart of a restless mass of people because few took the time to consult them and learn what they were doing.

What might we have learned had the technology been available to analyze the Southern migration to the big Northern cities? Suppose we had been able

"No one can possibly know what is about to happen: it is happening, each time, for the first time, for the only time."

— JAMES BALDWIN

to collect their motivations and dreams on a magnificent Web site and project out the course and pace of their migration. What might our cities and our country look like had the mayors and labor unions and the federal government planned ahead and aided the migrants' transition? Imagine what our attitudes and presumptions toward one another might be today had the migration been recognized for what it was: an internal migration of rural peasants looking to live out a dream—just like the Poles, the Irish, the Italians, the Swedes, the Germans, and the Lithuanians who came before them, and the Cubans, Koreans, Salvadorans, Hmong, and Laotians who came after them.

Had the migration been understood for what it was, there might have been places like Jane Addams's Hull House in Chicago, a model for helping immigrants to our big cities. Imagine similar places set up to ease the black migrants into the strange new world of the big Northern cities. If the migration were better understood, the trade unions might have been induced to admit this new group of internal immigrants into their ranks rather than to reject them as a temporary annoyance, inferior and not worth assimilating.

Now, in our own era, as we enter a new millennium, what demographic sea changes are occurring at this very moment that we are unable to see because they are occurring at the speed of a dripping faucet? We know that this is a country still in flux, its population still churning and being replenished by migration and immigration. Nearly one in every ten U.S. residents is an immigrant. The number of immigrants in the United States has tripled since 1970. And within these borders a typical American moves an average of every seven years—about ten or eleven times during his or her lifetime.

To gain a fuller understanding of our mobility and migration and its effects on our culture, the National Geographic Society used its World Wide Web site (nationalgeographic.com) to seek out the voices of the people and gather their experiences. The study was called Survey 2000. One of the survey's purposes was an assessment of American's sense of community in America at the turn of this century. One question, for example, asked whether the respondents thought their community was "a source of comfort." More than two-thirds said it was.

The Geographic's Survey 2000 was the largest such Web-based survey ever conducted. One aspect of it is especially pertinent to the Great Migration:

What we do

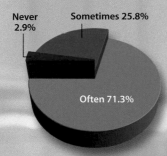

People who read books

Never 2.9%
Sometimes 25.8%
Often 71.3%

Survey 2000 also checked literary tastes. Mark Twain emerged as the No. 1 author throughout the United States.

People who participate in any sports activity

Never 30.1%
Sometimes 40.4%
Often 29.5%

The region with the highest proportion of "never" responses (35.1%) encompassed Arkansas, Louisiana, Oklahoma, and Texas.

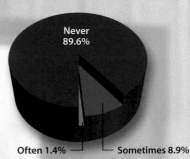

People who go to an auto or motorcycle race

Never 89.6%
Often 1.4%
Sometimes 8.9%

Asked about attending live theater performances, 39.9% of the respondents said they never did.

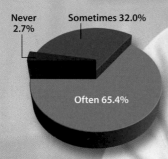

People who watch television

Never 2.7%
Sometimes 32.0%
Often 65.4%

The high "often" percentage reflects 1998 U.S. television average daily viewing time: 7 hours, 43 minutes of prime time; 1 hour, 13 minutes of late night time.

People who visit art museums or galleries

Never 23.1%
Sometimes 64.2%
Often 12.7%

The highest "never" (29.3%) came from the region made up of Kentucky, Tennessee, Alabama, and Mississippi; Pacific states registered the lowest "never": 20.6%

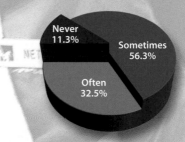

People who go to movies

Never 11.3%
Sometimes 56.3%
Often 32.5%

Of all the non-moviegoers, the Pacific states had the smallest percentage: 9.4%.

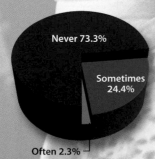

People who go to live ballet or dance performances

Never 73.3%
Sometimes 24.4%
Often 2.3%

New England dance aficionados had the highest "often" rate (3.2%). Respondents were told "school performances" did not count.

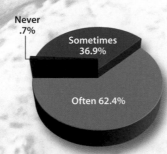

People who dine out

Never .7%
Sometimes 36.9%
Often 62.4%

Dining out was almost a universal activity, with few people from any area clicking on the "never" box.

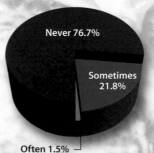

People who gamble

Never 76.7%
Sometimes 21.8%
Often 1.5%

Casino gambling, though a growing U.S. industry, won few "often" responses; support of state-run lotteries was not queried.

More African Americans participated in Survey 2000 than in the General Social Survey, a leading social science tool for the analysis of social change in contemporary America. Survey 2000 showed that, among those who responded, white Americans typically have lived longer at their current addresses than black Americans. Does this fact somehow stem from the Great Migration? Extensive analysis of the survey may offer an answer.

Because the World Wide Web does not know national boundaries, Americans were not the only ones answering Survey 2000 questions about themselves. Of the more than 80,000 people who participated, 40,642 were American adults. (Some 14,300 schoolchildren, the overwhelming majority of them Americans, also logged in for a survey geared to them.) Results shown on these pages have been sorted to reflect only the responses of adult Americans.

"Surveys provide useful data but do not give respondents the chance to express the richness and complexity of their own lives," a note in Survey 2000 says. So people were asked for their "Reflections" on the most significant moves of their lives. Numerous responses showed the enduring themes of migration and redemption—and the angst of being uprooted. A San Diego man reported an insight into the reality of immigration that he had noted in a casual encounter: "The other day, we had a meeting of people whose birthdays were in June. Of the fourteen people in the meeting, only two were born in the U.S."

A Maryland woman, born in Puerto Rico in 1952, left at the critical age of eight and a half. It was a traumatic migration experience. "I had become conscious there; it was my world," she wrote. "...I was yanked away from my world unwillingly to move to an alien country...with strange weather and strange food....I was miserable for years."

"When I was seven," wrote a 55-year-old San Diego electronic technician, "we moved to Idaho. We took the train (California Zephyr) from Grand Junction, Colorado, to Salt Lake, Utah, and continued on other trains to Spokane, Washington. I was thrilled and can still remember wanting to see what was over the next hill and around the bend. The result was that my father came to Idaho every spring at the end of school to drive us to Colorado and back to Idaho in the fall for school. We always took a different route and I could not get enough travel. So it was natural for me at age eighteen to join the Navy...."

A farm wife in Iowa wrote of a narrower world: "I have only moved a few miles in my life, but moving on to the home farm of my husband's parents proved to be the biggest mistake of our lives. It is hard when you know the people who used to live in your house and yard. They tend to notice if you change the wallpaper or cut down a tree."

A 51-year-old Colorado educator said his most significant move was "going to Vietnam. My beliefs in my country and my government were completely shattered." But, he added, "I have recovered my beliefs in my country."

"Mobility" was an elastic concept to some people. They did not see it as just a geographic phenomenon. An unemployed New York man wrote that to him, at 33, the most significant move was not moving from New York to Colorado and back again. "I stopped using drugs and alcohol," he said. "Definitely most significant move."

People who took the survey were also asked to look into the future and tell their predictions. What emerged was a millennial intersection of technology and spirituality, a wonder at the advances of the digital age and a fear that it could isolate and overtake us even as it liberates and binds us in a global e-village.

"I'm afraid I don't think the world will change for the better," a nurse wrote. "I anticipate more crime, fewer manners, worse grammar, less reading, more relying on technology to provide entertainment." A retired man from Ithaca, New York, foresaw "awful new TV shows." A teacher in Alabama predicted that we would all someday be wearing shorts. One person said of the future, "It's too big a question for me tonight."

A public school teacher—logging on from a remote Eskimo village in western Alaska—compared this moment in time to the moment when a man landed on the moon. "The village has no power, sewage, or water systems," she wrote. "We have no post office, although most weeks on Wednesday, a plane leaves off a mail sack….We have no stores. We have a radio telephone that cuts off in about fifteen minutes." But, she said, her school is on the Internet. "We have power Macs and a color printer, digital camera, laser disc player, FAX, satellite TV reception, and a VCR…."

"My students use the Internet every day and have learned so much about technology, the United States, and the world in the eight months that we have traveled the information highway, our only highway….I'm as excited about it as people were about Marco Polo, Christopher Columbus, and Neil Armstrong because technology will change my everyday world far more."

A man who makes his living on the leading edge of technology suggested that the most basic of human problems will defy technological answers, no

"If you don't understand yourself you don't understand anybody else."

—NIKKI GIOVANNI

matter how advanced, "I think that technology in a century will make the technology today seem primitive," he wrote. "I predict that there will be much turmoil between races and the rich and poor, and there will probably be a bigger gap between these groups within the next century, unless someone can come up with a way of getting people to realize that we are all stuck here together...."

The most significant move one man in his 50s said he had ever made was getting divorced, because "it gave me the chance to discover myself and do things for me rather than always for others." He had this to say about the future: "Fairer; less politics; less emphasis on power; more long-term thinking; acceptance of diversity; more caring for our planet....I see colonization of the moon and manned space travel to other parts of the solar system....I believe that we are evolving towards a more tolerant, closer world....We live in a modern world, but the hatred in this place is ancient and must be purged."

A rural respondent worried about the future of food production: "We live in a rural area with no public transportation, no real grocery store, no town hall (only town in our county without one), and maybe be losing our little library. Population has been dropping here for ten years or more, as there is nothing to keep the young people wanting to stay. The vast majority has no interest in agricultural occupations because they have no desire to get their hands dirty. One teen told me agricultural work is 'the dreaded farm.' If the trend continues, who will produce our food?"

Many people saw environmental problems ahead—destruction of the rain forests, global warming, depletion of the ozone layer. There was also a willingness to see this moment in human history through a wide-angle lens and to use the broadest of brush strokes in daring to paint the future, as if the future of all of humanity depended upon the decisions of our time.

One such visionary was a woman raised in New York City who has chosen to live the late 1990s trend known as "voluntary simplicity." She and her husband are rearing their children in a rural town of 1,800 people. She had much to say about the future and where we are as a species: "We are about to begin what may be the most crucial century in human history...a crossroad period between our adolescence and maturity as a multi-cultural civilization on Earth. If...we collectively fail to mature and accept this responsibility for ourselves as a species, the near-future may be a series of disasters, setbacks, and the end of us. If we get together to face the next challenges...we may survive."

A matter of taste

When was the last time you had a donut? Come on. Really…

Admitted donut eating varies widely from state to state. Few on the West Coast confessed—perhaps because they also had a high level of reported knowledge and interest in food. The food survey indicates that Americans eat more junk food than traditional regional favorites. The nation's favorite food: pizza.

"Never tried"　　　　"One of my favorite foods"

DONUT EATING

Drinkin', cheatin' and cryin': country music's home is South and Midwest

Here is how county western fared in various regions of the nation. The height of the bars indicates the proportion of respondents with a taste for country music. Despite the growing influence of nationwide media, regional variations in music prevail.

U.S. REGIONS
keyed by color

George Washington appears on the first U.S. adhesive stamp, issued by a private firm in 1842. Ever since, stamps have commemorated key leaders and events in American history.

CIRCA 1000
- First Europeans arrive. Leif Eriksson leads Viking sailors west from Greenland. Some winter in Newfoundland.

1492
Indian population about 850,000
- Columbus arrives.

1565
- Spanish found St. Augustine

1587
- About 120 English try colonizing Roanoke Island (now North Carolina). They disappear: the "Lost Colony."

1607
- At Jamestown (Virginia), some 100 men set up first permanent English settlement. By year's end, 38 survive.

1608
- First Poles and Dutch arrive.

1609
- Spanish build Governor's Palace, Santa Fe; becomes America's oldest surviving European building.

1612
- Virginian John Rolfe finds way to hybridize tobacco for export.

1613
- Dutch set up trading post on Manhattan Island.

1619
- Dutch ship brings 20 Africans to Jamestown to be sold.

1620
- *Mayflower* carries 102 Pilgrims to Massachusetts. They settle Plymouth. Half die in first winter.

1630
European population of colonies: 4,646
- Massachusetts Bay Company, under Gov. John Winthrop, brings some 1,000 colonists to New England.

1638
- John Harvard's will grants money, library to new seminary; it adopts his name.

1650
Colonial population: 50,368

1685
- William Penn's Quaker colony nears 9,000. Philadelphia, with 7,000 people, is the largest city in British North America.

1700
Colonial population: 205,888

1721
- For the first time in the colonies, a doctor gives inoculations against smallpox.

1773
- Colonists protest British taxes by dumping tea into the harbor: the Boston Tea Party.

1774
- First Continental Congress meets in Philadelphia.

1775
- In Massachusetts, Battle of Lexington and Concord. Americans repel British attempt to destroy stockpiled arms. British win Battle of Bunker (really Breed's) Hill.
- George Washington takes command of Continental Army; lays siege to Boston.
- Benedict Arnold and Ethan Allen take Fort Ticonderoga.

1776
- Declaration of Independence adopted July 2. British win at Long Island, occupy New York.
- On Christmas night Washington leads men across the Delaware River, attacks German mercenaries at Trenton.

1777
- Continental Congress adopts Stars and Stripes as flag.
- Washington wins at Princeton, halting capture of Philadelphia. British recapture Ticonderoga. Americans whip Hessians at Bennington. British take Philadelphia.
- Washington's army in winter quarters at Valley Forge.

1778
- France comes to Americans' aid.

1779
- Americans gain control of the Old Northwest (Illinois, Indiana).
- John Paul Jones captures HMS *Serapis* as his shattered *Bonhomme Richard* sinks.

1780
Population 2,780,400
- British battle in the Carolinas to control South.

- Benedict Arnold sells out to British.

1781
- Revolutionary War essentially ends on Oct. 19, when Gen. Cornwallis surrenders at Yorktown.

1783
- Treaty of peace with Britain signed and ratified.

1789
- U.S. Constitution ratified. George Washington inaugurated as first President.

1790
- Capital moves from New York to Philadelphia.
- First session of the Supreme Court.

1791
- Ratification of first ten amendments to the Constitution—the Bill of Rights.
- Vermont ends 14 years as separate republic, becomes 14th state.

1792
- Kentucky 15th state.

1793
- Congress passes Fugitive Slave Law. Now illegal to aid escaping slaves.
- Eli Whitney invents cotton gin.

1795
- 11th Amendment regulates suits against states.

1796
- John Adams, Washington's Vice President, elected President over Thomas Jefferson.
- Tennessee 16th state.

1800
Population: 5,308,483
- Thomas Jefferson and Aaron Burr tie 73-73 in electoral vote for President. Choice goes to House of Representatives, which picks Jefferson.
- Capital moves to Washington.

1803
- Jefferson buys Louisiana Territory from Napoleon.
- Ohio 17th state.
- Supreme Court, under Chief Justice John Marshall, establishes its right to declare act of Congress unconstitutional.

1804
- 12th Amendment changes method of electing President.

1807
- Robert Fulton's steamboat sails Hudson River.
- British frigate *Leopard* halts U.S. frigate *Chesapeake*; in tradition of impressing sailors, British take four men—three are American.

1808
- Congress bans import of African slaves.
- James Madison elected President.

1812
- Congress declares war on Britain.
- Despite unpopular war, Madison wins reelection.
- Louisiana 18th state.

1814
- Francis Scott Key watches bombardment of Fort McHenry, Baltimore, and writes the lyrics for "The Star-Spangled Banner."
- British march into Washington, burn Capitol and White House.
- Treaty of Ghent, ending war, signed Dec. 24.

1815
- Word of treaty doesn't arrive in time to stop Battle of New Orleans, only resounding American victory in war.

1816
- James Monroe elected President.
- Indiana 19th state.

1817
- Mississippi 20th state.

1818
- Connecticut is first state to ban property qualifications for voting.
- Illinois 21st state.

1819
- Alabama 22nd state.

1820
- Monroe reelected.
- Congress passes Missouri Compromise, admitting Maine (23rd state) as a free state, while Missouri (24th state) will be a slave state.

1823
- President Monroe reveals Monroe Doctrine, warning European powers away from the Western Hemisphere.

1824
- John Quincy Adams beats Andrew Jackson, hero of New Orleans, for President.

1828
- Andrew Jackson of new Democratic Party becomes President, unseating John Quincy Adams.

1830
- Robert L. Stevens invents T-rail, which becomes standard railroad track.
- Recent immigrants total about 150,000, starting a century of immigration that will add 32 million.
- Indian Removal Act allows President Jackson to move eastern tribes west of the Mississippi.

1831
- Nat Turner's slave rebellion ends quickly; 60 whites and about 100 slaves dead.
- Cyrus McCormick builds a successful reaper. In hours it harvests as much grain as two men can cut by hand in a day.

1832
- Jackson beats Sen. Henry Clay.

1836
- Texas declares itself republic free of Mexico. Siege at The Alamo in San Antonio.

- Jackson's Vice President, Martin Van Buren, elected President over William Henry Harrison.
- Arkansas 25th state.

1837
- Congress increases Supreme Court from 7 to 9.
- Michigan 26th state.
- John Deere invents plow that can break prairies' tough sod.

1838
- About 16,000 Cherokees are marched from Southern highlands to Indian Territory in what will become Oklahoma; about 4,000 die on "Trail of Tears."

1839
- Charles Goodyear, trying to find a way to make rubber manageable, accidently drops some on a hot stove. The blob solidifies: vulcanization.

1840
- William Henry Harrison beats Van Buren for new Whig Party, lives only a month—first President to die in office.

1841
- Vice President John Tyler, advocate of states' rights, becomes President.

1843
- Norbert Rillieux, "free man of color," patents equipment that speeds refining of sugarcane juice and produces purer granulated sugar.
- Gen. Santa Anna, Mexico's ruler, warns annexation of Texas will be an act of war.

1844
- James K. Polk, Tennessee governor, elected President over Henry Clay.
- Samuel F. B. Morse sends "What hath God wrought!" to test telegraph line between Washington and Baltimore.

1845
- Florida 27th state.
- Texas becomes 28th state after annexation.
- First organized baseball team: New York Knickerbockers.

1846
- California secedes from Mexico and is claimed by United States.
- Iowa 29th state.
- U.S.-Mexican War: Gen. Zachary Taylor wins battles at Palo Alto, Resaca de la Palma, and Monterrey.
- Elias Howe patents sewing machine.

1847
- Taylor's small army wins at Buena Vista.

1848

- By Treaty of Guadalupe Hidalgo, Mexico gives up claim to Texas, confirms Rio Grande as border, U.S. gets what will become California, Nevada, Utah, and parts of New Mexico, Colorado, Wyoming, and Arizona.
- Zachary Taylor elected President.
- Chinese imported to build railroads.
- Wisconsin 30th state.

1849

- Gold Rush in California.
- Walter Hunt, twisting a wire into an odd shape, invents the first modern safety pin.
- Elizabeth Blackwell is America's first female physician.

1850
Population: 23,191,876

- Vice President Millard Fillmore becomes President on death of Taylor.
- Levi Strauss, planning to make canvas tents for gold miners, finds they need rugged pants. His canvas pants are called "Levis."
- Isaac Singer invents improved sewing machine and sells it on "installment plan"; sales boom.
- 31st state, California, admitted as free state.

1852

- Franklin Pierce elected President over war hero Winfield Scott.
- Elisha Otis invents "safety" elevator—ratchets stop it if cable breaks.

1853

- Gadsden Purchase: Mexico sells territory that will become southern Arizona and New Mexico.

1855

- New York doctor makes patent medicine from raw petroleum, calls it "kerosene." It won't be used as a fuel for some years: kerosene lamp hasn't been invented.

1856

- James Buchanan elected President over explorer John Frémont of the new Republican Party.

1857

- Supreme Court's Dred Scott decision: ex-slave's residence in free territory does not make the slave free.

1858

- President Buchanan and Queen Victoria exchange messages to mark laying of transatlantic telegraph cable.
- Patent issued for pencil with an eraser.
- Minnesota 32nd state.

1859

- Abolitionist zealot John Brown raids Harpers Ferry armory.
- First successful oil well drilled at Titusville, Pennsylvania.
- Oregon 33rd state.

1860
Population: 31,443,321. When the Civil War begins, Northern states have about 23 million; Confederate population is some 9 million, including about 3 million slaves.

- Republican Abraham Lincoln elected President.
- South Carolina reacts by seceding from the Union.
- 2,500,000 more immigrants arrive from 1850 to 1860.

1861

- Mississippi, Florida, Alabama, Georgia, Louisiana, Texas join South Carolina to form Confederate States of America. Virginia, Arkansas, North Carolina, and Tennessee secede and join.
- Confederate troops fire on Fort Sumter, South Carolina.
- North is routed in Battle of Bull Run.
- Lincoln names Gen. George B. McClellan commander of the Army of the Potomac.
- Union Navy blockades Southern ports.
- Kansas admitted to Union as 34th state (free).
- Telegraph lines cross the country, putting Pony Express out of business.

1862

- Unknown Union general, Ulysses S. Grant, captures Forts Donelson and Henry, barely wins at bloody Shiloh.
- First ironclad warships, *Monitor* and *Merrimac*, fight inconclusive battle.
- McClellan's army, nearing Richmond, stopped by forces of Gen. Robert E. Lee.
- McClellan defeats Lee's invasion of Maryland at Antietam but lets Lee escape. McClellan replaced by Ambrose Burnside, who is defeated by Lee at Fredericksburg.
- Western counties of Virginia, loyal to Union, secede from the state.

1863

- Burnside replaced by Joseph Hooker, who is beaten at Chancellorsville. Hooker replaced by George Meade. He meets Lee's second invasion of North at Gettysburg, Pennsylvania, and wins the war's climactic battle.
- Lincoln issues Emancipation Proclamation, which gives freedom to slaves in Confederacy.
- Grant takes Vicksburg, controls Mississippi River, cutting Confederacy in two. Chattanooga taken, Chickamanga a victory for South; northern invasion of Georgia imminent.
- West Virginia 35th state.

1864

- Lincoln puts Grant in command of all Union armies. Army of the Potomac hammers toward Richmond, though held off by Lee's weary men at the Wilderness, Spotsylvania, Cold Harbor. Circling Richmond, Union troops dig in at Petersburg.
- Sherman starts march through Georgia, takes Atlanta, Savannah, and destroys resources.
- Nevada 36th state.

1865

- Grant takes Richmond. Lee surrenders at Appomattox. Civil War deaths: Union—364,000; Confederate—260,000.
- Five days after war's end, Lincoln assassinated by John Wilkes Booth. Vice President Andrew Johnson becomes President.
- 13th Amendment, abolishing slavery, ratified.
- Linus Yale patents a new kind of cylinder lock.

1867

- Secretary of State Seward arranges purchase of Alaska from Russia.
- Nebraska 37th state.

1868

- President Johnson impeached by House for abusing veto powers. The Senate acquits Johnson.
- Ulysses S. Grant elected President.
- 14th Amendment guarantees rights of citizens, regulates apportionment of Representatives.
- George Westinghouse tests air brake for trains.
- First American open-hearth steel furnace built.
- Patent issued for practical typewriter. Arrangement of keys will soon standardize and stay the same—even on computer keyboards.

1869

- First transcontinental railroad completed when tracks of Central Pacific and Union Pacific are joined by last spike—a gold one—at Promontory Point, Utah.

1870

- 15th Amendment gives vote to former slaves—men only.
- John D. Rockefeller incorporates Standard Oil Co. of Ohio.

1872

- After trying unsuccessfully to make rubber from Mexican chicle, a New Yorker markets it as chewing gum.
- Grant wins reelection.

1873

- Yale, Princeton, Columbia, and Rutgers formalize rules of new game: football.

1874

- Cartoonist Thomas Nast draws an elephant to symbolize a big, unstoppable "Republican Vote." He soon gives "stubborn" Democrats their donkey.
- Joseph Glidden, an Illinois farmer, patents barbed wire; it will fence in the West.

1876

- Alexander Graham Bell uses his invention, the telephone, to call assistant in another room: "Mr. Watson, come here! I want to see you."
- Lt. Col. George A. Custer leads 7th Cavalry in attack on Sioux. He and all men are killed.
- Colorado 38th state.
- Rutherford B. Hayes and Samuel Tilden run for President. Democrat Tilden wins popular vote; neither wins electoral vote.

1877

- Contested election ends in appointment of Republican-dominated Electoral Commission, which picks Hayes.
- Reconstruction era ends as last federal troops leave Dixie.
- Thomas Alva Edison recites "Mary Had a Little Lamb" into his "talking machine," the first phonograph.

1879

- Edison's incandescent lamp, first practical electric light bulb, glows for 40 hours.

Population: 50,155,783

- James A. Garfield becomes President in close race.

1881

- Garfield fatally shot by disappointed office-seeker.
- Chicago meat packer Gustavus F. Swift uses refrigerated railroad car to ship meat East.
- Black educator Booker T. Washington becomes President of Alabama's Tuskegee Institute.

1883

- Brooklyn Bridge opens.

1884

- Grover Cleveland elected President over Republican James G. Blaine despite scandal of admittedly siring illegitimate child.

1886

- Statue of Liberty, gift from French people, is dedicated.

1888

- Benjamin Harrison, grandson of President William Henry Harrison, loses popular vote to Cleveland, but wins electoral vote.

- Amateurs begin taking snapshots with George Eastman's Kodak camera.

1889

- Edison, using a strip of Eastman's film, makes first motion picture: a study of "Fred Ott's Sneeze."
- Humphrey O'Sullivan, Irish immigrant who had tacked pieces of rubber on his shoes to ease tired feet, patents the rubber heel.
- North Dakota, South Dakota, Montana, Washington—39th, 40th, 41st, 42nd states.

1890
Population: 62,947,714

- At Wounded Knee, South Dakota, troops of 7th Cavalry kill 300 Sioux—last major clash between whites and Indians.
- For the first time, machines (ancestors of computers) count people in a U. S. census.
- Idaho and Wyoming—43rd, 44th states.

1891

- Dr. James A. Naismith invents basketball at YMCA in Springfield, Massachusetts.
- American Express Company copyrights "travelers cheque."

1892

- President Harrison runs again, but Grover Cleveland elected—first President to win non-consecutive second term.
- New York's Ellis Island opens as immigrant gateway.
- Connecticut dentist puts toothpaste in tubes designed for artists' paints.

1893

- George W. G. Ferris invents a 250-foot-high rotating wheel with free-swinging cars to thrill visitors to Chicago World's Columbian Exposition.
- "Clasp Locker" or "Unlocker for shoes" demonstrated. Not until 1926 will it be called a zipper.

1896

- Former slave George Washington Carver begins 47 years of agricultural research. He develops more than 300 products from peanuts alone.
- Supreme Court legalizes "separate but equal" (segregated) facilities for black Americans.
- William McKinley elected President over William Jennings Bryan.
- Vaudeville shows include motion pictures for the first time.
- Utah 45th state.

1897

- Inventive food processors develop Jell-O, Grape Nuts, condensed soup, milk in glass bottles.
- First Boston Marathon.

1898
- Incited by destruction of battleship *Maine* in Havana harbor, and prodded by yellow journalism, America declares war on Spain. War-ending treaty grants Cuba independence, gives America Guam, Puerto Rico, and the Philippines.
- Battle deaths: 385; other deaths, mostly from disease: 2,061.
- America annexes Hawaii.

1900
Population: 75,994,575
- Army doctor Walter Reed proves *Aedes aegypti* mosquito spreads yellow fever. Work on Panama Canal speeds up as epidemics are curbed.

1901
- McKinley assassinated. Vice President Theodore Roosevelt succeeds.
- King C. Gillette markets safety razor with throwaway blades.

1903
- Orville and Wilbur Wright fly at Kitty Hawk, North Carolina.
- Henry Ford founds his company.
- Boston defeats Pittsburgh in first World Series.

1904
- Roosevelt elected President.
- Ice-cream vendor at St. Louis Exposition runs out of dishes, tries wrapping ice cream in waferlike Middle Eastern pastry from a nearby stall. The ice-cream cone catches on.

1905
- First nickelodeon opens in Pittsburgh.

1906
- Massive earthquake destroys much of San Francisco.

1907
- Lee de Forest patents grid vacuum tube, the key that unlocks radio.
- More than 1,250,000 immigrants (peak year).
- Oklahoma 46th state.

1908
- William Howard Taft elected President.

1909
- National Association for the Advancement of Colored People (NAACP) founded in New York.

1911
- Charles F. Kettering's self-starter replaces hand crank on cars. He gets a contract from Cadillac.

1912
- Democrat Woodrow Wilson wins election in which Roosevelt's Progressive Party splits Republicans.
- New Mexico and Arizona 47th and 48th states.

1913
- 16th Amendment legalizes federal income tax; 17th provides for popular election of senators.
- 60-story Woolworth Building soars over New York.

1914
- Panama Canal completed.
- Red-for-stop, green-for-go traffic lights—the world's first—begin operating in Cleveland.

1915
- *Lusitania* sunk by German U-boat; more than1,000 people die—including 124 Americans.

1916
- Wilson gains reelection for keeping America out of war.

1917
- U.S. declares war on Germany, reacting to continued submarine warfare by U-boats.
- Inhabitants of Puerto Rico granted U.S. citizenship.

1918
- U.S. supplies and fresh troops speed Allied victory. U.S. battle deaths: 53,402; and 63,114 from other causes.
- More than 500,000 Americans die in influenza epidemic.

1919
- Green Bay Packers professional football team founded.

1920
Population: 105,710,620
- 18th Amendment bans sale and consumption of alcoholic beverages;19th gives women the vote.
- Warren G. Harding elected President. His defeat of Ohio Gov. James M. Cox is transmitted by KDKA Pittsburgh in first broadcast by the first licensed U.S. commercial radio station.
- American Professional Football Association (later National Football League) sells team franchises for $100 each.

1921
- Johnson & Johnson introduce Band-Aids.

1923
- Harding dies, succeeded by Calvin Coolidge.
- Henry Luce founds *Time*.

1924
- Clarence Birdseye markets quick-frozen Birdseye Seafoods.
- Coolidge easily wins election.

1926
- Physicist Robert H. Goddard launches first liquid-fuel rocket.

1927
- Charles A. Lindbergh flies nonstop and solo from New York to Paris.
- Babe Ruth hits 60 home runs.

1928
- Herbert Hoover elected President.
- Mickey Mouse debuts in first talking cartoon, *Steamboat Willie*. Creator Walt Disney does Mickey's voice.

1929
- First U.S. shopping center opens in Kansas City, Missouri.
- October 29,"Black Thursday": New York Stock Market prices plummet by $14 billion. Great Depression begins.
- First mobile home on sale.

1930
- First self-serve supermarket, "King Kullen", opens in New York City.

1931
- New York's Empire State Building is world's tallest.

1932
- Franklin D. Roosevelt soundly defeats Hoover.

1933
- 21st Amendment repeals 18th (Prohibition).
- Peak of Great Depression: 12,830,000 unemployed (25% of workforce). Farmers abandon Dust Bowl for California.
- Chicago Bears 23, New York Giants 21 in first National Professional Football League Championship.
- First drive-in movie opens in New Jersey.

1934
- Dr. Francis E. Townsend offers old-age pension plan. It will evolve into Social Security.

1935
- "Monopoly," based on a 19th-century board game, goes on sale.

1937
- Chester F. Carlson invents copy process he calls Xerox ("dry writing"). But he can't get anyone interested in it.

1938
- DuPont begins selling its first nylon product, a toothbrush.

1939
- Television unveiled at New York World's Fair. Roosevelt talks on TV—a presidential first.
- World War II begins as Germany invades Poland.
- Igor Sikorsky flies his helicopter, the first made in America.

1940
Population: 131,669,275
- Roosevelt wins precedent-shattering third term.

1941
- Japan bombs main base of U.S. Pacific Fleet—Pearl Harbor, Hawaii. U.S. declares war on Japan; Germany declares war on U.S.

1942
- Japanese troops drive Americans from the Philippines. Off Midway, U.S. carriers defeat Japanese carriers in a pivotal battle. American forces invade Guadalcanal and North Africa.
- First controlled, self-sustained nuclear reaction takes place at University of Chicago.

1943
- Trudging the long road to victory, U.S. forces take Sicily, invade Italy, begin "island hopping" in Pacific.

1944
- D-Day begins the liberation of Europe. U.S. landings in Philippines begin the drive to Japan.
- GI Bill of Rights signed into law, allowing millions of servicemen, home from World War II, to attend college.
- Roosevelt wins fourth term.

1945
- Roosevelt dies. Vice President Harry Truman succeeds.
- Germany surrenders.
- World's first nuclear bomb is exploded near Alamogordo, New Mexico.
- A-bombs on Hiroshima and Nagasaki finish the war.
- U.S. battle deaths: 291,557; other deaths: 113,842.

1947
- Army Air Forces becomes United States Air Force, a separate service.
- Philippine Islands granted independence.
- ENIAC (Electronic Numerical Integrator and Computer) goes to work for U.S. Army.
- Three Bell Telephone engineers successfully test first transistor. It will replace vacuum tube and become the heart of the computer.
- Jackie Robinson signs with Brooklyn Dodgers—first African American in major leagues.

1948
- Truman, in an upset, elected President.
- Polaroid camera develops photograph in 60 seconds.

1949
- All armed services now part of Department of Defense.

1950
Population: 150,697,361
- North Korea invades South Korea. United Nations asks aid for South Korea. Truman sends in U.S. forces. Chinese troops enter the war.

1951
- 22nd Amendment limits President to two terms.

1952
- Dwight David Eisenhower elected President over Democratic candidate, Illinois governor Adlai E. Stevenson.
- Jonas Salk introduces first vaccine to fight polio.

1953
- Korean War ends with 33,629 U.S. battle deaths, 20,617 from other causes.

1954
- World's first nuclear powered submarine, *Nautilus*, launched.
- Contraceptive pill developed.

1955
- Disneyland, first theme park, opens in California.

1956
- Eisenhower, again facing Stevenson, wins second term.
- For 16 months, Elvis Presley has at least one song in top ten.

1958
- Explorer 1, first American satellite, launched.

1959
- Two new states: Alaska 49th, Hawaii 50th.
- Motown Records founded in Detroit.

1960
Population: 179,323,175
- John F. Kennedy is first Catholic to be elected President, narrowly beating Vice President Richard Nixon.
- Scientists show first laser (Light Amplification by Stimulation Emission of Radition).

1961
- 23rd Amendment gives vote to District of Columbia in presidential elections.
- Astronaut Alan Shepard, Jr., takes U.S. first ride in space.

1962
- Cuban missile crisis threatens nuclear war.
- Astronaut John Glenn orbits Earth.
- University of Mississippi admits, under federal order, its first black student, James Meredith.
- Rachel Carson's *Silent Spring* opens American eyes to the environment.
- American James D. Watson joins Englishmen Francis H.C. Crick and Maurice H.F. Wilkins, in winning Nobel Prize for determining the structure of deoxyribonucleic acid (DNA).

1963
- President Kennedy assassinated. Vice President Lyndon B. Johnson succeeds him.
- Martin Luther King, Jr., delivers "I Have a Dream" speech.

1964
- 24th Amendment bans poll taxes (aimed at black voters).
- Civil Rights Act and Wilderness Act become law.
- Draft hits 100,000 men as Vietnam involvement grows.
- Surgeon General links smoking to lung cancer.
- Johnson wins in landslide over Sen. Barry Goldwater.
- Robert Moog invents electronic music synthesizer.

1965
- Black Muslim leader Malcolm X assassinated in Harlem.
- First 3,500 U.S. combat troops, of what will be a 540,000-man force, land in South Vietnam.

1966
- Vietnam War escalates;. draft quota soars to 400,000.
- First black member of Cabinet, Robert Weaver, takes over new Department of Housing and Urban Development.
- Endangered Species Act signed into law.
- Edward Brooke (D-Mass.) elected first black Senator since Reconstruction days.

1967
- Demonstrations mount against Vietnam War.
- Thurgood Marshall is first black Supreme Court justice.
- First Super Bowl: Vince Lombardi's Green Bay Packers beat Kansas City Chiefs.

1968
- Tet Offensive by North Vietnamese escalates war again.
- Richard M. Nixon beats Vice President Hubert H. Humphrey.
- Martin Luther King, Jr., assassinated in Memphis.
- Robert Kennedy assassinated in Los Angeles.
- Democrat Shirley Chisholm is first black woman elected to House of Representatives.

First Moon Landing, 1969

1969
- Neil Armstrong and Buzz Aldrin walk on the moon.
- U.S. forces in Vietnam top half a million.
- Lottery replaces draft for 18-year-old men.
- More than 250,000 mass in Washington in war protest.
- 300,000 youths attend Woodstock Music Festival in Bethel, New York.
- "Sesame Street" debuts on TV.

1970
Population: 203,302,031
- As U.S. troops invade Cambodia, some 2 million college students protest. Ohio National Guardsmen kill four at Kent State University. At Jackson State University, Mississippi police kill two students.
- Washington jammed by the largest antiwar rally yet.
- Garry Trudeau's "Doonesbury," debuts; only comic strip to win the Pulitzer Prize.

1971
- 26th Amendment grants vote to 18-year-olds.
- Cigarette advertising on radio and TV ends.
- Microchip invented.

1972
- Burglars rifle Democratic National Committee headquarters in Washington's Watergate apartments; five arrested. Long ordeal of "Watergate" begins.
- Dow Jones closes above 1,000 for first time.

1973
- Cease-fire halts fighting in Vietnam, but bombing of Cambodia continues.
- Watergate hearings begin in Senate.
- Spiro Agnew resigns in disgrace as Vice President; replacement Gerald R. Ford is first to hold that office without election.
- Supreme Court rules abortion a legal right for women.
- U. S. spacecrafts Skylab 1 and Skylab 2 link up.
- Twin towers of New York World Trade Center now world's tallest buildings.

1974
- Facing three articles of impeachment, Nixon becomes first President to resign. Vice President Ford, as President, pardons Nixon.
- Sears Tower, Chicago, now world's tallest building.

1975
- Last Americans leave Vietnam as Saigon falls, ending nation's longest war. American deaths top 58,000.
- Apollo and Soviet Soyuz 19 spacecraft dock in space.

1976
- Jimmy Carter, Georgia governor, wins presidential election, beating Ford.
- Viking 1 and Viking 2, unmanned spacecraft, land on Mars, send back data.
- Episcopal Church approves ordination of women.
- Steve Jobs and Steve Wozniak build first Apple computer in a garage.

1977
- Carter pardons Vietnam War draft evaders.
- Department of Energy debuts.

1978
- Full diplomatic relations established with People's Republic of China.
- Marine Corps names its first female general, Brig. Gen. Margaret A. Brewer.

1979
- Sixty-six U.S. Embassy staff and Marines are taken hostage in Iran by Islamic militants under Ayatollah Khomeini; 52 will be held for 444 days.
- Department of Education established.
- Near meltdown destroys Three Mile Island nuclear power reactor near Harrisburg, Pennsylvania.

1980
Population: 226,504,825
- Rescue mission to free U.S. hostages goes wrong; eight soldiers die.
- Ronald Reagan, running against Carter, is elected President.
- Unmanned Voyager 1, skimming Saturn, reveals new details about the planet.
- Beatle John Lennon gunned down in New York City.

1981
- Iran releases 52 hostages.
- First reusable spaceship, the space shuttle Columbia, flies 36 orbits in 54 hours.
- Acquired Immune Deficiency Syndrome (AIDS) identified.
- Sandra Day O'Connor is first female Supreme Court Justice.

1982
- First artificial heart successfully implanted.

1983
- Unemployment rises above 12 million for the first time since the end of the Great Depression.
- Astronaut Sally Ride is the first American woman in space.
- Pioneer 10, launched in 1972, is first spacecraft to leave solar system and enter deep space.

1984
- Geraldine Ferraro is first woman nominated for Vice President by a major political party when chosen to run with Walter Mondale, Carter's Vice President. Reagan wins second term.

1986
- Space shuttle Challenger explodes shortly after liftoff; all seven astronauts, including teacher Christa McAuliff, killed instantly.
- "Irangate" scandal; President Reagan confirms secret arms deals occurred with Iran.

1987
- Soviet Premier Gorbachev and President Reagan agree to reduce size of nuclear arsenals.
- Mae Carol Jemison is first black female astronaut.

1988
- George Bush, Reagan's Vice President, beats Massachusetts governor Michael Dukakis.

1989
- Supertanker Exxon Valdez runs aground in Prince William Sound, Alaska; spills 11.2 million gallons of oil and blackens more than 700 miles of coastline.
- Gen. Colin Powell is first black chairman of the Joint Chiefs of Staff.
- U.S. forces invade Panama, overthrow corrupt Noriega regime.
- Virginians elect first black governor, L. Douglas Wilder, a Democrat.
- Democrat David Dinkins elected first black mayor of New York City.
- "Warmest year on record" say meteorologists, perhaps due to "greenhouse effect."

1990
Population: 248,765,170
- Operation Desert Shield launched after Iraq invades Kuwait; allied troops gather in neighboring Saudi Arabia.
- Hubble Space Telescope in orbit but malfunctioning; later repaired.
- Space probe Magellan orbits Venus and transmits radar scans of surface.

1991
- Dow Jones closes above 3,000 for first time.
- Operation Desert Storm begins when Saddam Hussein ignores UN deadline to pull his forces out of Kuwait; U.S. planes bomb Iraq. Ground forces liberate Kuwait in 100 hours.
- President Bush and Soviet Premier Gorbachev sign first nuclear arms reduction treaty (START for Strategic Arms Reduction Talks).
- Caught on videotape, four white LA policemen are indicted for beating black motorist Rodney King.

1992
- William Clinton, Arkansas governor, elected over Bush as Cold War ends.
- 27th Amendment is ratified prohibiting congressmen from raising their own pay within a session.
- Americans with Disabilities Act becomes law.
- U.S. troops guard food relief efforts in Somalia.
- Riots sweep Los Angeles after white policemen are cleared of beating Rodney King; More than 50 people killed and $1 billion property damage.

1993
- Terrorist bomb explodes in New York's World Trade Center killing six and injuring some 1,000.
- In Waco, Texas, cult leader David Koresh and more than 70 followers die in battle with federal agents.
- AIDS virus is the leading killer of men 25 to 44 years old.

1994
- With over one million behind bars, America has world's highest incarceration rate

1995
- U.S. resumes diplomatic relations with Vietnam.
- Car bomb explodes in Oklahoma City, killing 169 people.
- Dow Jones closes above 5,000 for first time.

1996
- First U.S. regulatory agency, the Interstate Commerce Commission, is abolished.
- Hubble Space Telescope transmits first pictures of Pluto.
- Defense of Marriage Act says no federal recognition for same-sex marriages.

1997
- Madeleine Albright is first female Secretary of State.
- Oklahoma City bomber Timothy McVeigh sentenced to death; accomplice Terry Nichols wins a separate trial.

1998
- President Clinton's affair with White House intern Monica Lewinsky triggers impeachment proceedings.
- Germany's Daimler-Benz AG buys Chrysler Corporation in the largest foreign takeover of a U.S. company.
- Male anti-impotence drug Viagra approved by FDA.

1999
- Clinton impeached for lying under oath about Lewinsky affair. Senate votes against conviction.
- In Yugoslavia, U.S. and other NATO warplanes bomb selected targets to stop systematic ethnic cleansing in province of Kosovo.
- Dow Jones closes above 10,000 for first time.
- One person or more in 40 percent of America's households has home or workplace access to the Internet.

Projected Population for 2050: 394,000,000

Index

397

Illustration credits

Contributors

Leslie Allen, is the author of *Liberty: The Statue and the American Dream* and a former National Geographic Society staffer. She is a frequent contributor to Society books. She also writes for *American Heritage* and other publications on social history and the environment.

Spencer R. Crew, director of the Smithsonian's National Museum of American History, is the author of *Black Life in Secondary Cities.* He taught history at the University of Maryland and was chair of the Department of Social and Cultural History at the National Museum of American History. He served as deputy director of the museum until he became director in 1994.

David Herbert Donald is a two-time winner of the Pulitzer Prize—for *Charles Sumner and the Coming of the Civil War* and *Look Homeward: A Life of Thomas Wolfe.* Donald is Harvard Professor Emeritus in American History and American Civilization. His works include *Why the North Won the Civil War, Gone for a Soldier, The Great Republic, Liberty and Union,* and *Lincoln.*

William H. Goetzmann, a professor of American Studies at the University of Texas, was awarded both the Pulitzer and Parkman Prizes for his *Exploration and Empire: the Explorer and Scientist in the Winning of the American West.* His other books include *Army Exploration in the American West 1803–1863, The Atlas of North American Exploration (*with Glymdwr Williams), and *Daniel Boone and the Opening of the Ohio Country* (with Seamus Cayan).

William Least Heat-Moon is the author of *Blue Highways: A Journey into America* and *PrairyEarth.* His latest book is *River-Horse, Across America by Boat.*

Charles Kaiser is the author of *1968 in America: Music, Politics, Chaos, Counterculture and the Shaping of a Generation* and *The Gay Metropolis: The Landmark History of Gay Life in America Since World War II.*

John Leonard is the television critic for *New York* magazine and a contributor to many other publications. He is the author of two collections of essays: *Smoke and Mirrors* and *The Last Innocent White Man in America.*

David Mindell, Professor of the History of Science and Technology at Massachusetts Institute of Technology, is the author of a forthcoming book on the Civil War ironclad *Monitor.* His special interest is the evolution of technology and its impact on society.

Edmund S. Morgan, Yale Sterling Professor Emeritus, is the author of *American Slavery American Freedom: The Ordeal of Colonial Virginia; The Challenge of the American Revolution; The Meaning of Independence; The Genius of George Washington; Inventing the People: The Rise of Popular Sovereignty in England and America;* and *Diary of Michael Wigglesworth 1653 1657: The Conscience of a Puritan.*

Edwards Park, former associate editor of *Smithsonian* magazine, has written frequently about the American Revolution and the early days of the Republic. He is the author of *Treasures of the Smithsonian, A New View from the Castle, The Glory of Flight: The Art of William S. Phillips, Angels Twenty: A Young American Flier a Long Way from Home,* and several other books. Before beginning his career at *Smithsonian* magazine he was associate director of the National Geographic's Book Service.

Howard Rheingold is the author of *Virtual Reality, The Virtual Community: Homesteading on the Electronic Frontier, Tools for Thought: The History and Future of Mind-Expanding Technology, The Millennium Whole Earth Catalog: Access to Tools & Ideas for the Twenty-First Century,* and *Secrets of the Super Net Searchers;* co-author of *Exploring the World of Lucid Dreaming* and *Higher Creativity: Liberating the Unconscious for Breakthrough Insights.* He is a frequent contributor to *Wired* magazine.

Richard Schickel, longtime film critic for *Time* and *Life,* has lectured on film at Yale and the University of Southern California. He is the author of numerous books, including *The Platinum Years; Harold Lloyd: The Shape of Laughter; The Men Who Made the Movies; Cary Grant, A Celebration; D.W. Griffith: An American Life; Intimate Strangers: The Culture of Celebrity; Schickel on Film;* and *Brando: A Life in Our Times.*

Geoffrey C. Ward, historian, screenwriter, and contributor to NATIONAL GEOGRAPHIC magazine, is the co-author of *The West: An Illustrated History; The Civil War: An Illustrated History;* and *Shadow Ball: The History of the Negro Leagues.* He also wrote *Before the Trumpet: Young Franklin Roosevelt 1882-1905,* and *A First-Class Temperament: The Emergence of Franklin Roosevelt.* Ward is an associate of prize-winning television producer Ken Burns. His latest book is *American Originals: The Private Worlds of Some Singular Men and Women.*

Isabel Wilkerson, a Pulitzer Prize-winning feature writer for the *New York Times,* is writing a book on the epic migration of African Americans that began during World War I. Her interest in migration is reflected in her role as a member of the Advisory Board on the National Geographic Society's Survey 2000.

We Americans: Celebrating a Nation, Its People, and Its Past
Edited by Thomas B. Allen and Charles O. Hyman

Published by The National Geographic Society
John M. Fahey, Jr. *President and Chief Executive Officer*
Gilbert M. Grosvenor *Chairman of the Board*
Nina D. Hoffman *Senior Vice President*

Prepared by The Book Division
William R. Gray *Vice President and Director*
Charles Kogod *Assistant Director*
Barbara A. Payne *Editorial Director and Managing Editor*
David Griffin *Design Director*

Staff for this book
Kevin Mulroy *Director, Adult Trade Publishing*
Thomas B. Allen *Text Editor*
Charles O. Hyman *Illustrations Editor*
Bill Marr *Art Director*
Kevin G. Craig *Assistant Editor*
Anne E. Withers *Researcher*
R. Gary Colbert *Production Director*
Richard S. Wain *Production Project Manager*
Sharon Kocsis Berry *Illustrations Assistant*
Peggy J. Candore *Assistant to the Director*
Dale-Marie Herring *Staff Assistant*
Kathleen Barber *Indexer*

Manufacturing and Quality Control
George V. White *Director*
John T. Dunn *Associate Director*
Vincent P. Ryan *Manager*
James J. Sorensen *Budget Analyst*

STARS AND STRIPES ROLL FOR WOMEN'S SUFFRAGE.

The world's largest nonprofit scientific and educational organization, the National Geographic Society was founded in 1888 "for the increase and diffusion of geographic knowledge." Since then it has supported scientific exploration and spread information to its more than nine million members worldwide.

The National Geographic Society educates and inspires millions every day through magazines, books, television programs, videos, maps and atlases, research grants, the National Geography Bee, teacher workshops, and innovative classroom materials.

The Society is supported through membership dues and income from the sale of its educational products. Members receive NATIONAL GEOGRAPHIC magazine—the Society's official journal—discounts on Society products, and other benefits.

For more information about the National Geographic Society and its educational programs and publications, please call 1-800-NGS-LINE (647-5463), or write to the following address:

National Geographic Society
1145 17th Street N.W.
Washington, D.C. 20036-4688 U.S.A.

Visit the Society's Web site at www.nationalgeographic.com

ACKNOWLEDGMENTS

The Smithsonian's National Museum of American History provided a great deal of help to the editors. We wish especially to thank the director, Spencer R. Crew; Valeska Hilbig, and Debora Scriber-Miller. Bill Bonner of the National Geographic Image Collection led us to many rare and several unpublished photographs. Kevin Kelly, editor of *Wired* magazine, helped us in the development of "Clicking Toward Y2K."

We also thank Edwards Park for his extraordinary work on the Time Line that begins on page 392. James Witte and Lisa M. Amoroso, both of Northwestern University, were of immense help in preparing the Survey 2000 information that begins on page 382. The data was expertly transformed into graphics (pages 383, 387, and 391) by Dennis Lowe.

The editors also acknowledge the invaluable assistance of contributing editor K. M. Kostyal, and the editorial assistance of Victoria Cooper and Howard Robinson.